HANDBOOK FOR

CHRISTIAN MATURITY

HANDBOOK FOR

CHRISTIAN MATURITY

by
BILL BRIGHT

**A Compilation of
Ten Basic Steps
Toward Christian Maturity**

Campus Crusade for Christ International
San Bernardino, California 92414

HANDBOOK FOR CHRISTIAN MATURITY
A Compilation of Ten Basic Steps Toward Christian Maturity

A Campus Crusade for Christ Book
Published by
HERE'S LIFE PUBLISHERS, INC.
P. O. Box 1576
San Bernardino, CA 92402

Library of Congress Catalogue Card 81-67817
ISBN 0-86605-010-8
HLP Product No. 35-112-2

Manufactured in the United States of America.

FOR MORE INFORMATION, WRITE:

L. I. F. E. — P O Box A399. Sydney South 2000. Australia
Campus Crusade for Christ of Canada — Box 368. Abbottsford. B C . V25 4N9. Canada
Campus Crusade for Christ — 103 Friar Street; Reading RGI IEP. Berkshire. England
Campus Crusade for Christ — 28 Westmoreland St . Dublin 2. Ireland
Lay Institute for Evangelism — P O Box 8786. Auckland 3. New Zealand
Life Ministry — P O Box / Bus 91015. Auckland Park 2006. Republic of So. Africa
Campus Crusade for Christ, Int'l. — Arrowhead Springs. San Bernardino. CA 92414. U S A.

FOREWORD

By Bill Bright

The greatest spiritual awakening of all time is taking place today. More people are hearing the gospel; more people are receiving Christ; more people are committed to helping fulfill the Great Commission than at any other time since the church was born almost 2,000 years ago.

Here in the United States, one-third of all adults identify themselves as born again, evangelical Christians, according to the Gallup Poll. Every Sunday, more than 85 million people are in church, and 125 million people listen to Christian radio and television programs regularly, according to the National Religious Broadcasters.

But we have a problem — a very serious problem. These encouraging, unprecedented statistics are not reflected in the life of our nation. Our Lord has commanded us to be the salt of the earth and the light of the world. But there is little evidence of the influence of Christianity in the media, in education, in government and in other major areas of influence. What has gone wrong?

As a part of our ministry, we take hundreds of thousands of surveys — working with pastors, other Christian leaders and students. The statistics compiled as a result of these surveys are cause for great alarm and concern, as we discover that more than 50% of the members of the churches in America are not sure of salvation (in some churches that figure might be 5%; in others, 95%, depending on the denomination and the leadership of the church). Ninety-five percent of the members do not understand the ministry of the Holy Spirit, and 98% are not regularly sharing their faith in Christ.

It is for the purpose of helping to meet this critical need that the *Handbook for Christian Maturity* has been written. An immature, surrendered Christian can be used by the Lord in limited ways. But as the Christian grows in maturity his effectiveness also grows. To be an influence for Christ in his community or in the world, he must learn how to grow spiritually. His knowledge of how to introduce men and women to the Savior must increase and he must be able to help other believers reach a higher level of maturity in Christ. An in-depth study of God's Word is a major factor in accomplishing these things.

The Bible study series, called *Ten Basic Steps Toward Christian Maturity*, were especially designed and written to help Christians gain this necessary growth. As a result, individuals and groups alike have been stimulated to explore the riches of God's Word and find spiritual nourishment.

Written originally with the college student in mind, these

5

booklets have been equally effective with adults and youth. They have been used by churches, home Bible study groups, military and prison chaplains and many high school groups.

Now, the need for a single volume has become evident. So the *Ten Basic Steps* booklets have been revised and compiled into this *Handbook for Christian Maturity*. The entire work has been redesigned especially for use by the individual Christian in his private Bible study and in his spiritual growth.

When used with the *Teacher's Manual*, the *Handbook* also can be used effectively in a group situation, as the *Steps* booklets are. These two books — the *Handbook* and the *Teacher's Manual* are so prepared that even inexperienced first-time teachers can lead and teach the Bible studies successfully.

Feelings of hopelessness and inadequacy are sensed often in the face of the desperate needs evident in the world today. An understanding of the material in this *Handbook for Christian Maturity* will help to dispel these feelings and will challenge the concerned Christian to seek new heights in communicating his faith.

Nearly every major doctrine of Christianity has been carefully considered and clearly presented. Any person seeking spiritual truth will be generously rewarded as he or she reads and studies these pages. Christians will be strengthened as they allow the teachings to change their lives.

Our prayer is that this book will bless and enrich your life, and that you will be further encouraged to grow to full maturity in Jesus Christ. We trust also that the effectiveness of your personal witness for Him will be greatly enhanced.

HANDBOOK FOR CHRISTIAN MATURITY

TABLE OF CONTENTS

INTRODUCTION

Inquisitive, intellectually minded, concerned people investigate a great many things to varying degrees, but frequently give little thought and even less time to Bible study. Yet the Bible undoubtedly has had a more profound effect on history than any other book. It has played a major part in the development of western culture, influencing national and international affairs, and affecting even matters of everyday life in ways of which we are not aware. In order for any individual to be properly informed and well-educated, he must have at least a general knowledge of the Bible and its teachings. That knowledge can be acquired only through carrying out a consistent plan of study.

The HANDBOOK FOR CHRISTIAN MATURITY is designed to give you an efficient means for a systematic study of the Christian faith as taught in the Bible. The course consists of a broad survey of Christianity. It will give you an understanding of the nature, privileges and responsibilities of the Christian way of life. It also discloses the secret of the available transforming power which can enable you to live that life abundantly.

In this study several things will be emphasized:

The distinctiveness of Christianity. There is a breach between God and man which Christianity calls sin. No religion makes any provision that is acceptable to God for that breach. Christianity, however, does provide for it — not in what man can do for God (which religions attempt to do and which is never good enough) but in what God did for man when He sent His Son Jesus Christ, to die on the cross.

The distinctive claims of Christ. Many people feel that Christ was only a good moral teacher, but this study will make clear that He claimed to be no less than deity. He is either the true God or He is a liar and an impostor.

The abundant life God has for every Christian through the power of the Holy Spirit. The lives of many people have been utterly transformed through an understanding of the doctrine of the filling of the Holy Spirit. (See Step 3, The Christian and the Holy Spirit.)

The benefit from your study therefore should be two-fold:

First, your study should communicate knowledge. Without a knowledge of at least some biblical teaching no one can become a Christian, and no Christian can live a victorious life. A great many people reject Christianity and a great many Christians are miserable, defeated and frustrated simply because of ignorance. The Psalmist said, "The entrance of Thy Words giveth light" (Psalm 119:130), and Jesus taught that "the truth shall make you free" (John 8:32).

light" (Psalm 119:130), and Jesus taught that "the truth shall make you free" (John 8:32).

Second, your study should communicate power to your life. Hebrews 4:12 says that "the Word of God is quick and powerful, and sharper than any two-edged sword, piercing even to the dividing asunder of soul and spirit, and of the joints and marrow, and is a discerner of the thoughts and intents of the heart." The Bible differs from all other books — it is a living book, and through it the life and power of God are communicated to the life of an individual. Men and women by the thousands, including Augustine, Luther, Wesley and many others, have changed history because God used the Bible to change them.

As you or your group begin to use this HANDBOOK FOR CHRISTIAN MATURITY as a guide for your study of the Bible, you undoubtedly will become aware of a number of changes coming over you. You will be shown how to receive Christ as your Savior and be given an opportunity to invite Him into your life if you have not already done so. If you have already taken that step, you will probably notice your Christian living becoming more consistent. You will grow in love for others, your devotion to Christ will deepen, and you will sense an increase in your desire to share your faith.

If you are a new Christian, this HANDBOOK is designed to help you gain a good general knowledge of the Bible, acquainting you with the major doctrines of the Christian faith. It should assist you in your spiritual growth and help you find solutions to the problems you face.

If you are an older, more mature Christian, you will acquire the tools you need to help another person find Christ or to help a weak Christian grow in his faith. Your own commitment will be affirmed and intensified, and you will have an effective devotional and study plan.

A faithful study of this HANDBOOK FOR CHRISTIAN MATURITY will prepare you for a more comprehensive ministry, giving you a thorough understanding of the biblical principles upon which your faith is based. it will focus and strengthen your purpose in life. And it will show you the way to continual appropriation of the power of the Holy Spirit enabling you to live a more joyous, triumphant Christian life.

INSTRUCTIONS
FOR INDIVIDUAL STUDY OF THE
HANDBOOK FOR CHRISTIAN MATURITY

This course of study is designed to give you a broad survey of Christianity. You will meet its central figure, Jesus Christ, and you will study its authoritative literature, the Holy Bible. You will learn of the nature, privileges and responsibilities of the Christian way of life, and you will discover the secret of its power to transform men and give them a continually abundant life.

The study is divided into 11 parts or steps, correlated with the 11 booklets of the *Ten Basic Steps Toward Christian Maturity* (each of the ten steps plus an introductory study).

SUMMARY OF THE STEPS

Introduction: The Uniqueness of Jesus

This Introductory Step toward Christian maturity presents the person of Jesus Christ. It explains who He is, His earthly life, His death, resurrection and continuing ministry in the lives of all believers. A special emphasis is given to the importance of the church of Jesus Christ.

Step 1: The Christian Adventure

Step 1 deals with various facets of the Christian walk, i.e., the Christian's certainty, the Christ-controlled life, principles of growth, the Christian's authority and the importance of the church to the believer.

Step 2: The Christian and the Abundant Life

Step 2 describes the Christian way of life — what it is, and how it works out practically. It discusses problems of sin and temptation and the warfare of life. It points the way to Christian victory and the abundant life.

Step 3: The Christian and the Holy Spirit

Step 3 is a discussion of the Holy Spirit, who is the third member of the Godhead, or Trinity. This lesson teaches us who the Holy Spirit is and how He works in the lives of individuals. It shows us how we may have Him working in our own lives and what the results will be. It teaches us how we may have His power continually energizing us.

Step 4: The Christian and Prayer

Step 4 introduces us to prayer — communion with God. It gives us suggestions regarding a time of meditation. It discusses the purpose, privileges, procedures and promises in prayer, and the power to be derived from it.

Step 5: The Christian and His Bible

In Step 5 we turn to an analysis of the Bible itself. We learn of its composition, authority, central theme and character, and its power to help us. We also will learn methods of studying it and the spiritual needs that are met from such a study. A plan for memorizing the names of the books of the Bible is included.

Step 6: The Christian and Obedience

Step 6 teaches us what the Bible says about obedience. It discusses such matters as finding and doing God's will, personal purity, security, fears, use of the tongue and the problems of insincerity.

Step 7: The Christian and Witnessing

Step 7 deals with the subject of sharing Christianity with others. We will see how Jesus did it and its relationship to the Word of God, prayer and the Holy Spirit. We will also learn of the value and place of the personal testimony. This step concludes with important information on how to share Christ with others and with a reproduction of the Four Spiritual Laws.

Step 8: The Christian and Stewardship

Stewardship is discussed in Step 8. This subject speaks of God's claim upon every individual and upon everything that makes up that individual's life. It discusses consecration of the spiritual and physical aspects of one's life, as well as all of the material things that he possesses. The nature and responsibilities of the Christian steward are defined. A letter written to Paul V. Brown, on the subject of "How to know the will of God for your life according to the 'Sound Mind Principle' of Scripture," is reproduced at the close of this step.

Step 9: Highlights of the Old Testament

Step 9 is a brief survey of the highlights of the Old Testament. It discusses the history of Israel, through which God revealed Himself to the world. It tells of the creation and fall of man, the promise of the Messiah (God's deliverer), Abraham (father of the Jews), Moses, law and grace, Joshua and deliverance, David and forgiveness, Elijah and the power of the Holy Spirit, and Jeremiah, the prophet of God.

Step 10: Highlights of the New Testament

The tenth, and final, step gives us highlights of the New Testament. It reviews each of the New Testament books and gives a brief survey of its contents.

These steps toward Christian maturity are formulated to help you mature and become established in your relationship with Christ. Each step reveals a different facet of Christian life and truth and contains lessons for daily study.

ORGANIZATION OF THE HANDBOOK STUDIES

In the opening pages of each step you will find preparatory material. Sometimes it will be quite short and other times it will contain a great deal of information. Read this through carefully before proceeding with the individual studies. It will give you a clearer perspective on the subjects to be covered.

There are six or seven lessons in each step plus a review or "Recap" lesson. At the end of some of the steps you will find more supplementary material. Be sure to read this and make it your own.

Each lesson is divided into three sections, the Introduction, the Bible Study and the Life Application.

The Introduction is comprised of the stated Objective for that lesson, a Scripture verse or two to memorize and an appropriate Bible reading. The main goal for each lesson is stated in the Objective and should be kept in mind as you continue through the lesson. Memorizing the key verses of Scripture is one of the most effective ways to assimilate the Word of God as an aid to Christian growth.

In each lesson you will be instructed to read important Scripture passages. Some will be for general reading; most will be about the topic to be studied. By doing this reading you will become acquainted with many important portions of the Bible. As you read, select your favorite verse and add it to the verses already listed to be memorized.

Casual Bible reading uncovers valuable spiritual facts that lie near the surface. But to understand the deeper truths requires study. Often the difference between reading and study is a pen. Every lesson in this Handbook contains a study of important topics with an opportunity for you to record your answers to the questions. We recommend that you spend a minimum of 30 minutes each day, preferably in the morning, in Bible study, meditation and prayer.

MEMORIZATION

The memory verses have been provided to help you in your walk with Christ. As you study, you will find that by "binding certain truths on the table of your heart" you will be enabled to meet each situation as it arises. "Wherewithal shall a young man cleanse his way? By taking heed thereto according to Thy Word" (Psalm 119:9).

It is suggested that you learn each verse in connection with the corresponding lesson of the first step by writing it out on a small card. Cards for memorization can be obtained from any bookstore or printshop or they can be made by cutting down filing cards.

Retain the verses, reviewing daily, and then as you begin the next step, start memorizing these verses in the same way. When you have finished that step, continue with the following step, writing out each verse. Remember, a regular review and systematic method are essential in your daily walk.

The importance of memorizing as a means of study cannot be overemphasized. The Lord has commanded that we learn His Word. Proverbs 7:1-3 says, "My son, keep my words, and lay up my commandments with thee. Keep my commandments and live; and my law as the apple of thine eye. Bind them upon thy fingers, write them upon the table of thine heart."

As you memorize, you will experience some of the joy, victory and power which the memorized Word gives to the Christian's walk. Strive diligently to finish all the studies in the Handbook, and later, as you develop your own Bible study, continue to have a systematic method of memorization of God's Word.

HOW TO STUDY THE LESSONS

Plan a specific time and place in which to work on these studies. Make an appointment with God, then keep it.

Be sure you have a pen or pencil and your Bible along with this Handbook.

Begin with prayer for God's wisdom.

Read over the entire lesson.

Meditate on the Objective to determine how it will fit into your particular circumstances or life.

Commit the suggested verse or verses to memory.

Read the suggested Scripture passages.

Proceed to the Bible Study, trusting God to use it to teach you. Work carefully and prayerfully, thinking through the questions, answering each as completely as possible.

When you come to the Life Application section, be honest with yourself as you answer the questions and apply them to your own life.

Continuing in an attitude of prayer, read through the lesson again and re-evaluate your Life Application answers. Do they need changing? Or adjusting? Review the memory work. Consider the Objective again and determine if it has been accomplished. If not, what do you need to do?

Close with a prayer of thanksgiving, and with one of commitment, surrender, or whatever is necessary to bring you to the point of growth which God has revealed to you that you are now ready for.

As you complete each of the 11 steps, spend a little extra time on the Recap to make sure you understand every lesson thoroughly. If you don't, go back, ask God for wisdom again and go through whatever lesson(s) you need, repeating until you do understand and are able to appropriate the truths for yourself.

These studies are not intended as a complete development of Christian beliefs. However, a careful study of the material will give you, with God's help, a sufficient understanding of how you may know and appropriate God's plan for your life. If fully appropriated, the spiritual truths contained here will assure you of the full and abundant life which Jesus promised in John 10:10.

The rate of speed with which you complete the studies in the book is entirely up to you, but we encourage you not to go too fast. Give yourself time to think about the lessons, meditate on them and absorb the truths presented. Allow them to become a part of your life. Spend time in prayer with your Lord and enjoy His presence. Give God a chance to speak to you, and let the Holy Spirit teach you.

SUMMARY OF THE BOOKS OF THE BIBLE

OLD TESTAMENT

"The Old Testament was written to create an anticipation of, and pave the way for the coming of Christ. It is the story of the Hebrew nation, largely dealing with events and exigencies of its own time. But all through the story there runs unceasing expectance of the coming of ONE MAJESTIC PERSON, who will rule and do a great and wonderful work in the whole world. This person, long before He arrived, came to be known as the MESSIAH. The predictions of His coming constitute the Messianic strain of the Old Testament. They form the golden thread extending through, and binding together, its many and diverse books into one amazing unity" (*Bible Handbook*, Halley, Henry H., page 346).

THE PENTATEUCH is the Greek word for the first five books of the Old Testament, written by Moses, also called "the Law."

Genesis means "book of beginnings." It contains the story of the creation of the world, the fall of man, the flood, the calling out of Abraham and the formation of the Hebrew nation. The main characters are Adam, Noah, Abraham, Isaac, Jacob and Joseph.

Exodus means "going out." It contains the Egyptian bondage of the Hebrews, their deliverance through Moses, the giving of the Law and the building of the tabernacle.

Leviticus means "pertaining to Levites." That is, the book contains the system of laws administered by the Levitical Priesthood under which the Hebrew nation lived. It is a book full of rules and regulations.

Numbers means "numbering," and it contains the numbering of the Hebrews (about 2 million people). They were placed into tribes and were given specific tasks. It also contains the story of their wanderings in the wilderness (for 40 years) because of the unbelief that God would cast out the heathen people so that they could enter the "promised land."

Deuteronomy means "this is the copy (or repetition) of the law." It consists of the parting counsels of Moses delivered to the Jews in view of their impending entrance upon their covenanted possession, the promised land. During the 40 years of wilderness wanderings, a new generation of people had arisen. They, along with Joshua and Caleb (of the past generation), were the only ones allowed to enter the land (Deuteronomy 1:21-39).

The HISTORICAL BOOKS tell of the rise and fall of the Commonwealth of Israel.

Joshua means "Jehovah saves." It contains the conquest of Canaan (the promised land), the crossing of the Jordan, the fall of Jericho, the victories over the Canaanites, the sun made to stand still and the tribes settled in the land.

Judges contains the theme "every man did that which was right in his own eyes." There was no king, no system of government, no monarchy. The Israelites were to live in the land and serve God, but they failed. The country was infiltrated with heathen people and idolatry abounded.

Ruth is the story of the faithfulness and love of a woman. Its purpose: 1) to show that during times of apostasy (time of the judges) there were individuals serving God; 2) to show the founding of the Messianic family; 3) to illustrate the principle of redemption.

1 Samuel presents the personal history of Samuel, last of the Judges. It also contains the establishment of a monarchy under Saul, the failure of Saul and the introduction of David.

2 Samuel marks the restoration of order through the enthroning of God's king, David. God established the great Davidic Covenant out of which the eternal kingdom of the Messiah was to come.

1 Kings contains the reign of Solomon, the building of the temple and the division of the kingdom under Rehoboam and Jeroboam. (Rehoboam was head of the Southern Kingdom, commonly called Judah, and its main center was Jerusalem. Jeroboam was head of the Northern Kingdom, commonly called Israel, and its main center was Samaria.)

2 Kings contains the story of the two kingdoms and their final captivity. The Southern Kingdom (Judah) was conquered and brought into captivity by Babylon. The Northern Kingdom (Israel) was conquered and brought into captivity by Assyria.

1 Chronicles contains the reign of David. It is told from a religious point of view.

2 Chronicles contains the reign of Solomon, and the reigns of Rehoboam, Jeroboam and other kings who followed. It is told from a religious point of view.

Ezra is the story of the return of a Jewish remnant to Jerusalem, the restoration of law and ritual, and the rebuilding of the temple.

Nehemiah is the story of the rebuilding of the walls of Jerusalem and the restoration of civil authority.

Esther was a Jewess who became queen of Persia. Though a remnant had returned to Jerusalem, the majority of the nation had preferred to remain under the Persian rule. This book is the story of how Esther, the queen (through the providence of God), kept the Jewish nation from being exterminated.

The POETICAL BOOKS are the books of the human experiences of the people of God under the various exercises of earthly life.

Job is in the form of a dramatic poem. It is probably the oldest of the books of the Old Testament and deals with the problem: "Why do the godly suffer?"

Psalms is the Hebrew hymnbook. The great themes of the Psalms are: The Messiah, Jehovah, the Law, Creation, the future of Israel and the exercises of the renewed heart in suffering, in joy, in perplexity. The Psalms were to be used in private and public worship.

Proverbs consists of wise sayings about life, especially emphasizing righteousness and the fear of God.

Ecclesiastes is the book of man's reasonings about life and the vanity of it without God.

Song of Solomon is the story of the love of a bride and a bridegroom, symbolic of the love of Christ for the church.

PROPHETICAL BOOKS: Prophets were men raised up of God in times of apostasy. They were primarily revivalists and patriots, speaking on behalf of God to the heart and conscience of the nation. The prophetic messages have a twofold character: first, that which was local and for the prophet's time; second, that which was predictive of the divine purpose in the future.

Major Prophets — so called because of the size of the books:

Isaiah is considered to be "the Prince of the Old Testament prophets." He was thoroughly imbued with the idea that his nation was to be a Messianic Nation to the world. He prophesied to Judah, the Southern Kingdom.

Jeremiah's ministry extended over the last 40 years of the kingdom of Judah, the destruction of Jerusalem and the deportation of its inhabitants to Babylon. His orders constitute a stern warning to Judah to abandon idolatry and apostasy to escape the inevitable consequence of Babylonian captivity.

Lamentations consists of five poems lamenting the destruction of Jerusalem at the time of the Babylonian captivity. It was written by Jeremiah.

Ezekiel prophesied during the Babylonian captivity. His

mission was to instruct the Israelites that God was just in permitting the captivity of His people, and that eventually the nation would be restored.

Daniel prophesied during the Babylonian captivity. His book is indispensable to New Testament prophecy, the themes of which are: the apostasy of the church, the great tribulation, the return of Christ, the resurrections, and the judgments. His vision sweeps the whole course of Gentile world-rule to its end in catastrophe, and to the setting up of the Messianic kingdom.

Minor Prophets — so called because the books are shorter:

Hosea was a prophet to the Northern Kingdom (Israel) at the same time Isaiah was prophesying to the Southern Kingdom. His book is the prophecy of God's unchanging love for Israel; and Israel is pictured as an adulterous wife, shortly to be put away, but eventually to be purified and restored.

Joel was a prophet to the Southern Kingdom. He warns the nation to repent in the light of approaching judgment. He also stirs up the faithful among the people to believe the promises of God involving coming salvation and destruction of the enemies of God's Kingdom.

Amos prophesied to the Northern Kingdom when it was at its height. Fiery denunciation of luxurious living and the idolatry and moral depravity of Israel were the subjects of his messages.

Obadiah is a denunciation of the Edomites (bitter enemies of the Jews), predicting their forthcoming decimation.

Jonah was a prophet called of God to testify to Nineveh, the capital of the Assyrian Empire. The book teaches that God's grace goes beyond His chosen people, and that it reaches out to embrace the heathen nations.

Micah was a message to both Israel and Judah, stressing their sins, their destruction and their restoration.

Nahum was a message of judgment to Nineveh, predicting its destruction. Jonah's was a message of mercy; Nahum's, a message of doom. Together they illustrate God's way of dealing with nations; extending grace, but punishing continued sin by judgment.

Habakkuk was a prophet who was more concerned that the holiness of Jehovah should be vindicated than that Israel should escape judgment. It is written on the eve of the Babylonian captivity.

Zephaniah prophesied right before the Babylonian captivity. He told of the judgments which were to come;

captivity for Israel and eventually the judgment of nations, followed by the blessings of the kingdom and the Messiah.

Haggai prophesied when the remnant of Jews returned to Jerusalem after 70 years of captivity. The theme of his message is the building of the unfinished temple.

Zechariah was a prophet to the remnant which returned after the 70 years. Much of his message deals with the first and second comings of the Messiah.

Malachi is the last of the prophets to the restored remnant. He also predicts both comings of the Messiah and the love of God for His disobedient people.

THE NEW TESTAMENT

THE FOUR GOSPELS

The four Gospels, Matthew, Mark, Luke and John, record the eternal being, human ancestry, birth, death, resurrection and ascension of Jesus the Christ, Son of God and Son of Man. They reveal incidents of His life and incidents from His words and works. Taken together, they set forth, not a biography, but a personality. These Gospels, though designedly incomplete as a story, are devinely perfect as a revelation from God, and as such their greatest importance is to set forth a person, Jesus Christ, that the world may trust in Him. These narratives can be compared to the evangelist, who seldom seeks to describe Christ, but rather to make Him known.

Although God Himself inspired every word, He permitted the personality of each human writer to be reflected. They told the same story, but each in his own way. That accounts for the variation in certain incidents recorded. There is no cause for the accusation of contradictions, but rather many writers giving testimony provide much more authority to what is written and prove beyond doubt that there was never any collusion among them.

The Gospel of Matthew, written by Matthew, a Jew of Galilee and a hated tax-collector under the Roman government, was written for the Jews to prove that Christ was their promised King and the fulfillment of Old Testament prophecies of a coming Messiah.

The Gospel of Mark, written by John Mark (called either name), who was an associate of the apostles and mentioned in the writings of Paul and Luke. This Gospel sets forth Jesus as the mighty worker, records many miracles He performed and seems directed to the Gentile reader. The emphasis here is on what Christ did rather than the things He said, and shows Jesus as the great Conqueror, as well as Servant of the Lord.

The Gospel of Luke depicts Him as the Son of Man as well as the divine Savior. The style is orderly and classical, appealing to the Greek love for beauty, culture and philosophy. Luke, called the "beloved physician" by Paul, is the author.

The Gospel of John, written by the most intimate personal friend of Jesus, the apostle John, places great emphasis on Christ as the Son of God, co-equal with the Father and Holy Spirit as deity. The content is chiefly Jesus' discourses and conversations. The principal words are "believe" and "life."

EARLY CHURCH HISTORY

The Acts of the Apostles — is one of the most important books in the whole New Testament, because God makes it clear to man how His work is to be carried forth in the power of the Holy Spirit. With the promised coming of Pentecost and the fulfillment of God's Word to men, the apostles and every phase of their ministry are transformed by a new authority and boldness. Christ had said, "I will pray to the Father, and He shall give you another Comforter, that He may abide with you forever" (John 14:16). Meak, fearful men, whose own handicaps often marred the work of God, are transformed into true disciples, full of wisdom and power given at the coming of the Holy Spirit.

In addition to the descent of the Holy Spirit at Pentecost (Acts 2), other major themes include the ascension and promised return of the Lord Jesus; Peter's use of the keys to the kingdom; the conversion and powerful ministry of the apostle Paul; the beginnings of the true church as the body of Christ and the calling out of the people for the Lord; the taking of the gospel to the Gentiles in the house of Cornelius and their reception of the Holy Spirit; and the conversion of thousands to Christ and their careful establishment in the faith — all accomplished in the power of the Spirit.

The writer does not name himself, but this book, along with the Gospel of Luke, is accepted as the work of Luke.

THE EPISTLES OF PAUL

Key thoughts of these Epistles:

Romans — the nature of Christ's work, the whole body of redemptive truth and full doctrines of grace.

1 and 2 Corinthians — Christian conduct and answers to disorders in the churches; Paul's vindication of his apostleship.

Galatians — the complete gospel and salvation by grace

alone, not dependent upon human obedience to the law. Pure grace!

Ephesians — the unity of the church; the believer's position; the truth concerning the body of Christ and the walk according to one's position in Christ.

Philippians — a missionary epistle and Christian experience within the believer.

Colossians — the deity of Jesus Christ and Paul's answer to two major problems: legalism and false mysticism.

1 and 2 Thessalonians — the second coming of Christ and the confirmation of young disciples.

1 and 2 Timothy — church order, sound faith and discipline; the personal walk and testimony of the believer.

Titus — the divine order of the local churches, especially dealing with the churches of Crete.

Philemon — the conversion of a runaway slave, Onesimus, and the teaching of practical righteousness, brotherhood and love.

OTHER EPISTLES

Key thoughts of these Epistles:

Hebrews — Christ, the Mediator of a New Covenant; contrasting the good things of Judaism and the better things of Christ, thus confirming Jewish Christians; a great book of doctrine.

James — the necessity of good works to show forth a living faith; some patterns of Christian conduct.

1 and 2 Peter — the foundation of the Christian faith with emphasis on the atonement; encouragements for a persecuted church; prediction of apostasy.

1, 2, 3 John — Love, caution against false teachers and those who reject John's authority.

Jude — imminent apostasy and how to detect and deal with it.

ROPHECY

Revelation — the final triumph of Jesus Christ as the complete fulfillment to every individual and nation; the close of the age and the coming glory of God in its full revelation; the seven churches, the tribulation, the second advent, the doom of those who reject Christ and the ultimate reward for those who do receive Him; heaven and eternity with God.

Review

Old Testament

Historical — 17 books — Rise and fall of the Hebrew Nation.

Poetical — 5 books — Literature of the Nation's Golden Age.

Prophetic — 17 books — Literature of the Nation's Dark Days.

New Testament

Gospels — 4 books — The MAN whom the Nation produced.

Acts — 1 book — His reign among all nations begins.

Epistles — 21 books — His teaching and principles.

Revelation — 1 book — Forecast of His universal dominion.

The Uniqueness of Jesus

THE UNIQUENESS OF JESUS CHRIST

Who, in your opinion, is the most outstanding personality of all time?

I once directed some similar questions to a brilliant young medical student. He was from another land, and had been a devout follower of one of the great Eastern religions. My first questions were: "John, who in your opinion is the greatest leader that the world has ever known? Who has done the most good for mankind?" After a moment of hesitation, John replied, 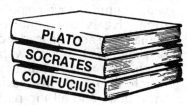 "I am sure that Jesus of Nazareth has done more good than anyone who has ever lived. I would say that He is the greatest leader."

Unique Personality

Then I asked, "Who do you think is the greatest teacher?" No doubt he thought of Socrates, Aristotle, Plato, Confucius and the other great philosophers of ancient and modern times. But he answered, "The greatest teacher is Jesus of Nazareth."

Finally I asked, "John, in your opinion, who has lived the most holy life of anyone who has ever lived?" To this question his reply was immediate. Obviously the world knows and he knew that in all recorded history, there has never been anyone like Jesus of Nazareth.

Visit any part of the world today and talk to adherents of any religion. No matter how devout they may be or how committed to their particular religion, if they know anything of the facts, they, too, will have to acknowledge that there has never been a man like Jesus of Nazareth. He is the unique personality of all time.

Worldwide Influence

He is the One who has changed the whole course of history. Even the date on your morning newspaper gives witness to the

27

fact that Jesus of Nazareth, the Christ, lived on this earth nearly two thousand years ago. "B.C." means "before Christ";"A.D.," *anno domini*, is the Latin phrase meaning, "in the year of our Lord."

Trace the life and influence of Jesus Christ and you will observe that His message always effects great changes in the lives of people and nations. History is HIS STORY — the story of the life of one man. Remove Jesus of Nazareth from history, and it would be a completely different story.

One writer described Jesus' influence in this way: "Nineteen wide centuries have come and gone and today He is the centerpiece of the human race and the leader of the column of progress. I am far within the mark when I say that all the armies that ever marched and all the navies that ever were built, and all the parliaments that ever have sat, and all the kings that ever reigned put together have not affected the life of man upon this earth as power-fully as has that one solitary life, Jesus of Nazareth."

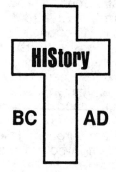

Though Jesus has influenced the whole world, I would call your attention especially to the effect He has had on society's view toward women. Aristotle said, "Society would be completely disorganized if women were on an equality with their husbands, just as it would be if slaves were on an equality with their masters." Socrates asked fellow Athenians, "To whom do you talk less than to your wife?" Plato recommended that women be held in common by men and that their children should be cared for by the state.

But Christ put an end to all of this. The New Testament declares that in Christ there is neither male nor female, slave nor free. Wherever Christ has gone, the sacredness of marriage, women's rights and suffrage have been acknowledged; institutions of higher learning have been established; child labor laws have been enacted; slavery has been abolished; and a multitude of other changes have been made for the good of mankind.

Personal Influence

It has been my privilege to visit hundreds of campuses where I have talked to thousands of college men and women about Jesus of Nazareth. Naturally, I have met professors and students alike who are militantly antagonistic toward Christ. Some of them contend that Jesus Christ is just a myth or that He is a great man and nothing more.

One such skeptic was Dr. Cyril E. M. Joad, one of the world's greatest philosophers, who was for years head of the Philosophy Department at the University of London. Dr. Joad and his colleagues, Julian Huxley, Bertrand Russell and H. G. Wells, have probably done more to undermine the faith of the collegiate world of the last generation than has any other one group. Dr. Joad believed that Jesus was only a man, and that God was a part of the universe. Should the universe be destroyed, he taught, God would also be destroyed. He subscribed to what is known as the "life-force philosophy" of Shaw. Dr. Joad believed that there is no such thing as sin, that man was destined for a Utopia. With sufficient time, he felt that man would have heaven on earth. Dr. Joad was militant in his antagonism against Christianity and wrote many books which have made a great impact upon the atheistic thinking of the student world during the last generation.

In 1948, the magazine section of the *Los Angeles Times* carried a picture of that venerable old scholar, and with it a statement concerning the dramatic change that had taken place in his life. It told how for many years he had been antagonistic toward Christianity. He had once denied sin, but now he had come to believe that sin was a reality. Two world wars and the imminence of another had demonstrated conclusively to him that man was indeed sinful. Now he believed that the only explanation for sin was found in the Word of God, and the only solution was found in the cross of Jesus Christ. Before his death, Dr. Joad became a zealous follower of the Savior.

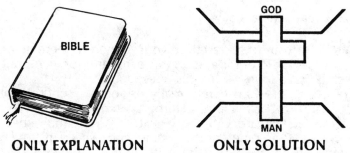

ONLY EXPLANATION   **ONLY SOLUTION**

Another example is Lew Wallace, a famous general and a literary genius. He and his friend, Robert Ingersoll, covenanted together to write a book that would forever destroy the myth of Christianity. Mr. Wallace tells how for two years he studied in the leading libraries of Europe and America, seeking information that would enable him to write the book that would destroy Christianity. While writing the second chapter of his volume, he found himself on his knees crying out to Jesus saying, "My Lord, and my God." The evidence for the deity of Christ was overwhelmingly conclusive. He could no longer deny that Jesus Christ was the Son of God. The One whom he had determined to expose as a fraud had captured him. Later Lew Wallace wrote *Ben Hur*, probably the greatest novel ever written concerning the times of Christ.

Another confirmed skeptic was the late C. S. Lewis, professor at Oxford University. For years he was an agnostic who denied the deity of Christ. Later he became a devout follower of Christ and wrote many outstanding books advocating his belief in Him as Savior. In his famous book, *The Case for Christianity*, he makes this statement: "A man who was merely a man and said the sort of things Jesus said, wouldn't be a great moral teacher. He would either be a lunatic on the level with a man who says he's a poached egg — or else he would be the devil of hell; you must take your choice. Either this was, and is, the Son of God, or else a madman or something worse. You can shut Him up for a demon; or you can fall at His feet and call Him Lord and God. But don't come up with any patronizing nonsense about His being a great moral teacher. He hasn't left that alternative open to us."

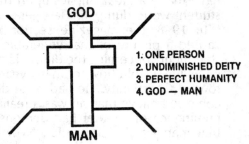

GOD

MAN

1. ONE PERSON
2. UNDIMINISHED DEITY
3. PERFECT HUMANITY
4. GOD — MAN

What Great Scholars Say

Who is Jesus of Nazareth to you? A myth? A mere man? Or the Son of God? Your life upon this earth and for all eternity is affected by your answer to this question.

Some ask, "Is Christianity really established upon positive historical facts?" Dr. Clifford Herbert Moore, for many years a professor at Harvard University, states, "Christianity knew its Savior and Redeemer not as some god whose history was contained in a mythical faith, with rude, primitive and even offensive elements. The Christian's faith is founded on positive, historical and acceptable facts."

A long list could be made of such outstanding scholars who are devout followers of Christ. For example, Dr. William Lyon Phelps, who was a professor at Yale University for 40 years and was one of the most distinguished professors in the history of our country, expressed his confidence in the historical evidence concerning the deity of the Lord Jesus Christ and regularly shared his personal faith in Christ as Savior.

But some of the world's greatest scholars do not believe that Jesus is the Son of God, our Savior. I am appalled when I talk about Christ to many of these men of learning, for I discover that nearly always they are ignorant of the basic truths of the gospel. Have you ever read any of the writings of Ingersoll, Thomas Paine and other well-known skeptics? You would be amazed to discover that, invariably, these men are taking issue with something that they do not fully understand. They have erected straw men, labeled them Christianity, and have then proceeded to destroy their own creations.

I have yet to meet a person who has honestly considered the overwhelming evidence concerning Jesus of Nazareth who does not admit that He is the Son of God. As I have said, I meet some who do not believe He is the Son of God. But as we have talked and reasoned together, they have been honest in confessing, "I have not taken the time to read the Bible or to consider the historical facts concerning Jesus." Their resentment has been based upon an unfortunate childhood experience, upon the inconsistency of some Christian or perhaps upon the influence of a college professor; but always they have admitted that they have not honestly considered the person of Jesus Christ and His claims on their lives.

Concerning Jesus of Nazareth Paul says in Colossians 1:15-20, "And He (Christ) is the image of the invisible God, the first-born of all creation. For in Him all things were created, both in heaven and on earth, visible

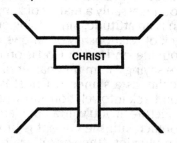

and invisible. . . . For it was the Father's good pleasure for all the fullness to dwell in Him, and through Him to reconcile all things to Himself, having made peace through the blood of His cross; through Him, I say, whether things on earth or things in heaven." In Hebrews 1:1, 2 we are told, "God, after He spoke long ago to the fathers in the prophets in many portions and in many ways, in these last days has spoken to us in His Son, whom He appointed heir of all things, through whom also He made the world." In Colossians 2:3 Paul states, "In whom (Christ) are hidden all the treasures of wisdom and knowledge."

There are many things that Jesus can do for us that no one

else can do, but I want to concentrate on four specific things. First of all, He is the only one who can *pardon* man from his sin. Second, He alone can give *purpose* for life. Third, only He can give *peace* to a troubled heart. Finally, Jesus alone can give us *power* to live an abundant life.

Pardons Sin

The Bible tells us that God is a *holy* God and that man is *sinful*. There is a great gulf between the two and man cannot bridge this gulf. The Bible says that all have sinned and come short of the glory of God. The wages of sin is death — eternal separation from God; but the gift of God is eternal life through Jesus Christ our Lord. Because man is sinful, he cannot bridge this gulf between himself and God, no matter how good he is. God bridges the chasm to man through His Son, Jesus Christ. The Scripture says, "For God so loved the world that He gave His only begotton Son, that whoever believes in Him should not perish, but have eternal life" (John 3:16).

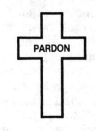

Now, let us define our terms. What do we mean by sin? Sin is not necessarily a matter of lying, stealing or immorality. Basically sin is an attitude. Sin is going one's own independent way. It is a lack of relationship or fellowship with God. There is a throne in your life, and either God is on that throne or you are on it. If you are saying, "I am the master of my life, I will do as I please," you qualify as a sinner. If Christ is on that throne, He has brought you back into relationship with Himself.

Picture, if you will, a floor lamp. Pull the plug out of the socket; contact with the current is broken, and the light goes out. Push the plug into the socket again; the light goes on. The current is constant, the variable is the plug. Man can be compared with that plug. Because we do not have fellowship with God, we walk in darkness. We have chosen to go our own way — we are guilty of sin.

Now, what is God's provision? In the Old Testament, the Israelites brought their sacrifices to the priest — the lamb, the dove and the bullock. These animals had to be perfect, without spot or blemish — the best in the flock. The sin of the one making the sacrifice was transferred to the innocent lamb. The animal was slain, the blood was sprinkled by the priest on the altar as a temporary covering for his sins. This pictured the coming of God's one special lamb, whose blood would not temporarily cover man's sins, but would wash them away forever. God sent His only Son, the Lamb of God, without spot or blemish, to give His life, to shed His blood upon the cross for the forgiveness of our sins. "Without the shedding of blood," we are told in the Scriptures, "there is no forgiveness" (Hebrews 9:22).

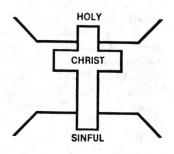

As one studies the most popular religions of the world, he becomes aware that no provision is made for the forgiveness of sin apart from the cross of Jesus Christ. Basically most religions embrace the philosophy of good works as a means to salvation. Man subscribes to the concept that if his good works outweigh his bad works, he will go to heaven. But if his bad works outweigh his good works, he will go to hell, if there is a hell. Of course, he does not know until this life is over whether he will go to heaven or to hell. What a tragedy! How inadequate is such a religion or philosophy. God has promised that we can know Him, and have fellowship with Him *now* and for all eternity, through His Son, the Lord Jesus Christ.

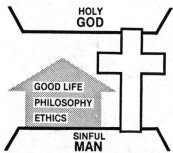

After I had finished speaking at a midwestern university campus, a group of students remained to learn how they could become Christians. Among them was a young Hindu lad from India who was pacing up and down, very angry and impatient. As we talked he said, "I resent you Christians. I resent the arrogance with which you say that you have the only way to God. I believe that Christianity is *one* way, but only one way. Hinduism is another. Buddhism, Shintoism and others are all ways to God."

I called his attention to the writings of the great Hindu leader Mahatma Gandhi, who, for all of his devotion to his religion, states in his autobiography, "It is a constant torture to me that I am still so far from Him whom I know to be my very life and being. I know it is my own wretchedness and wickedness that keep me from Him." This gifted young man said that he had once believed that Gandhi was God but, of course, he no longer believed this. In addition to being devout, he was unusually brilliant. He was completing his double doctorate — a doctorate in physics and a doctorate in chemistry. As we talked together, his anger began to subside, and he began to see that Christianity *is* different. He saw that it was not just another man-made religion or philosophy, but that it made provision for man's basic need, which is forgiveness of sin. He admitted also that he had not found the answer to his needs, though he was a devout follower of his religion, diligent in the reading of the sacred Hindu writings, and faithful in his times of prayer and all the ritual of his faith. He had to confess that he had never found God. I called his attention to the difference in the lives of his Christian friends. He admitted that they had something that he did not possess. It was obvious that that "something" was the living Savior who had come to live within them and had forgiven them of their sins.

For nearly an hour we discussed the difference between Christianity and the religions of the world. Take Buddha out of Buddhism, Mohammed out of Islam, and in like manner the founders of the various religions out of their religious systems, and little would be changed. But take Christ out of Christianity and there would be nothing left.

Finally, the light came on. Now this young Hindu understood the great truth of pardon for sin through our Savior's sacrifice on the cross. Quietly he bowed his head. This dear young scholar who had sought after God with all of his heart now prayed that Jesus of Nazareth, the risen, living Son of God, would come into his heart, would pardon his sin and become his Lord and Master. The Bible says, "There is no other name under heaven that has been given among men, by which we must be saved" (Acts 4:12). Only Jesus can pardon sin.

PURPOSE

Gives Purpose

Not only is Jesus of Nazareth unique as the only one who can *pardon* our sins, but He is also unique as the only one who gives *purpose, peace* and *power* to life.

Let us consider *purpose.* You will remember, according to the Bible, in Colossians 1:16, it was through the Son that God made the whole universe, and to the Son He has said that all creation shall ultimately belong. One can readily see that God has created everything for a purpose. There is order, system and design to the whole creation.

Man is the highest expression of God's creation. Man is the only part of creation with intelligence. God created man with a free will, with a right of choice. He can say "yes" or "no" to God, and for the most part man has chosen to say "no." Those who have said "no" have never discovered God's purpose for their lives.

No building contractor would think of constructing a beautiful building without consulting the blueprint of the architect, the designer. How can we be so foolish as to try to build our lives without first consulting the great architect of life, the One who created us for a wonderful purpose? The Bible says, "The steps of a man are established by the Lord" (Psalm 37:23). "And we know that God causes all things to work together for good to those who love God, to those who are called according to His purpose" (Romans 8:28).

There are great benefits to be derived from being where God wants you to be and doing what God wants you to do. God does not stand over us with a big stick. Rather, He has established His laws to govern the whole of creation and, if we violate these laws, we must pay the consequences; even as a man who violates the law of gravity must pay the consequences, or the man who violates the laws of traffic must pay the penalty. Failure to adhere to the laws of traffic endangers not only the life of the one who violates the law, but also the lives of others. We *do not break God's laws — they break us.*

Take, for example, the matter of marriage. The Bureau of the Census reported in 1979 that 1,170 out of each 2,359 marriages in this country end in divorce.* That's nearly one out of two! That one/two ratio was corroborated by a consumer report in the June 22, 1981 issue of *U.S. News and World Report* (page 12).

Yet it is a well-established fact that a Christian husband and wife who daily read the Bible and pray together will experience a remarkably high degree of stability in their marriage.

Why the great contrast? Jesus Christ makes the difference. He brings real purpose to marriage. With these facts before us, who would dare take the gamble of marriage without Christ? You say, "I don't understand. How can Christ make such a great difference?" Simply in this way: If you are on the throne of your life, your ego and the ego of the one whom you marry will war against one another. Friction is inevitable. However, if Christ is on the throne of the lives of both husband and wife, He will not war against Himself and there will be peace. Discord will turn to harmony and hate will turn to love. Many times I have had the

---

* Statistical Abstract of the United States, U.S. Department of Commerce.

privilege of kneeling in prayer with men and women who have been on the verge of divorce. Their lives were in shambles, their homes places of discord and friction. But as they have given their lives to Jesus Christ, harmony, peace and love have come into their homes and hearts. Of course, the same truth applies to individuals as well, for no man is complete without Christ.

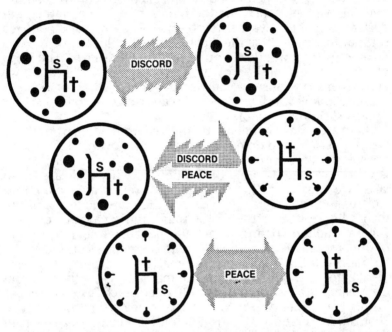

I have found through the years that people who know Jesus Christ have a purpose for life. Those who do not know Him are like a ship upon a rough sea without rudder and without sail, drifting with the tide. No matter how brilliant you might be or how successful as an athlete, as a student, as a business or a professional person, unless you know Jesus Christ, you will never know real purpose in life. God has made us for Himself, and, as St. Augustine said centuries ago, "Thou has made us for Thyself, O God, and our hearts are restless until they find their rest in Thee."

H. G. Wells, famous historian and philosopher, said at the age of 61: "I have no peace. All life is at the end of its tether." The poet Lord Byron said, "My days are in the yellow leaf, the flowers and fruits of life are gone, the worm and the canker, and the grief are mine alone." Thoreau, great literary genius, said, "Most men live lives of quiet desperation." Ralph Barton, one of the top cartoonists of the nation, left this note pinned to his pillow before he took his life: "I have had few difficulties, many friends, great successes; I have gone from wife to wife, and from house to house, visited great countries of the world, but I am fed up with inventing devices to fill up 24 hours of the day." Pascal, French physicist and philosopher, put it this way, "There is a God-shaped vacuum in the heart of every man which only God can fill through His Son, Jesus Christ."

Dare I say that there is a vacuum in your life? I do not know you. But in all honesty, in the quiet of your own heart, if you do not know Jesus Christ, you are saying today, "Yes, there is a vacuum; I am not satisfied with my life." And you never will be until you invite Christ to show you the very purpose for which He created you. There is no one else who ever lived who can do this — no religion, no philosophy, no man. Jesus said, "I am the way, and the truth, and the life; no one comes to the Father, but through Me" (John 14:6). As you are introduced to Him, He will show you that purpose for which He created you.

Gives Peace

Jesus alone can *pardon* sin. Jesus alone can give *purpose* to life. Third, Jesus of Nazareth is the only One who can give you *peace*. He is the Prince of Peace. There will never be peace in

the individual heart or at the peace tables of the world until the Prince of Peace reigns supreme in the hearts of men. In John 14:27, Jesus says, "Peace I leave with you; My peace I give to you; not as the world gives, do I give to you. Let not your heart be troubled, nor let it be fearful." In Matthew 11:28, He says, "Come to Me, all who are weary and heavy laden, and I will give you rest."

Perhaps you are now experiencing fears and frustrations in your life. Perhaps you are worried about your grades, your social life, your finances, problems in your home. You say, "Of course. Everyone has these problems." Yes, and the Christian is not exempt. Becoming a Christian does not mean that you will suddenly be ushered into a utopian situation, but *rather* you will have One with you who said, "Peace, be still; lo, I am with you always, even unto the end of the world, upon every occasion and at all times I am with you. I will never leave you, nor forsake you. My peace I give you."

Some time ago I was asked to be one of the speakers at an International Christian Leadership Conference in Washington, D. C. On this occasion I was speaking at a conference of which the famous Presidential Prayer Breakfast is a part. A young naval commander, who was representing the Pentagon at the breakfast, was an old fraternity brother and debate colleague of mine during my college days. He sought me out and we talked together. He told me the story of a tragedy that had recently taken place in his life through the loss of a child. He asked if I would come and talk with him and his dear wife.

As we talked together that evening, they both invited Jesus Christ to be their Savior and Lord. As Christ came into their lives, they experienced a wonderful peace. Their lives were changed. The following year I was invited to return to Washington where again I had the privilege of participating in the International Christian Leadership program. Again my commander friend was present, representing the Pentagon. Tragedy of tragedies, he told me that shortly after my previous visit, another of their children became ill. She had cancer of the nervous system, which resulted in her death. I shall never forget that day as Frank and I talked together. With a warm, understanding smile, he said, "Though I do not understand it, as dearly as we loved our little child and as much as we hated to see her go, during the time of her illness and after she was gone, the presence of the Lord Jesus Christ was so real! We do not understand it, but through it all we had a peace that passes all knowledge."

Gives Power

Heartache and sorrow will come into your life, too, but Christ, the Prince of Peace, waits to sit upon the throne of your life and to give you His *pardon*, His *purpose* and His *peace*. Yet even pardon, purpose, and peace are not all that Christ can give, for Jesus of Nazareth is the only One who can give you *power* to live a new life.

Frequently men and women will say to me, "I would like to become a Christian, but if I do, I am sure that I will never be able to live the life. You don't know the mistakes that I have made, the resentments that I have, the tendencies to sin, the immorality, the heavy drinking, the cruel tongue and many, many other problems. I do not believe I could live the Christian life."

But as these people have given their lives to Christ, they have discovered that the Christian life is a supernatural life. You and I *cannot* live it, no matter how good we are. Jesus Christ literally comes to live within us, and He lives His life *in* and *through* us.

Therefore, it is no longer what we do, but what *He* does, because He is the One who provides the power and we are merely the instruments through which He releases that power.

This is what Jesus taught a man named Nicodemus who came to see Him one night (John 3:1-21). Nicodemus was a ruler of the Jews. He was a good, moral and ethical religious leader. He asked Christ, "Rabbi, (meaning Teacher), we know that you have come from God as a teacher; for no one can do these signs that you do unless God is with him."

Jesus said to Nicodemus, "Truly, truly, I say to you, unless one is born again, he cannot see the kingdom of God." Nicodemus did not know what He meant. He asked if he must enter his mother's womb the second time to be born. Jesus replied, in essence, "No, you are born once in the flesh, but in order to enter the kingdom of God you must be born of the Spirit." You see, we are born with a physical body to live on a physical plane. But the kingdom of God is a spiritual kingdom and God is a spiritual being. If we are to have fellowship with Him, we must become spiritual creatures.

Picture a caterpillar crawling in the dirt. It is just an ugly, hairy worm. If you could communicate with this caterpillar, you might say, "Why do you crawl in the dirt? Why don't you fly like the butterfly?" No doubt it would reply, "It is impossible for me to fly for I am earthbound; I can only crawl in the dust." Then you might suggest, "Let us perform an operation. We will attach some butterfly wings to your body." But that would do no good. Then you could say, "Why don't you take a course in aviation? Then you will be able to fly. But all this is to no avail.

So it is with people who try to become Christians by good works, such as good conduct, church attendance, reading the Bible, praying, etc — rather than the way of the new birth, as Jesus commanded.

One day the caterpillar weaves about its body a cocoon, and later, out of that cocoon, emerges a beautiful butterfly. We do not understand fully what has taken place. We only know that where once a worm crawled in the dust, now a butterfly soars in the heavens. So it is in the life of a Christian; this new birth takes place when Jesus of Nazareth, the risen Lord and Savior, comes to live within you.

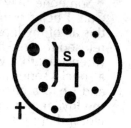

Intellect, Emotions and Will

I said earlier that there is a throne in every life. If you are on that throne deciding what to do with your life, it is quite likely that you are not a Christian. Christ knocks at the door. In Revelation 3:20 He says, "Behold, I stand at the door and knock" (the door of your heart, your will, your intellect, your emotions). He promises, "If you will open the door, I will come in and have fellowship with you and you with Me." The Bible says that as many as receive Jesus, to them God gives the power to become His sons. And if any man is in Christ or if Christ is in any man, he is a new creature; old things are passed away and all things are new. Commitment to Christ involves the surrender of the intellect, the emotions and the will — the total person.

Let us say for the sake of illustration that you had heard many fine compliments about a certain person of the opposite sex. You could hardly wait to meet that person. The actual meeting was even more exciting. Intellectually you liked what you saw — you liked his looks, his personality, his many other qualities. You liked everything about him. Was this enough to launch a marriage? No. There is more to marriage than mutual respect and admiration.

As you spent more and more time together, you became better acquainted. Then it happened. Cupid found his mark, and you were in love. Is this marriage? No. There is more to marriage than the intellect and the emotions. One day you become engaged and the wedding day arrives. How exciting!

Intellectually, you believe that he or she is the most wonderful person in all of the world. Emotionally, your heart beats twice as fast when you are together; but now something even more important is about to take place. As the two of you exchange vows before the minister or the one of authority, you commit your *wills*, one to the other. The marriage is not a true marriage if there is no mutual giving of one to the other. *There you have it — a marriage relationship involves the intellect, the heart and the will.*

So it is in becoming a Christian — one must give himself wholly to Christ — intellect, emotions and will.

Someone may say, "I believe that Jesus Christ is the Son of God. I believe that He died for my sins. Why, I have believed this all of my life. Am I not a Christian?" Not if that person has refused to yield his will to Him. Another may say, "I remember when I heard a wonderful sermon at a youth retreat or during a special series of meetings in our church. My heart was stirred and I had a great emotional experience. I even responded to the invitation to go forward for counsel. Am I not a Christian?" Not if that person has never relinquished the throne of his life, his will, to Christ. Still another may say, "I go to church regularly,

I read my Bible and pray daily. I try to live a good life. Am I not a Christian?" Not unless he has surrendered his will to Christ.

The surrender of the will is the key to becoming a Christian and the secret to living a victorious Christian life.

An outstanding young athlete and social leader wanted to become a Christian, but like so many, he was afraid to surrender his will to the will of God. He had worked out detailed plans for his life but was reluctant to become a Christian, for fear God would change those plans.

As we talked together, I explained that God loved him dearly — so much that He sent His only begotten Son to die on the cross for his sins and that God had a wonderful plan for his life. I asked, "Don't you think you can trust One who loves you this much and who is infinitely wiser than any man?"

"I had not thought of it that way," he said. "I will trust Him."

As we prayed together, he invited Christ into his heart as Savior and Lord. Yes, his life was changed. But you may be sure that he has no regrets, for he is now devoting all of his time to challenging others to become Christians also.

Your Opportunity

At this moment, if you have not already received Christ as your Savior and Lord, Jesus is knocking at the door of your heart (your intellect, your emotions, your will — your total personality). Will you, in the quiet of this moment, surrender your will to Him? Invite Him to come into your life to live His life in you, to *pardon* your sin, to give *purpose* to your life, to give you His *peace* and *power.*

Though the Lord is "not willing that any should perish," (2 Peter 3:9), He will not force His way into your life. He comes only by personal invitation. Just deciding to do something is not enough. All decisions are valueless until accompanied by action.

Bow your head just now and in this moment of decision, pray: "Lord Jesus, come into my life. Pardon my sin. I surrender my will — the throne of my life — to You. Show me Your purpose for my life. Give me Your peace and power that I may please and honor You. Amen!"

According to Scripture we are promised, "As many as received Him, to them He gave the right to become children of God"

(John 1:12). When you receive Christ, you become a child of God. We are also told in 1 John 5:11, 12, "God has given to us eternal life, and this life is in His Son. He who has the Son has the life." When you receive Christ, you have eternal life here and now.

As you receive Christ into your life, you begin the great adventure for which He created you. And as you continue in obedience to His commands, you will experience the fulfillment of His promise of an abundant life. May I encourage you to study the Word of God, the Bible, diligently and to become active in the vital Christian fellowship of a local church?

The *Ten Basic Steps Toward Christian Maturity* have helped thousands of students and adults to a more vital and fruitful relationship with Christ. Daily study of this material will prove rewarding to you also. May God bless and keep you in this great adventure with Christ our Savior.

WHO CHRIST IS, AND WHAT HE HAS DONE

Christ is the exact likeness of the unseen God. He existed before God made anything at all, and, in fact, Christ Himself is the Creator who made everything in heaven and earth, the things we can see and the things we can't; the spirit world with its kings and kingdoms, its rulers and authorities; all were made by Christ for His own use and glory. He was before all else began and it is His power that holds everything together. He is the Head of the body made up of His people — that is, His church — which He began; and He is the Leader of all those who arise from the dead, so that He is first in everything; for God wanted all of Himself to be in His Son.

It was through what His Son did that God cleared a path for everything to come to Him — all things in heaven and on earth — for Christ's death on the cross has made peace with God for all by His blood. This includes you who were once so far away from God. You were His enemies and hated Him and were separated from Him by your evil thoughts and actions, yet now He has brought you back as His friends. He has done this through the death on the cross of His own human body, and now as a result Christ has brought you into the very presence of God, and you are standing there before Him with nothing left against you — nothing left that He could even chide you for; the only condition is that you fully believe the truth, standing in it steadfast and firm, strong in the Lord, convinced of the Good News that Jesus died for you, and never shifting from trusting Him to save you. This is the wonderful news that came to each of you and is now spreading all over the world. (Col. 1:15-20 LB).

LESSON ONE

WHO IS JESUS CHRIST?

Introduction

OBJECTIVE: To personally recognize Jesus Christ as the Son of God.

TO MEMORIZE: John 14:6.

It has been said that if one could know what would occur five minutes in the future, he would need but two weeks to rule the world. The Bible miraculously foretells hundreds of events. Minute details are recorded. In many cases, prophecies preceded their fulfillment by hundreds, sometimes thousands of years. Some prophecies related to cities and countries, such as Tyre, Jericho, Samaria, Jerusalem, Palestine, Moab and Babylon. Other prophecies related to specific individuals.

Jesus Christ is the subject of more than 300 Old Testament prophecies. His birth nearly 2,000 years ago and events of His life had been foretold by many individual prophets over a period of 1,500 years. History confirms that even the smallest detail came about just as predicted. It confirms beyond a doubt that Jesus is the true Messiah, the Son of God and Savior of the world.

The following are some amazing predictions concerning Jesus Christ, together with the record of their fulfillment:

His birth: Isaiah 7:14; Matthew 1:18, 22, 23.
His birthplace: Micah 5:2; Luke 2:4, 6, 7.
His childhood in Egypt: Hosea 11:1; Matthew 2:14, 15.
The purpose for His death: Isaiah 53:4-6; 2 Corinthians 5:21; 1 Peter 2:24.
His betrayal: Zechariah 11:12, 13; 13:6; Matthew 26:14-16; 27:3-10.
His crucifixion: Psalm 22; Matthew 27.
His resurrection: Psalm 16:9, 10; Acts 2:31.

Bible Study

A. *Jesus' claims concerning who He is:*

State in your words the claims Christ made concerning Himself in the following verses:

1. John 10:30 _____
   What did those who heard what Jesus said understand
   Him to mean? _____

   _____

2. John 14:7 _____

   _____

3. Matthew 28:18 _____

   _____

4. John 14:8, 9 _____

   _____

5. John 14:6 _____

   _____

B. *What others said about who He was:*
   1. His followers:
      Peter (Matthew 16:16) _____

      _____

      How did Christ respond to what Peter said (v. 17)? _____

      _____

      Martha (John 11:27) _____

      _____

      Thomas (John 20:28) _____

      _____

      How does Christ's response to what Thomas said (v. 27)
      apply to you? _____

      _____

      _____

   2. His enemies:
      John 10:33 _____

      _____

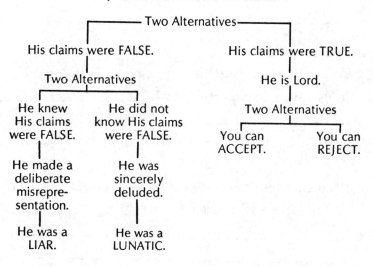

JESUS CLAIMED TO BE GOD.

Two Alternatives

His claims were FALSE. / His claims were TRUE.

His claims were FALSE.
Two Alternatives
He knew His claims were FALSE. / He did not know His claims were FALSE.
He made a deliberate misrepresentation. / He was sincerely deluded.
He was a LIAR. / He was a LUNATIC.

His claims were TRUE.
He is Lord.
Two Alternatives
You can ACCEPT. / You can REJECT.

C. *Importance of the truth about His identity*

According to the above passages, Jesus claimed actually to be God. He made the kinds of claims that only a person who presumed he was God would make and He was termed God by both friends and enemies without ever attempting to deny it. He even commended His followers for thinking thus.

1. Suppose Jesus Christ were not God. If He knew He was not God and that none of those claims were true, what could we conclude about Him? _____

_____

2. Suppose Jesus were sincerely wrong. Suppose He sincerely believed all these fantastic claims, even though they were not true. What could we conclude about Him?

_____

3. Does either of the above answers make sense to you?____
   Why or why not? _____

_____

4. Who do *you* believe Jesus is and on what do you base that

belief? _____

_____

Life Application

1. Why is it important that you personally recognize Jesus Christ for who He really is? _____

   _____

2. Have you invited Jesus Christ into your life? (See "Your Opportunity," page 41.)

3. What changes do you expect to experience in your life as a result of your trusting Christ? _____

   _____

   _____

   _____

LESSON TWO

THE EARTHLY LIFE OF JESUS CHRIST

Introduction

OBJECTIVE: To see that Christ's earthly life confirmed His deity.

TO MEMORIZE: John 1:12.

Bible Study

A. *The entrance of Jesus Christ into the world*

HEAVEN

GOD
BECAME
MAN

1. On the basis of His statement in John 17:5, where was Jesus Christ before He came into the world? ____

   _____

   _____

2. Read Matthew 1:18-23. In your own words summarize the circumstances which surrounded Jesus' birth. ____

   _____

   _____

   _____

   _____

   The New Testament passes over the next 30 years of Jesus' life almost in silence. Apparently the gospel writers were more anxious to portray what kind of a man Jesus was than to give us a chronological biography.

B. *The character of Jesus Christ:*

1. What do you learn about Jesus' character from the following:

   Mark 1:40-42 _____

   _____

   Luke 23:33, 34 _____

   _____

John 2:13-17 _____

_____

John 13:1-5 _____

_____

2. "The character of Jesus has not only been the highest
   pattern of virtue, but the strongest incentive to its practice,
   and has exerted so deep an influence that it may be truly
   said that the simple record of three short years of active
   life has done more to regenerate and to soften mankind
   than all the disquisitions of philosophers and than all the
   exhortations of moralists."

W. E. H. Lecky,
History of European Morals

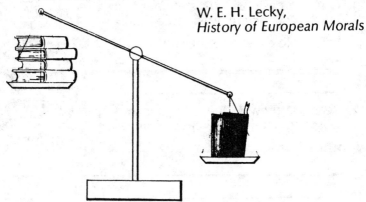

C. *Jesus Christ as a teacher:*

   1. What was some of the *content* of Christ's teaching about:

      a. The new birth in John 3:1-8? _____

      b. His claims about Himself?

         John 10:11 _____

         John 13:13, 14 _____

         John 15:1, 5 _____

         Matthew 5:17 _____

         John 11:25, 26 _____

         Which of these claims do you feel is most important
         and why? _____

   c. His demands of those who would follow Him?

     Mark 8:38 _____

     Matthew 9:9 _____

     Matthew 11:29 _____

     Luke 9:23 _____

     Matthew 19:28 _____

     Which of these demands do you find it easiest to follow? _____

     _____

     How do you think Jesus wants you to deal with the difficult ones? _____

     _____

2. Read carefully Matthew 7:7-12 from the Sermon on the Mount. In what verse do you find the following teaching methods illustrated?

   Effective repetition of ideas _____

   Relevant illustrations _____

   Practical application _____

   Clear summarization _____

3. What was even more important than Christ's effective teaching methods (Matthew 7:29)? _____

   Where did He get this authority (John 13:49, 50)?_____

   _____

Life Application

Give at least three reasons you feel you can trust Jesus' teachings:

_____

_____

_____

_____

_____

LESSON THREE

THE DEATH OF JESUS CHRIST

Introduction

OBJECTIVE: To understand the meaning of Christ's death on the cross; and the importance of receiving Christ as Savior and Lord.

TO MEMORIZE: Romans 5:8.

NOTE: The Bible teaches that death means separation, not cessation of existence. *Physical death* is separation of the soul (the immaterial or spiritual part of man) from the body (the material part of man) with the resulting decomposition of the body. *Spiritual death* is the separation of man from God. Both physical and spiritual death are the results of sin.

Actually, man was created to have fellowship with God, but because of his stubborn self-will, he chose to go his own independent way, and the fellowship was broken. Remember the floor lamp? (See page 32). Pull the plug from the socket and the light goes out. This is what the Bible says has happened to man.

The results of this separation are not only gross sins like murder, immorality, stealing, etc., but also worry, irritability, lack of purpose in life, frustration, desire to escape reality and fear of death. These and many other conditions are evidence that man is cut off from God, the only One who can give him the power to live an abundant life.

Bible Study

A. *The need for the death of Jesus Christ:*

1. Read carefully Romans 3:10-12 and 3:23.

   How many times does the writer use terms like "all," "none," or their equivalents? _____

   Why do you think he repeats these terms so much? _____

   _____

   What does this tell you about moral, respectable people?

   _____

2. What is the result of sin (Romans 6:23)? _____

B. *The result of the death of Christ:*

   1. Read 2 Corinthians 5:21 carefully.

     How good does it say Christ was? _____

     _____

     But what happened to Him when He died?_____

     _____

     What was the result for you? _____

     _____

   2. How did Christ feel about such a death (Hebrews 12:2)?

     _____

   3. What did Christ teach concerning His death (Mark 8:31,32)?

     _____

   4. Why did He die for us (1 Peter 3:18)? _____

     _____

C. *Significance of the death of Christ:*

   1. What is the only thing we can do to make sure that the death of Christ applies to us so we can be saved (Acts 16:31)? _____

   2. Why can't we work for salvation (Ephesians 2:8, 9)? _____

     _____

Life Application

   1. Read John 3:18 carefully.

     What two kinds of people are described here? _____

     _____

     What is the only reason that one kind is condemned?

     _____

     According to what the Bible says here, are you condemned or uncondemned? _____

   2. According to 1 John 5:11, 12, do you have eternal life?

     _____

(Do not confuse 1 John, the Epistle, near the end of the New Testament, with the Gospel of John.)

3. According to that same passage, how can you know?

_____

_____

4. Have you made the decision to accept Christ's death on the cross for you, and have you accepted Him into your life as Savior and Lord? _____

LESSON FOUR

THE RESURRECTION OF JESUS CHRIST

Introduction

OBJECTIVE: To recognize the importance of Christ's resurrection, and how it relates to us personally.

TO MEMORIZE: 1 Corinthians 15:3, 4.

Jesus' crucifixion had apparently disbanded and demoralized His followers. That little band was now terror-stricken and scattered. His enemies were celebrating their victory. But three days after His crucifixion a miracle occurred: Jesus rose from the dead.

Within a few weeks His once cowardly followers were fearlessly proclaiming His resurrection, a fact that changed the entire course of history. Followers of Jesus Christ were not those who followed the ethical code of a dead founder, but rather those who had vital contact with a living Lord. Jesus Christ lives today, and anxiously waits to work in the lives of those who will trust Him.

THE REAL DIFFERENCE

"The great difference between present-day Christianity and that of which we read in these letters is that to us it is primarily a performance, to them it was a real experience. We are likely to reduce the Christian religion to a code, or at best a rule of heart and life. To these men it is quite plainly the invasion of their lives by a new quality of life altogether. They do not hesitate to describe this as Christ 'living in' them.

"Mere moral reformation will hardly explain the transformation and the exuberant vitality of these men's lives — even if we could prove a motive for such reformation, and certainly the world around offered little encouragement to the early Christians! We are practically driven to accept their own explanation, which is that their little human lives had, through Christ, been linked up with the very life of God.

"Many Christians today talk about the 'difficulties of our times' as though we should have to wait for better ones before the Christian religion can take root. It is heartening to remember that this faith took root and flourished amazingly in conditions that would have killed anything less vital in a matter of weeks.

"These early Christians were on fire with the conviction that they had become, through Christ, literally sons of God; they were pioneers of a new humanity, founders of a new kingdom. They still speak to us across the centuries. Perhaps if we believed what they believed, we might achieve what they achieved."

J. B. Phillips, Foreword to *Letters to Young Churches*

Bible Study

A. *Four proofs that Jesus actually rose from the dead*

1. *First Proof: The resurrection was foretold by Jesus Christ, the Son of God.*

What had Jesus told His disciples in Luke 18:31-33?

_____

If Jesus had clearly stated He would rise from the dead, and then had failed to do so, what would this say about

Him? _____

_____

2. *Second Proof: The resurrection of Christ is the only reasonable explanation for the empty tomb.*

What did Jesus' friends do to make certain His body would not be taken

(Mark 15:46)? _____

_____

_____

What did Jesus's enemies do to make sure His body would not be taken

(Matthew 27:62-66)? _____

_____

_____

But on Sunday morning the tomb was *EMPTY!*

NOTE: If Jesus had not been killed, but only weakened and wounded by crucifixion, the stone and the soldiers would have prevented His escape from the tomb. If Jesus' friends had tried to steal His body, the stone and the soldiers would likewise have prevented them. Jesus' enemies would never have taken the body since absence of His body from the tomb would only serve to encourage belief in His resurrection. **Only His resurrection can account for the empty tomb!**

3. *Third Proof: The resurrection is the only reasonable explanation for the appearance of Jesus Christ to His disciples.*

List all the individuals or groups who actually saw the risen Christ, according to what the apostle Paul wrote in 1 Corinthians 15:4-8: _____

_____

_____

If Christ did not rise from the dead, what should we then conclude about all these witnesses (1 Corinthians 15:15)?

_____

Does the above answer make sense to you? _____

Why or why not? _____

_____

What else would be true, if Christ did not rise from the dead (1 Corinthians 15:17)? _____

_____

When Christ appeared to His followers, what things did He do to prove it was not an hallucination (Luke 24:36-43)? _____

_____

4. *Fourth Proof: The resurrection is the only reasonable explanation for the beginning of the Christian church.*

Within a few weeks after Jesus' resurrection, Peter preached at Pentecost, and the Christian church began.

What was the main subject of his sermon (Acts 2:14-36)?

_____

_____

If Jesus' body were still in the tomb, how do you think his audience would have responded to this sermon?

_____

_____

But how did they respond (Acts 2:37, 38, 41, 42)? _____

_____

_____

B. *The results of the resurrection*

　1. What does the resurrection tell us about:

　　a. Jesus Christ (Romans 1:4)? _____

　　　_____

　　b. The power God can now exercise in our lives (Ephesians 1:19, 20)? _____

　　　_____

　　c. What will eventually happen to our bodies (Philippians 3:21)? _____

　　　_____

　2. If we can believe the miracle of the resurrection, why do you think it would be logical to believe in all the other miracles Jesus performed? _____

　　_____

Life Application

Hebrews 13:8 says Jesus is the same today and can transform your life.

1. How can your life be different if you allow Jesus to transform it? _____

　_____

2. How do you think His "resurrection life" can be seen in you on a daily basis?_____

_____

_____

3. How would your life be different from what it is if Jesus had not risen from the dead? _____

_____

_____

Thomas Arnold, for 14 years the renowned headmaster of Rugby, author of the famous three-volume *History of Rome,* and a man appointed to the chair of Modern History at Oxford, gave the following testimony to his own persuasion of the historic trustworthiness of the resurrection narrative:

"The evidence for our Lord's life and death and resurrection may be, and often has been, shown to be satisfactory; it is good according to the common rules for distinguishing good evidence from bad. Thousands and tens of thousands of persons have gone through it piece by piece, as carefully as every judge summing up a most important case. I have myself done it many times over, not to persuade others but to satisfy myself. I have been used for many years to study the histories of other times, and to examine and weigh the evidence of those who have written about them, and I know of no one fact in the history of mankind which is proved by better and fuller evidence of every sort, to the understanding of a fair inquirer, than the great sign which God hath given us that Christ died and rose again from the dead."

LESSON FIVE

JESUS CHRIST LIVING IN THE CHRISTIAN

Introduction

OBJECTIVE: To show the importance of total surrender to Christ.

TO MEMORIZE: Revelation 3:20.

Note that Chapters 2 and 3 of Revelation are addressed to churches. This serves to emphasize the fact that merely to be a church member offers no guarantee of a right relationship with Jesus Christ. Notice in Revelation 3:20 that the reference is to individuals, not to a group as a whole. "If *anyone* hears, I will come in to *him*, and eat with *him*, and *he* with Me."

When you invite Jesus Christ to come into your heart and life to be your Savior and Lord, confessing your sin and need of forgiveness, He answers your prayer. He enters your heart and life. Why?

One of the main reasons is so that He can empower you. The Christian life is more than difficult; it is humanly impossible. Jesus Christ alone can live it. When He is within you, He wants to live the Christian life that only He can live through you. He wants to think with your mind, express Himself through your emotions, and speak through your voice, though you may be unconscious of it.

Thus the Christian life is not the Christian trying to imitate Christ. It is Christ imparting His life to and living His life through the Christian. The Christian life is not what you do for Christ; it is what He does for and through you. The Christ-controlled life always produces the fruit of the Spirit as listed in Galatians 5:22-23.

- Love
- Joy
- Peace
- Patience
- Kindness
- Faithfulness
- Goodness

- Christ centered
- Empowered by H.S.
- Introduces others to Christ
- Effective prayer life
- Understands God's Word
- Trusts God
- Obeys God

Bible Study

A. *The need for Jesus Christ to live in the Christian:*

1. What do you think Jesus was not willing to entrust to men and why not (John 2:24, 25)? _____

   _____

2. What kinds of things are in our hearts (Mark 7:21, 22)?

   _____

   _____

3. How did the apostle Paul, one of the world's greatest Christians, evaluate his human nature (Romans 7:18)?

   _____

   _____

4. What is our condition apart from Jesus Christ (John 15:4, 5)? _____

B. *The fact that Jesus Christ lives in the Christian:*

1. Paraphrase Revelation 3:20 (restate in your own words):

   _____

   _____

   NOTE: The word "sup" in some translations is Old English for "eat" or "dine" — hence the idea of "fellowship" in its original meaning.

2. What guarantee does Jesus Christ give in this verse, and how can we believe Him? _____

   _____

3. How do you know that Jesus Christ has entered your life?

   _____

4. How do you know Jesus Christ will never leave you, even if you sin (Hebrews 13:5)? _____

   _____

5. But if you do sin, how can you renew your fellowship

with Him (1 John 1:9)? _____

_____

NOTE: *Salvation* differs from *fellowship*. Salvation is being forgiven of sins and having eternal life. Fellowship with Christ is our daily relationship, or communion with Him. Through sin we may often lose our fellowship. In the same way, a child may lose fellowship with his father through dis-obedience, but he does not lose his relationship as a son. See also John 10:27-29.

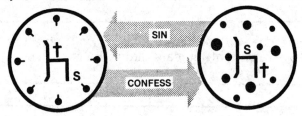

C. *Jesus Christ at home within the Christian:*

When Jesus Christ is within us, what can He do as we face the following problems:

1. Emptiness (John 6:35)?   _____

_____

2. Anxiety (John 14:27)?   _____

_____

3. Unhappiness (John 15:11)?   _____

_____

4. Lack of power (Philippians 4:13)?   _____

_____

Life Application

1. What must we do so that He can live His victorious life through us (Romans 6:13; 12:1, 3)?   _____

_____

2. Read and meditate on John 3:16. On the basis of this verse, why do you think we should give control of our lives to God?   _____

_____

As non-Christians or carnal Christians examine their lives, they find that they are filled with many areas of activity — studies, finances, social life, home life, business, travel — but with no real purpose or meaning. The reason is that such individuals control these areas themselves, instead of allowing Jesus Christ to control them.

There is a throne in each life (see diagram). Until Jesus Christ comes into a life, the self, or the person's own ego, is on the throne. But when Jesus comes in, He wants to assume His place of authority on this throne. You must step down and relinquish the authority of your life to Him. As you can see from the diagram, when Christ becomes the controller of your life, He becomes Lord of every activity, and that results in purpose and harmony.

LESSON SIX

THE CHURCH OF JESUS CHRIST

Introduction

OBJECTIVE: To show the importance of the church in the Christian's life.

TO MEMORIZE: Hebrews 10:25.

Bible Study

The Bible describes the church in two senses: (1) as the *universal* church, which refers to all true Christians, and (2) as the *local* church, which is an individual group of Christians who gather for worship, instruction and mutual encouragement.

A. *The universal church*

1. Paul frequently compares the church to a body.

   Who is the only head (Ephesians 5:23)? _____

   Who are the members (1 Corinthians 12:27)? _____

2. How does Christ see the church (1 Corinthians 12:12, 13)?

   _____

3. As members of His body, how should we feel toward each other (1 Corinthians 12:25, 26)? _____

   _____

   Name some specific ways we can express these feelings.

   _____

   _____

4. Read carefully Acts 1:5-11.

   According to verse 8, what is to be the church's great concern? _____

Where does the Bible say Jesus went physically (v. 9)?

_____

Describe in your own words how Jesus will come again for His church (verse 11). _____

_____

Who knows when that will be (verse 7)? (See also Mark 12:32, 33). _____

_____

The Bible teaches that though Jesus is spiritually present in our hearts, He is also with God the Father in heaven. In the future, He will return to judge the world and rule the nations (Matthew 25:31, 32; 24:36). In the meantime, the church is to be His witness on earth and bring as many people as possible into a living relationship with Him.

5. In light of this, what should be one of your main purposes while here on earth? _____

_____

_____

_____

B. *The local church*

1. What are Christians *not* to do (Hebrews 10:25)? _____

_____

NOTE: The "assembling of ourselves together" refers to the regular meeting of the local church. The Bible *commands* Christians to attend church regularly.

2. We are saved by faith. But the church has two simple, yet meaningful, ordinances we are to observe — baptism and communion.

According to Matthew 28:18, 19, why should we be baptized? _____

_____

What is the purpose of the communion service (1 Corinthians 11:23-26)? _____

_____

3. Write your own one-sentence description of each of the following local churches:

The church in Jerusalem (Acts 4:32, 33) _____

_____

_____

The church in Thessalonica (1 Thessalonians 1:6-10) ____

_____

_____

The church in Laodicea (Revelation 3:14-17) _____

_____

_____

As this shows, some New Testament churches were dynamic; others powerless. So it is today. Not all churches are vital churches, and great variety exists even within a single denomination. In order to stimulate your Christian growth, you should attend a church that exalts Christ, teaches the Bible, explains clearly what a Christian is and how to become one, and provides vital fellowship.

Life Application

1. Give at least two reasons it is important for us to be a part

   of a local church. _____

   _____

   _____

   _____

   _____

2. If you are not now involved in a local church, what kind of church will you seek and when will you begin attending?

   _____

   _____

   _____

LESSON SEVEN

RECAP

Review verses memorized.

What do you think is the most important way in which Jesus Christ is different from other people? _____

_____

Who is Jesus Christ to you? _____

_____

Why do you suppose Jesus' enemies did not want to believe His claims about who He was? _____

_____

What does it mean to you now to have Jesus living within you?

_____

_____

How does your present relationship with Christ correspond to your present relationship with your local church? _____

_____

How should it?_____

_____

STEP ONE
The Christian Adventure

THE CHRISTIAN ADVENTURE WITH JESUS CHRIST

With all due respect to the leaders of various religions, it should be noted that Jesus is the only one who ever claimed to be God. Mohammed claimed to be a prophet of God. His body, like that of any mortal being, remains in the grave. So do the bodies of Buddha, Confucius, Zoroaster and the founders and leaders of other religions.

Jesus of Nazareth is unique in many ways. Minute details of His life were foretold by Old Testament prophets hundreds of years before His birth. In life and in example, He remains without a peer. Crucified because He claimed to be God, He confirmed His claims by His resurrection. History supports the fact of His resurrection.

He is recognized as the greatest figure of history by everyone who knows the facts, and He is alive!

What does all this mean to you today? The practical benefits of the resurrection of Jesus Christ are obvious. If you have trusted Him, He has taken up residence in your life, wants you to yield complete control to Him and to invite Him to be the Lord of every area of your life.

The Bible tells us in Colossians 1:15, 16 that "He (Christ) is the image of the invisible God, the first-born of all creation. For in Him all things were created, both in the heavens and on earth, visible and invisible, whether thrones or dominions or rulers or authorities — all things have been created through Him and for Him." This creative act included man.

Since we were created by Jesus Christ, God the Son, He alone holds the answer to the basic questions of life: Where did I come from? Why am I here? Where am I going?

With the One who created you in control of your life, you will receive a new quality of life, *His resurrection life*. In exchange for your life of defeat and frustration, Christ will give you His life of victory, purpose and power. You will no longer be a creature of chance. You will be a child of God.

To many people, Christianity is something to be endured in anticipation of heaven. But this is not the way our Lord intended it. He meant for your Christian life to be victorious, fruitful and exciting. To know Jesus Christ personally as Savior and Lord is the greatest privilege and adventure that man can ever experience.

LESSON ONE

THE CHRISTIAN'S CERTAINTY

Introduction

OBJECTIVE: To give assurance to the new Christian of eternal life and Christ's presence in his life.

TO MEMORIZE: 1 John 5:13.

TO READ: John 3:1-20 and 1 John 5:9-15.

Believers of Old Testament times looked forward to the coming of their Messiah. New Testament believers look back to the cross and the resurrection. Both of these events are culminated in the unique life of Jesus Christ which is the basis for Christian confidence.

Jesus' death on the cross and His bodily resurrection from the dead prove that He was God's promised Messiah of the Old Testament, the Savior of the world.

To believe in Jesus Christ as the Savior of the world is to believe in a living person. People often ask, "What is the meaning of belief?" The Amplified New Testament expresses the full meaning of the term "believe" as "adhere to, trust in and rely on." The Gospel of John has been called the "Gospel of Belief." The word "believe" occurs many times in the book of John. Chapter 20, verse 31, expresses the purpose of that book: "But these have been written, that you may believe that Jesus is the Christ, the Son of God; and that believing you may have life in His name."

Bible Study

A. *Christian certainty*

   1. What must one do to become a Christian (John 1:12)?

---

2. To be a son of God is to be born of whom (John 1:13)?

_____

3. To believe in Jesus Christ is to possess _____
   and to be free from _____ (John 5:24).

4. What did Christ do with our sins (1 Peter 2:24, 25)? _____

   _____

   How should this affect your life? _____

5. What three things characterize Jesus' sheep (John 10:27)?

   _____

   _____

6. What is your relationship with Christ, as He Himself
   states in John 10:28-30? _____

   _____

   _____

7. What are the implications of failing to believe the
   testimony that God has given regarding His Son (1 John
   5:10, 11)? _____

   _____

   _____

B. *New life*

1. In John 3:3, 7, what did Jesus tell Nicodemus about
   seeing and entering the kingdom of God? _____

   _____

2. At physical birth one receives many things of which he is
   not aware; e.g., family name, privileges, wealth, love, care
   and protection. At spiritual birth one becomes a son of
   God, receives eternal life, a divine inheritance and God's
   love, care and protection. God has given us these definite
   things because of His great love. God's gifts are never
   based on man's changing emotions, but on His unchanging
   Word.

   In your own words describe what you have, according to
   these verses:

Ephesians 1:7 ———————————————————

Romans 5:1 ————————————————————

Romans 3:22 ———————————————————

Colossians 1:27b ——————————————————

3. As you begin to live the Christian life, what three evidences in your life will assure you that you know Jesus Christ?

———————————————(1 John 2:3).

———————————————— (1 John 3:14).

———————————————— (Romans 8:16).

Life Application

On the basis of Lesson One:

1. Who is Jesus Christ to you? ————————————

2. What is your relationship to God? ————————

3. What kind of life do you now possess? ————————

4. What about your sins? ————————————————

5. Why are you sure (or doubtful) of your salvation? ———

————————————————————————

6. What changes in your life do you believe have taken place

because of Christ? ————————————————

————————————————————————

————————————————————————

————————————————————————

————————————————————————

LESSON TWO

THE PERSON OF JESUS CHRIST

Introduction

OBJECTIVE: To confirm through biblical evidence that Christ is deity — God in human form.

TO MEMORIZE: John 1:18.

TO READ: Philippians 2:5-11.

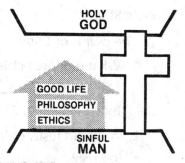

The Bible explains that God Himself became a man to give mankind a concrete, definite and tangible idea of *what kind of person God is.* "Christ is the image of the invisible God" (Colossians 1:15). (See also John 1:18). Jesus was God incarnate — God in human form. Perhaps the most succinct statement about the deity and humanity of Christ was made by Byron, the poet, when he said, "If ever a man were God or God were man, Jesus was both."

"At the beginning God expressed Himself. That personal expression, that Word, was with God, and was God, and He existed with God from the beginning. All creation took place through Him, and none took place without Him. In Him appeared life and this life was the light of mankind. The light still shines in the darkness and the darkness has never put it out.

"A man called John was sent by God as a witness to the light, so that any man who heard his testimony might believe in the light. This man was not himself the light: he was sent simply as a personal witness to that light. That was the true light which shines upon every man as He comes into the world. He came into the world — the world He had created — and the world failed to recognize Him.

"He came into His own creation, and His own people would not accept Him. Yet, wherever men did accept Him, He gave them the power to become sons of God. These were the men who truly believed in Him, and their birth depended not on the course of nature nor on any impulse or plan of man, but on God. So the Word of God became a human being and lived among us. We saw His splendor (the splendor as of a father's only son), full of grace and truth" (John 1:1-15, Phillips).

"For God has allowed us to know the secret of His plan, and it is this: He purposes in His sovereign will that all human history shall be consummated in Christ, that everything that exists in heaven or earth shall find its perfection and fulfillment in Him. And here is the staggering thing — that in all which will one day belong to Him, we have been promised a share" (Ephesians 1:9-11, Phillips).

Bible Study

A. *The claims of Christ*

  1. What did Jesus claim for Himself in the following verses?

    Mark 14:61, 62 _____

    John 6:38; 8:42, 58 _____

  2. What did Jesus claim to do in the following verses?

    John 5:22 _____

    Matthew 9:6 _____

    John 6:47 _____

  3. What did Jesus predict in the following verses?

    Mark 9:31 _____

    Luke 18:31-33 _____

    John 14:1-3 _____

B. *Contemporary opinions about Christ*

  1. His enemies

    Pilate (Matthew 27:24) _____

    Judas (Matthew 27:4) _____

    The Roman soldier (Matthew 27:54) _____

  2. His friends

    John the Baptist (John 1:29) _____

    Peter (1 Peter 2:22) _____

    Paul (2 Corinthians 5:21) _____

    Disciples (Matthew 8:27) _____

C. *The deity of Christ*

1. In John 5:17, 18, whom did Jesus Christ claim to be?

_____

2. Paul described Jesus as _____(Titus 2:13).

3. In the following verses, what characteristics of Jesus are attributes of an omnipotent God?

John 2:24_____

Matthew 8:26, 27 _____

John 11:43-45_____

4. What was the most significant sign of Christ's deity (1 Corinthians 15:3-8)? _____

_____

D. *The compassion of Christ*

1. How does Jesus' attitude contrast with the attitude of His contemporaries toward:

adults (Matthew 14:15-21)? _____

_____

children (Mark 10:13-16)? _____

_____

those who offend (Luke 9:51-56)? _____

_____

2. Why did the following people love Christ?

The widow of Nain (Luke 7:11-15)? _____

_____

The sinful woman (Luke 7:47) _____

_____

Mary and Martha (John 11:33-44) _____

_____

The disciples (John 14:1-3, 27; 16:24) _____

_____

3. How do you feel about Him and why? _____

_____

_____

E. *The death of Christ*

1. Describe the purpose of Christ's death as it is related in 1 Peter 2:24. _____

_____

2. How did Christ's death affect your relationship with God (Colossians 1:21, 22; Romans 5:10, 11)? _____

_____

3. Describe the effect of Christ's death with respect to God's holiness (Romans 3:25; 1 John 2:2; 4:10). _____

_____

F. *The resurrection of Christ*

1. What event did Jesus Christ predict in John 2:19-21? Summarize the details. _____

_____

_____

2. Three days after Christ's death, of what were the disciples reminded (Luke 24:6)? (Read Luke 24:1-9.) _____

_____

3. According to the apostle Paul, where was it recorded that Christ would rise from the dead on the third day (1 Corinthians 15:4)? _____

4. For a period of six weeks after His resurrection, Jesus Christ walked and talked with many individuals and groups. As recorded in 1 Corinthians 15:5-8, who saw Him? List them here.

_____   _____

_____   _____

_____   _____

5. Read 1 Corinthians 15:12-26 and state how it would affect your life if Christ were not resurrected. _____

_____

_____

G. *The visible return of Christ*

After spending approximately six weeks giving His disciples final instructions, Christ ascended into heaven (Acts 1:1-9).

1. Describe the way in which Christ will return to earth (Matthew 24:30; Acts 1:11). _____

_____

_____

2. How does this compare with the first time Christ came to the earth? _____

_____

_____

3. What will happen to the Christian when Christ comes for him (1 Corinthians 15:51, 52; Philippians 3:20, 21)?_____

_____

_____

4. According to Matthew 24:6-8, what will be the condition of the earth when Christ returns? _____

_____

5. What did Jesus say will happen to those who are not Christians when He returns (2 Thessalonians 1:7-9)?

_____

_____

6. How does this motivate your present life, as you wait expectantly for His visible return (1 John 3:2, 3)? _____

_____

_____

Life Application

1. Contrast your relationship to Christ with your relationship to any other human being. _____

   _____

   _____

2. Compare man's use of profanity to God's honored use of the name of Jesus in Philippians 2:9-11. _____

   _____

   _____

3. Write a brief statement answering, "In what way does this study of the deity of Christ make me appreciate my relationship with Him more deeply?" _____

   _____

   _____

   _____

   _____

   _____

   _____

   _____

   _____

   _____

   _____

   _____

LESSON THREE

THE CHRIST-CONTROLLED LIFE

Introduction

OBJECTIVE: To show how the indwelling life of Christ, not our own efforts, is the key to the Christian life.

TO MEMORIZE: Philippians 4:13.

TO READ: 1 Corinthians 2:11 - 3:5; Galatians 5:16-24.

There are many misconceptions concerning the Christian life. Some feel that once they have admitted Jesus Christ into their lives by faith, it is up to them to try their best to live a life that is pleasing to God. Others feel that Christ has entered their lives to help them live and work for God's glory. Perhaps these two ideas of Christian living 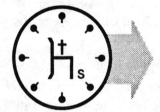 look good on the surface, but there is a basic weakness in each concept that actually undermines the basis of vital Christian living.

In light of Romans 7:18, Galatians 2:20 and Romans 1:17, what do you think the basic approach should be, rather than trying or seeking help?

_____

_____

_____

It has been said, "The Christian life is not hard; it is impossible." Only one person has ever lived the Christian life, and that was Jesus Christ. He desires to go on today living His life through Christians whom He indwells. J. B. Phillips, in the preface (p. xiv) to his translation of part of the New Testament, *Letters to Young Churches,* said:

"The great difference between present-day Christianity and that of which we read in these letters is that to us it is primarily a performance; to them it was a real experience. We are apt to reduce the Christian religion to a code, or at best a rule of heart and life. To those men it is quite plainly the invasion of their lives by a new quality of life altogether. They do not hesitate to describe this as Christ 'living in' them."

Prior to his death, Christ told His disciples that it was best for Him to leave them in order that the Spirit of God might come to dwell in each of them (John 14:16-20; 16:7). In other words, Christ was physically departing from His disciples in order that He might always be present spiritually within each of them.

Today when a person places his faith in Christ, Christ comes to dwell within him by means of the Holy Spirit (Romans 8:9). His purpose for dwelling in us is that *He might live His life through us.* Many Christians are trying to operate on their own finite power when there is an infinite power available.

One may ask, "How can I experience the victorious life of Christ?" In this lesson we will examine the three types of persons in the world today — the non-Christian (natural man), the spiritual Christian and the carnal Christian.

Bible Study

A. *The non-Christian or natural man*

This first circle represents the life of the person who has never received Christ as Lord and Savior. Christ stands outside the door of the life, seeking entrance (Revelation 3:20).

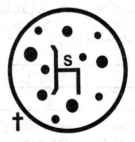

SELF-DIRECTED LIFE
S · Self is on the throne
† · Christ is outside the life
**• · Interests are directed
by self, often resulting in
discord and frustration**

1. What adjective do you think best describes the man who does not understand the things of the Spirit of God (1 Corinthians 2:14)? _____

_____

2. What terms describe "self" in the following verses?

Romans 6:6 _____

Galatians 5:16, 17 _____

3. List at least three characteristics of the man without Christ, as described in Ephesians 2:1-3.

_____

_____

_____

4. What is the condition of the heart of the natural man (Jeremiah 17:9)? _____

_____

_____

5. List the 13 sins that Jesus said come from the heart of man (Mark 7:20-23). _____

_____

_____

_____

6. Summarize the relationship between God and the non-Christian (John 3:36). _____

_____

7. How, then, does one become a Christian (John 1:12; Revelation 3:20)? _____

_____

_____

B. *The spiritual or Christ-controlled Christian*
   This second circle represents the life of the person who has

- Love
- Joy
- Peace
- Patience
- Kindness
- Faithfulness
- Goodness

- Christ centered
- Empowered by H.S.
- Introduces others to Christ
- Effective prayer life
- Understands God's Word
- Trusts God
- Obeys God

invited Jesus Christ to come into his life and who is allowing Him to control and empower his life. Christ is occupying His rightful place on the throne of the life. Self has been dethroned.

1. List the characteristics of a life controlled by the Spirit of God (Galatians 5:22, 23). _____

   _____

2. In what sense could the Spirit-controlled life be called the "exchanged life" (Galatians 2:20)? _____

   _____

3. Where does the Christian receive the power to live this otherwise impossible life (Philippians 4:13)? _____

   _____

4. What does the spiritual Christian have that will enable him to understand the things of God (1 Corinthians 2:14-16)? _____

   _____

C. *The carnal Christian and the solution to carnality*

   In 1 Corinthians 3:1-3, the apostle Paul addresses the Christians as "carnal" (self-centered), rather than "spiritual" (Christ-centered). The following diagram represents a life in which ego has asserted itself. It has usurped the throne of the life, and Christ has stepped down. The result is the loss of the individual's fellowship with God though he is still a Christian.

- LEGALISTIC ATTITUDE
- IMPURE THOUGHTS
- JEALOUSY
- GUILT
- WORRY
- DISCOURAGEMENT
- CRITICAL SPIRIT
- FRUSTATION
- AIMLESSNESS

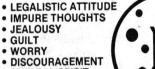

- IGNORANCE OF HIS SPIRITUAL HERITAGE
- UNBELIEF
- DISOBEDIENCE
- LOSS OF LOVE FOR GOD AND FOR OTHERS
- POOR PRAYER
- NO DESIRE FOR BIBLE STUDY

1. Describe the carnal Christian as presented in 1 Corinthians 3:1-3. _____

   _____

   _____

   _____

   Name five or six practices that result from carnality (Galatians 5:19-21). _____

   _____

   _____

   _____

   Summarize in your own words the relationship between the carnal mind and God, as described in Romans 8:7.

   _____

   _____

2. The solution to carnality (the self-controlled life) is threefold:

   We must *confess* our sins — recognize that we have been rulers of our own lives. When we do confess them, what will God do (1 John 1:9)? _____

   _____

   Read Proverbs 28:13. What is the result of not admitting sin? _____

   _____

   What is the result of admitting sin? _____

   _____

   We must *surrender* or yield the throne to Christ. State in your own words how Paul describes the act of presenting ourselves to God in Romans 12:1, 2. _____

   _____

   _____

   By *faith* we must *recognize* that Christ assumed control of our lives upon our invitation.

How can you be sure that if you ask Jesus Christ to assume His rightful place on the throne of your life, He will do so (1 John 5:14, 15)? _____

_____

Do you really want Him to take control of your life?

_____

We receive the Lord Jesus Christ by faith. How then do we allow Him to control our lives moment by moment (Colossians 2:6)? _____

_____

Give three reasons faith is so important (Hebrews 11:6; Romans 14:23; Romans 1:17)? _____

_____

_____

Life Application

The secret of the abundant life is to allow Jesus Christ to control one's life moment by moment. When one realizes he has sinned, he should confess his sin immediately, thank God for forgiving him and continue to walk in fellowship with God.

1. List areas of your life that you feel should be brought under the control of Jesus Christ: _____

_____

_____

_____

2. To make 1 John 1:9 meaningful in your life:

Make a list of your sins and failures on a separate sheet of paper.

Claim 1 John 1:9 for your own life by writing the words of the verse over the list.

Thank God for His forgiveness and cleansing, and then destroy the list.

LESSON FOUR

THE FIVE PRINCIPLES OF GROWTH

Introduction

OBJECTIVE: To understand the essentials of Christian growth and put them into practice.

TO MEMORIZE: 2 Timothy 2:15.

Deciding to receive Jesus Christ as one's personal Lord and Savior is the most important choice a person will ever make. It is an act of faith which starts a whole new life. Just as physical life requires, air, food, rest and exercise, so does spiritual life require certain things for growth and development. This lesson deals with five principles of growth. If these are followed, one can know that he will grow toward spiritual maturity in Christ.

Bible Study

A. *Principle one: we must study God's Word*

Read James 1:18-27.

One would not think of going without physical food for a week or for even a day. It is necessary for physical life. Without food, one becomes weakened and eventually may become ill. Lack of spiritual food produces the same results in our spiritual lives.

1. What is the food of the young Christian (1 Peter 2:2)?

   _____

2. Jesus said, "Man shall not live by bread alone." How did He say that we should live and be nourished (Matthew 4:4)? _____

   _____

3. List the two characteristics of the workman of whom God approves, according to 2 Timothy 2:15. _____

4. What did Jesus say about those who read and believe God's Word (John 8:31)? _____

5. When does the man who is spiritually mature meditate on the Word of God (Psalm 1:2, 3)? _____

6. In what specific ways do you expect God's Word to affect you? _____

B. *Principle two: we must pray*

Read Matthew 26:31-75.

Prayer is the inspiring experience of conversing with and praising God as our loving heavenly Father. Few experiences can equal prayer in empowering Christians and lifting them above their problems. Many times lack of character can be traced to prayerlessness. When it is hardest to pray, one should pray hardest. Study the above passage and answer the following questions:

1. What was Jesus' command in Matthew 26:41? _____

   Why did He command it? _____
2. Why did Peter fail to resist temptation? _____

3. What was the most serious result of Peter's prayerlessness? _____

4. Why did Christ experience inner power to face the

severest test of His life? _____

_____

5. How often are we to pray (1 Thessalonians 5:17)? _____

_____

Prayer without ceasing involves conversing with our heavenly Father in a simple and free way throughout the day. Our prayer life should be such that we come to know the Lord Jesus in a personal way. Our prayer life becomes effective as our relationship with Christ becomes more intimate.

"And I will do — I Myself will grant — whatever you may ask in My name (presenting all I AM) so that the Father may be glorified and extolled in (through) the Son. (Yes) I will grant — will do for you — whatever you shall ask in My name (presenting all I AM)" John 14:13, 14, Amplified New Testament.

C. *Principle three: we must fellowship with other Christians*

Read 1 Corinthians 12:12-27.

Fellowship is spending time and doing things with others who love Christ. Just as several logs burn brightly together,

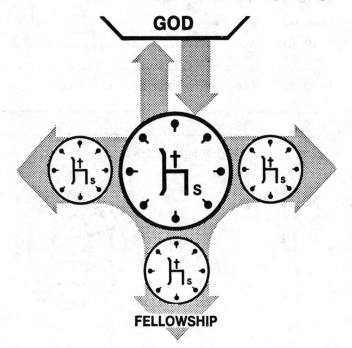

but the fire goes out of one placed alone on the cold hearth, so do Christians need to work together or the fire of enthusiasm will go out. Fellowship is vital for Christian growth. That is why church attendance is important.

1. As God's children, what should we not neglect (Hebrews 10:23-25)? _____

_____

2. According to the above verses, what should we do for one another? _____

_____

3. The new believers in Acts 2:42 continued steadfastly in what four things? _____

_____

_____

_____

4. If you spend 90% of your time with non-Christians and 10% with Christians, you know which group will have the greater influence on your life.

   How can you increase your own time of fellowship with other Christians? _____

_____

5. In what ways do you profit from Christian fellowship?

_____

_____

D. *Principle four: we must witness for Christ*

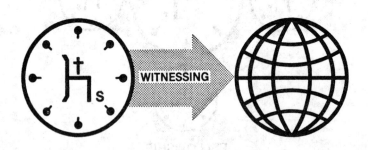

Read Acts 26:12-29.

A witness is a person who tells what he has seen and heard. heard. He shares his own personal experience. Anyone who has a vital personal relationship with Christ can be a witness for Him. Witnessing is the overflow of the Christian life. As our lives are filled with the presence of the Lord Jesus, we cannot help but share Him with those with whom we come in contact. A vital Christian life is contagious.

1. What is the greatest thing that has ever happened to you?

   _____

   _____

   What, then, is the greatest thing you can do for another

   person? _____

2. In Romans 1:14-16, Paul tells us his own attitude concerning the matter of sharing the gospel with others.
   Using his three "I am's" as the keys to the passage,
   describe his attitude in your own words.

   _____

   _____

   _____

   _____

   _____

3. Compare your own attitude concerning witnessing with
   that of Paul's. _____

   _____

   _____

4. What did Peter tell us we should always be ready to do
   (1 Peter 3:15)? _____

5. What was Jesus' promise in Acts 1:8? _____

   _____

6. Name at least three people to whom you can witness in

the power of Christ. _____

_____

It is the privilege and responsibility of every Christian to reach "his world" with the message of Christ. (If you would like to receive information regarding how to witness effectively for Christ, write to Campus Crusade for Christ, Arrowhead Springs, San Bernardino, Ca 92414. Ask for speciallly prepared materials concerning witnessing for Christ.

E. *Principle five: we must obey God*

Read Romans 6:14-23.

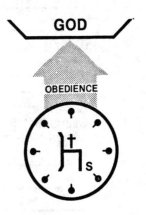

The key to rapid growth in the Christian life is instantaneous obedience to the will of God. Knowing the principles of growth is of no value unless we actually apply them to our lives. This is why obedience is a basic necessity to all Christian growth. To be disobedient to the One who loves us and who alone knows what is really best for us would be sheer folly. Remember that He is even more desirous than you are that you have an abundant life.

1. What did Christ teach concerning the possibility of serving more

   than one master (Matthew 6:24)? _____

_____

2. How much are you to love the Lord (Matthew 22:37)?

_____

3. How can you prove that you love Him (John 14:21)?

_____

4. What will be the result of keeping Christ's commandments (John 15:10-11)? _____

_____

5. What would you say God's standard life is for those who

say they are abiding in Christ (1 John 2:6)? _____

_____

6. Where do we get the power to obey God (Philippians 2:13)? _____

_____

7. In light of Christ's illustration in Luke 6:46-49, why do you think obedience to Christ is imperative for your life?

_____

_____

_____

Life Application

We may look at these five principles of growth in the following way: The first two relate to our *vertical* relationship with God. Through the Bible, God communicates — reveals Himself — to us. Through prayer we communicate with Him. The next two principles relate to our *horizontal* relationship with men. In fellowship, we Christians communicate with each other concerning our Savior and the bond that He gives us with one another. In witnessing, we communicate with non-Christians concerning our Savior, what He has done for us, and what He

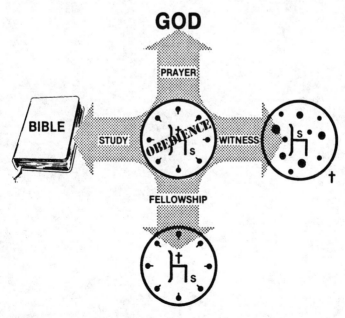

desires to do for them.

The fifth principle, *obedience*, is the catalyst for growth. As you obey Christ, you will experience increasing joy, peace and fellowship with Him, and you will become increasingly mature in the Christian life.

"Have this attitude in yourselves which was also in Christ Jesus, who . . . (became) *obedient* to the point of death, even death on a cross" (Philippians 2:5-8).

CHART

On this chart, list the five key principles of Christian growth, a key verse relating to each one, and at least one way you can apply each principle to your own life.

PRINCIPLE	KEY VERSE	HOW TO APPLY

LESSON FIVE

THE CHRISTIAN'S AUTHORITY

Introduction

OBJECTIVE: To understand the role and the power of the Bible in our daily Christian lives.

TO MEMORIZE: 1 Thessalonians 2:13.

TO READ: Psalm 119:97-104.

Ultimately our views of the authority of the Bible and of the incarnation of Christ are related. For instance, in John 10:34-36, Christ taught that the Old Testament was totally accurate. In Matthew 4:4-7, 10, He quoted it as being authoritative. Furthermore, He taught His followers that He was speaking God's own words (John 3:34) and that His words would not pass away, but would be eternally authoritative (Matthew 24:35).

He even said that the Holy Spirit would bring to mind what He said so that the disciples would preach and write accurately, not depending only upon memory and human understanding (John 16:12-15). Obviously, then, high views of the incarnation and of the inspiration of the Old and New Testaments are related.

A high view of inspiration should be related to personal Bible study and meditation. Even though you believe in the Bible as a unique, written message from God, you would defeat the purpose of God if you failed to apply biblical truths to your life.

Bible Study

A. *Biblical claims of authority*

   1. What were the attitudes of the following prophets concerning their writings?

      Isaiah 43:1-12 _____

      Jeremiah 23:1-8 _____

      Ezekiel 36:32-38 _____

2. What were the attitudes of the following authors toward other writers of Scripture?

Paul (Romans 3:1, 2) _____

Peter (2 Peter 1:19-21) _____

The writer of Hebrews (1:1) _____

B. *Purpose of personal Bible study*

1. Name some practical results of a thorough study of the word of God (2 Timothy 3:15-17). _____

_____

_____

_____

2. In Acts 20:32, Paul says that the Word of God is able to do what two things?

_____

_____

3. What should be the effect upon your own life of reading the Bible (James 1:22-25)? _____

_____

_____

_____

_____

_____

C. *Preparations for personal Bible study*

1. Set aside a definite time.

When did Moses meet with God (Exodus 34:2-4)? _____

_____

When did Christ meet with God (Mark 1:35)? _____

_____

When is the best time for you? _____

_____

2. Find a definite place.

   Where did Christ pray (Mark 1:35)? _____

   What is the value of being alone? _____

   _____

3. Employ these tools:
   Modern translation of the Bible.
   Notebook and pen.
   Dictionary.

OBSERVATION   **INTERPRETATION**   **APPLICATION**

D. *Procedure for personal Bible study*

   Three major steps to methodical Bible study.

   1. Observation: "What does the passage say?"
      Read quickly for content.
      Read again carefully, underlining key words and phrases.

   2. Interpretation: "What does the passage mean?"
      Ask God to give you understanding of the passage.
      Consult a dictionary or modern translation for the precise meaning of words.
      Ask: Who? What? Where? When? Why? How?

   3. Application: Ask yourself, "What does the passage mean to me and how can it be applied to my life?"

      Make a list of:
      Attitudes to be changed   Sins to confess and forsake
      Actions to take or avoid   Examples to follow
      Promises to claim   Other personal applications

Life Application

1. What has been your view of the Bible before this? _____

_____

_____

_____

2. Study Luke 19:1-10 and apply the Bible study method you have just learned.

   What does the passage say? _____

   _____

   What does it mean? _____

   _____

   How does this apply to you? _____

   _____

   Can you now use this method of ?ible study for other Scripture passages? _____

3. What changes in your life do you expect as you proceed with more in-depth Bible study?_____

   _____

   _____

   _____

LESSON SIX

THE CHURCH

Introduction

OBJECTIVE: To realize the importance of involvement in a local church.

TO MEMORIZE: Colossians 1:18.

TO READ: Acts 2:41-47.

In the Greek New Testament the word for church is *ecclesia,* which comes from two Greek words with the root meaning of "to call out." In usage, the meaning was "assembly," and was adopted in New Testament times to refer to the church in two ways. One refers to the local assembly or congregation of Christians meeting together for worship, Bible study, teaching and service. The other is the universal church composed of every believer in Jesus Christ.

Bible Study

A. *Composition of the church*

1. What did the early Christians do that we should do also?

   Acts 2:41, 42 _____

   Acts 4:31, 8:4 _____

   Acts 5:41, 42 _____

2. As God's children, how do we obey the instruction given in Hebrews 10:25? _____

   _____

3. The entire church is compared to a _____ which Christ is the _____ and the individual believers are the _____ (Colossians 1:18; 1 Corinthians 12:27).

4. Read 1 Thessalonians 1:1-10, then list some qualities

God desires for members of any church.

_____

_____

_____

B. *Ordinances of the church*
   1. What do you believe baptism accomplishes (Matthew
      28:19)? _____

      _____

      Who is eligible for baptism? _____
      What was the significance of *your* baptism? _____

      _____

   2. What is the meaning of the communion service
      (1 Corinthians 11:23-26)? _____

      _____

      How do *you* prepare to observe the Lord's Supper?

      _____

      _____

C. *Purposes of the church*
   1. What should be one of the basic purposes of a church
      (2 Timothy 4:2)? _____

      _____

   2. List several of your own reasons for joining a church.

      _____

      _____

      _____

   3. What should the church believe about Christ?
      His birth (Matthew 1:23) _____
      His deity (John 1:14)   _____
      His death (1 Peter 2:24)   _____
      His resurrection (1 Corinthians 15:3, 4) _____

His second coming (1 Thessalonians 4:16, 17) _____

4. Whom did God give, besides prophets and apostles, to strengthen the church members (Ephesians 4:11, 12)?

_____

_____

Life Application

1. If you are not already in a local church, prayerfully list two or three you will visit in the next month, with the purpose of planning to join one. _____

_____

_____

2. Suggestions for making your church worship more meaningful:

   Bow for silent prayer before the service begins. Pray — for yourself, for the minister, for those taking part in the service and for those worshipping — that Christ will be very real to all, and that those who do not know Christ may come to know Him.

   Always take your Bible. Underline portions that are made especially meaningful by the sermons.

   Meditate upon the words of the hymns.

   Take notes on the sermon and apply them to your life.

   Can you list some other ways? _____

_____

_____

3. If you are a part of a local church, ask God to show you ways in which you can be more used by Him by being of service in the church. List the ways He reveals to you. _____

_____

_____

LESSON SEVEN

RECAP

Review verses memorized.

Reread: John 3:1-20; 1 John 5:9-15; Romans 6:14-23.

1. Assurance of salvation:

    Suppose you have just made the great discovery of knowing Jesus Christ personally and you know you have eternal life. In your enthusiasm you tell your roommate you have become a Christian and have eternal life. He replies, "That is mere presumption on your part. No one can know he has eternal life." How would you answer him? What verse would you

    use as your authority? _____

    _____

2. How may a Christian be restored to fellowship after he has

    sinned? What Scripture reference is your authority? _____

    _____

3. Name some of the qualities of a Christ-controlled life.

    _____

    _____

    _____

    _____

4. List the five principles of growth.

    _____

    _____

5. What are the three major steps in methodical Bible study?

    _____

    _____

    _____

6. List at least three ways Scripture may be applied to your life.

_____

_____

_____

7. Name some characteristics of a New Testament church.

_____

_____

_____

8. Match the titles with the appropriate references:

The humiliation and exaltation of Christ	Philippians 2:5-11
The meaning of the resurrection for us	Acts 2:41-47
The value of the Word of God to us	1 Corinthians 2:11; 3:5
The fruit of the Spirit	Psalm 119:97-104
The spiritual and carnal Christians	Psalm 63
Reading the Bible for growth	Galatians 5:16-24
A psalm relating to prayer	James 1:18-27
The early church	1 Corinthians 15:12-26

Life Application

Ask yourself these questions and write the answers. "In what specific ways is my life different now from what it was when I began this study about the Christian adventure?" _____

_____

_____

"In what areas do I need to obey Scripture more?" _____

_____

_____

The Christian
and the Abundant Life

TOWARD CHRISTIAN MATURITY

The Christian life is a life of victory, joy, peace and purposeful living. Jesus said, "I came that they might have life, and might have it abundantly" (John 10:10). True, there are many professing Christians who are defeated and discouraged, but this is not the New Testament norm. Picture the apostle Paul and Silas imprisoned in Philippi. They were beaten and cast into the inner prison where their feet were locked in the stocks. Yet they prayed and sang praises unto God. Their confidence was not in themselves. Their confidence and trust were in the true living God whom they loved, worshipped and served.

Picture the disciples and thousands of other first-century Christians singing praises to God as they were burned at the stake, crucified or fed to the lions. They faced horrible deaths with courage and joy because of their vital, personal relationship with Christ, remembering that "the servant is not greater than his Lord." Such dedication to Christ is not limited to the disciples and early Christians. Down through the centuries, there have been — and still are — many thousands of Christians who have dedicated their very lives to Christ. They are living the abundant life which Christ promised. You may not find it necessary to die for Christ, but are you willing to live for Him?

Referring to the world crisis of his time, Sir Winston Churchill once said, "This generation may well live to see the end of what we now call civilization." As civilization stands on the brink of extermination, *the desperate need of this hour is men and women who are utterly abandoned to Jesus Christ — Christians who are willing to serve Him at any cost.*

"The more I think of and pray about the state of religion in this country, and all over the world, the deeper my conviction becomes that the low state of the spiritual life of Christians is due to the fact that they do not realize that the aim and object of conversion is to bring the soul, even here on earth, to a daily fellowship with the Father in heaven. When once this truth has been accepted, the believer will perceive how indispensable it is to the spiritual life of a Christian to take time each day with God's Word and in prayer to wait upon God for His presence and His love to be revealed.

101

"It is not enough at conversion to accept forgiveness of sins, or even to surrender to God. That is only a beginning. The young believer must understand that he has no power of his own to maintain his spiritual life. No, he needs each day to receive new grace from heaven through fellowship with the Lord Jesus. This cannot be obtained by a hasty prayer, nor a superficial reading of a few verses from God's Word. He must take time quietly and deliberately to come into God's presence, to feel his own weakness and his need, and to wait upon God through His Holy Spirit, to renew the heavenly light and life in his heart. Then he may rightly expect to be kept by the power of Christ throughout the day, and all its temptations.

"Many of God's children long for a better life, but do not realize the need of giving God time day by day in their inner chamber through His Spirit to renew and sanctify their lives.

"Meditate on this thought: The feeble state of my spiritual life is mainly due to the lack of time day by day in fellowship with God."

— Andrew Murray

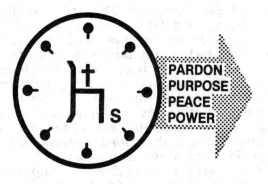

PARDON
PURPOSE
PEACE
POWER

LESSON ONE

WHAT IS THE CHRISTIAN LIFE?

Introduction

OBJECTIVE: To show the difference between our new life in Christ, and the old life.

TO MEMORIZE: 2 Corinthians 5:17.

TO READ: John 1-3.

The Christian life begins with spiritual birth (John 3:6) through faith in the Lord Jesus Christ (Ephesians 2:8, 9). The Christian life is a personal, daily relationship between the believer and Christ. This life is lived by faith. *Faith is trust. We trust our lives to Christ's keeping because He has proven Himself trustworthy by His life, His death, His resurrection and His abiding presence.*

Bible Study

A. *A new creation*

1. On the basis of 2 Corinthians 5:17, what has happened to you? _____

   What are some evidences in your life of new things having come, and old things having passed away? _____

   _____

   _____

2. To what does the Bible compare this experience of newness (John 3:3)? _____

3. How was your new birth accomplished (John 3:16; 1:12, 13)? _____

   _____

4. According to Ephesians 2:8, 9, what did you do to merit this gift? _____

   _____

B. *A new relationship with God*

    1. What are you called (1 Peter 2:2)? _____

    What should be your desire? _____

    2. What is your new relationship with God (John 1:12)?

    _____

    3. What does it mean to you to be a partaker of the divine nature (2 Peter 1:4)? _____

    4. How do you know that you are God's child (Galatians 4:6; Romans 8:16)? _____

    _____

C. *A new motivation*

    1. How does the love of Christ motivate you (2 Corinthians 5:14)? _____

    2. What has replaced self as the most important factor (verse 15)? _____

    3. Two things have happened in your life to give you new motivation, according to Colossians 3:1-3:

    What has happened to your old life according to verse 2?

    _____

    What will motivate you to seek those things which are above, according to verse 1? _____

    _____

D. *A new relationship to mankind*

    1. What is new about your relationship to people (1 John 3:11, 14)? _____

    2. How can you show that you are a follower of Christ (John 13:35)? _____

    3. Read 2 Corinthians 5:18-21. What ministry has been given to you (verse 18)? _____

    We are called _____ for Christ (verse 20).

4. As an ambassador for Christ, what is the greatest thing that you can do (Matthew 4:19)? _____

   _____

   Name at least three ways you can do that in your own life.

   _____

   _____

5. How can your friends benefit from the message you, as an ambassador for Christ, deliver to them (1 John 1:3, 4)?

   _____

   _____

Life Application

1. What is the greatest change you have seen in your life since you became a new creation in Christ Jesus? _____

   _____

2. In your new relationship with God, what now can be your response toward problems, disappointments and frustrations (1 Peter 5:7; Romans 8:28)? _____

   _____

3. How will your goals be changed as a result of your new motivation? _____

   _____

4. What now is your responsibility to other men and women, and how will you carry it out? _____

   _____

   _____

5. List two changes you would like to see in your life now that you are a Christian, and ask God to bring those changes about. _____

   _____

   _____

LESSON TWO

AN APPRAISAL OF
YOUR OWN SPIRITUAL LIFE

Introduction

OBJECTIVE: To evaluate your relationship with Christ.

TO MEMORIZE: Galatians 6:7.

TO READ: John 4-6.

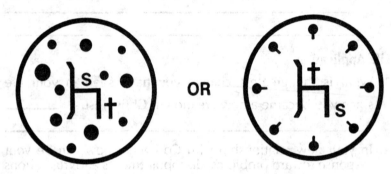

Bible Study

Meditate upon each question as well as upon the answer. Make this a personal appraisal of your spiritual condition.

A. *Types of soil*

Read the parable of the sower in Matthew 13:1-23; Mark 4:3-20; Luke 8:4-15.

1. To what does the seed refer (Mark 4:14)? _____

2. What are the four kinds of soil referred to in Matthew 13:4-8? _____

_____

B. *Making soil productive*

1. What does each kind of soil represent?

   Compare verse 4 with 18, 19. _____

_____

Compare verses 5, 6 with 20, 21. _____

_____

Compare verse 7 with 22. _____

_____

Compare verse 8 with 23. _____

_____

2. What must happen for the roadside soil to be changed (Hebrews 3:15)? _____

_____

3. How can unproductive, rocky ground be made productive? (See 1 Corinthians 10:13 and Proverbs 29:25). _____

_____

4. How can individuals described as thorny soil become vital and effective Christians (1 Peter 5:7, Matthew 6:19-21)? _____

_____

C. *Result of dwelling in good soil*

1. What condition in a Christian results in abundance of fruit (Mark 4:20; Luke 8:15)? _____

_____

2. What type of soil do most of the professing Christians whom you know represent? _____

_____

3. What type of soil would you say your life now represents?

_____

4. What type of soil do you want your life to represent?

_____

Life Application

1. How must the soil of your life be changed to become good ground or to increase in its fruitfulness? _____

_____

_____

2. What can you do?_____

_____

3. What must you trust Christ to do? _____

_____

LESSON THREE

ABUNDANT LIVING

Introduction

OBJECTIVE: To learn how practical the "abundant life" is.

TO MEMORIZE: John 10:10.

TO READ: John 7-9.

Jesus said, "I came that they might have life, and might have it abundantly" (John 10:10b).

"As you therefore have received Christ Jesus the Lord so walk in Him" (Colossians 2:6). *We have received Christ by faith and we are admonished to live by faith.*

YOU HAVE BEEN SAVED FROM THE PENALTY OF SIN (John 3:18; Ephesians 2:8).

YOU ARE BEING SAVED FROM THE POWER OF SIN (Jude 24, 25; 2 Thessalonians 3:3).

YOU SHALL BE SAVED FROM THE PRESENCE OF SIN (1 John 3:2; Philippians 3:21; 1 Corinthians 15:51, 52).

You have trusted God for payment of your penalty for sin and for eternal life. Why not trust Him now for power over sin? Remember that you received Christ by faith, so you should now walk in faith.

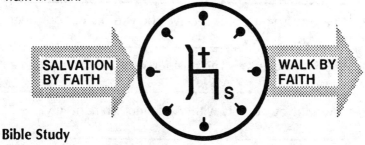

SALVATION BY FAITH → ← WALK BY FAITH

Bible Study

A. *The basis of abundant living*

Read Romans 6:1-16.

1. What do you *know* happened to you when you became a Christian (verse 6)? _____

_____

2. According to verse 11, what must you do? _____

_____

3. What does verse 13 tell you your responsibility is? _____

_____

4. According to verse 16, man is either a servant of sin or of righteousness.

   What determines his allegiance? _____

_____

   What is your choice?   _____

_____

   Review Romans 6:6, 11, 13 and 16 and note the progression: *Know* that you have been crucified with Christ; *reckon* yourself dead to sin and alive to Jesus Christ; *yield* yourself unto God; *obey* God. (See Directory of Terms.)

B. *The practice of abundant living*

   Read Psalm 37:1-7, 34.

   1. What is to be your attitude toward worry (verse 1)? _____

_____

   2. What is to be your attitude toward the Lord (verse 3)?

_____

   3. What must you do to receive the desires of your heart (verse 4)? _____

   4. Why is it necessary to consider verse 5 when you plan your future? _____

   5. How will you comply with the admonishment in verse 7?

_____

   6. What does verse 34 mean to you? _____

   Now, review each of the above references and note the progression: *Fret not* thyself, *trust* in the Lord, *delight* thyself in the Lord, *commit* thy way unto the Lord, *rest* in the Lord, *wait* on the Lord. (See Directory of Terms.)

The secret of the abundant life is contained in these words: *know, reckon, yield, obey, fret not, trust, delight, commit, rest* and *wait.* (Underline these key words in your Bible in Romans 6 and in Psalm 37.)

Directory of terms:

Know — To be fully assured of a fact.

Reckon — To act upon a fact, to consider it, to depend upon it instead of upon feelings.

Yield — To give up, to surrender, to submit.

Obey — To put instructions into effect, to comply with, to trust.

Trust — To rely on wholeheartedly.

Delight — To take great pleasure or joy.

Commit — To place in trust or charge, to entrust.

Wait — To anticipate with confident expectancy.

Life Application

1. In the chart below, list which key words of the abundant life you are now applying, and which you need to begin to apply, through the power of Christ:

KEY WORDS	APPLYING NOW	NEED TO APPLY
KNOW		
RECKON		
YIELD		
OBEY		
TRUST		
DELIGHT		
COMMIT		
WAIT		

2. How do you plan to go about applying these? Be specific.

_____

_____

_____

_____

LESSON FOUR

THE ABIDING LIFE

Introduction

OBJECTIVE: To understand and begin *abiding* in Christ.

TO MEMORIZE: John 15:7, 16.

TO READ: John 10-12.

The abiding life is one of the most significant phases of the Christian life. To have real abiding joy, we must learn to abide in Christ constantly. Many people never find the secret to a joyous life; consequently they feel the Lord has let them down. The Christian who is not enjoying his Christian experience should be taught the truth of God's Word. "These things have I spoken unto you that My *joy* might remain in you, and that your *joy*

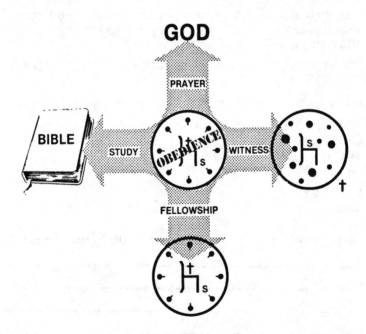

might be full." The abiding life brings lasting joy. Abiding in Christ also makes our lives fruitful; our prayers are answered. We are obedient to Him because He lives in and through us.

Bible Study

A. *The abiding life explained*

To abide in Christ is to live in conscious dependence upon Him, recognizing that it is His life, His power, His wisdom, His resources, His strength and His ability, operating through you, which enable you to live according to His will. "I can do all things through Him who strengthens me," but apart from Him I can do nothing (Philippians 4:13; John 15:5). The Christian believes, "I am strong enough for all things, due to Christ's strength."

1. Jesus referred to Himself as the _____ and

   Christians as the _____ in John 15:5.

   What is the relationship between Christ and you, as

   illustrated in that verse? _____

   _____

   _____

2. Why does Jesus prune every branch that bears fruit

   (John 15:2)? _____

   _____

   What are some experiences that have constituted "pruning" in your life as a Christian? (See Hebrews 12:6;

   Romans 5:3-5.) _____

   _____

   _____

   _____

B. *The results of abiding in Christ*

1. Read John 15:7-11.

   List two necessary qualifications for effective prayer

   according to verse 7. _____

_____

_____

2. Jesus glorified God. Can you glorify God? How (verse 8)?
_____

3. Christ commands us to continue in His love. How great do you believe this love to be (verse 9)? _____

How are we to abide in Christ's love (verse 10)? _____
_____

How do you think the result promised in verse 11 will be revealed in your life today? _____
_____

4. What has Christ chosen us to do (John 15:16)? _____
_____

What is meant by "fruit"? _____
_____

5. Will you be able to do what Christ expects of you? _____
_____

How do you know? _____
_____

6. Why do you think Jesus chose this particular way to illustrate our abiding in Him?_____
_____
_____

Life Application

1. Write briefly what you need to do to begin abiding in Christ more consistently. _____
_____
_____

2. What do you think He will do as a result? _____

_____

_____

"Abiding is the key to Christian experience by which the divine attributes are transplanted into human soil, to the transforming of character and conduct."
— Norman B. Harrison

LESSON FIVE

THE CLEANSED LIFE

Introduction

OBJECTIVE: To learn the importance and means of living a cleansed life, moment by moment.

TO MEMORIZE: 1 John 1:9.

TO READ: John 13-15.

God does not fill a dirty vessel with His power and love. Cleansing precedes filling. We often yearn for spiritual power and do not have it because of impure motives, double motives or unconfessed sin. To be filled vessels, we must be cleansed vessels.

This lesson explains how your life can have power. The first step is to be cleansed from sin and filled with the Spirit of God.

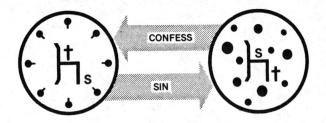

Bible Study

A. *Being "out of fellowship" with God*

Study the diagram at the beginning of this lesson:

1. What characterizes a person who is not in fellowship with God (James 1:8)? _____

2. Read Isaiah 59:2. What is the result of sin in one's life?

   _____

   _____

3. Do you think sin in your life has affected your relation-

ship with God? _____ How? _____

_____

_____

B. *How to be cleansed*

   1. What is the condition for cleansing and forgiveness
      (1 John 1:9)? _____

      _____

      The word "confess" means to "say the same thing as
      another — to agree with God." When God brings to your
      attention the fact that something you have done is sin,
      you are to confess — agree with God — say the same thing
      that God says about it. Do not just say, "I have sinned,"
      but state what the sin was and agree with God, looking at
      it from His viewpoint. Then determine that you will put it
      out of your life and will not do it again.

   2. What two things did the psalmist do about his sin in
      Psalm 32:5? _____

      _____

      According to Proverbs 28:13, what is the result of not
      admitting sin? _____

      _____

      Of admitting sin? _____

      _____

C. *Living "in fellowship" with God*

   1. Notice in the diagram that, when we confess our sins, God
      restores us to fellowship. Walking in fellowship with the
      Father and the Son is referred to as "walking in the light."

      Read 1 John 1:7 and list two results promised: _____

      _____

      _____

   2. When we are in fellowship with God, some things are
      happening within us. According to Philippians 2:13 and
      4:13 what are they? _____

_____

_____

_____

3. What is this power within us and what is its result
   (Romans 8:9; Galatians 5:22, 23)? _____

_____

4. What should be our attitude when temptations come
   (Romans 6:11-13)? _____

_____

Why (Colossians 3:3)? _____

What responses does that make possible? _____

_____

_____

Life Application

1. In your own words write what you will do when you find
   anything that breaks the fellowship between you and the
   Lord. _____

_____

_____

_____

2. Summarize the reasons it is so important to confess sin as
   soon as you are aware of it. _____

_____

_____

_____

3. List any sin in your life right now which needs to be confessed. Then, confess the sin, and thank God for His
   complete forgiveness. _____

_____

_____

LESSON SIX

THE CHRISTIAN ARMOR AND WARFARE

Introduction

OBJECTIVE: To learn of spiritual warfare and how to use the things God has provided for the battle.

TO MEMORIZE: Ephesians 6:10-12.

TO READ: John 16-18.

Bible Study

Describe in your own words, the picture depicted in Paul's command given in Ephesians 6:10-18.

HELMET OF SALVATION

BREAST PLATE OF RIGHTEOUSNESS

BELT OF TRUTH

SHIELD OF FAITH

SWORD OF THE SPIRIT (WORD OF GOD)

SHOES TO SPREAD THE GOSPEL OF PEACE

_____

_____

_____

_____

_____

_____

A. We are on the battlefield

1. What two things will putting on the whole armor of God help you to do (verses 11-13)? _____

_____

_____

2. Christians are engaged in warfare.

Who are the enemies?	How should you respond to these enemies?
James 4:4 _____	Romans 12:2 _____
Galatians 5:17 _____	Galatians 5:16 _____
1 Peter 5:8 _____	James 4:7 _____

3. Name the five protective pieces of armor God provides and expects you to wear (Ephesians 6:14-17)._____

_____

_____

_____

4. How can you employ the sword of God's Word (verse 17) for defense against temptation (Psalm 119:9, 11)? _____

_____

_____

5. List some ways the sword of God's Word can be used in an offensive action (2 Timothy 3:16, 17). _____

_____

_____

_____

6. How can you stay alert and always be prepared (Ephesians 6:18; Colossians 4:2)? _____

_____

B. *We are more than conquerors through Christ!*

1. When you consider the pieces of armor and weapons provided, who can you conclude is really fighting the battle (Ephesians 6:10)? _____

_____

2. Why can you always expect God to be the winner (1 John 4:4)? _____

_____

3. What does Romans 8:31 suggest to you regarding your attitude toward adversity and temptation? _____

_____

_____

_____

Life Application

1. Describe a specific situation in your life right now in which you need to employ a spiritual "weapon." _____

_____

_____

2. Which weapon(s) will you use and how? _____

_____

3. What result(s) do you expect? _____

_____

LESSON SEVEN

ATTITUDE

Introduction

OBJECTIVE: To begin to look at life consistently from God's perspective.

TO MEMORIZE: 2 Corinthians 1:3, 4.

TO READ: John 19-21.

When two Christians face the same tragedy, one may become depressed and defeated while the other is drawn closer to God. What do you think is the reason for this?_____

_____

_____

_____

In this study you will learn about unrecognized blessings. Sometimes Christians feel that God has let them down when they find themselves without money, health, prestige, or in severe straits. Such an attitude leads to coldness of heart, prayerlessness, distrust, worry and selfish living. Attitude makes the difference.

Bible Study

A. *God's people in trouble*

In Exodus 14:1-4, the Israelites experienced an unrecognized blessing. As you read, notice the human viewpoint of the people and God's viewpoint as seen in Moses.

1. How did the Israelites react to apparent danger (Exodus 14:10-12)? _____

_____

2. Notice how Moses reacted. Why do you think he

commanded the people as he did (Exodus 14:13, 14)?

_____

_____

3. State the blessings God wrought in their hearts and minds through this experience (Exodus 14:31). _____

_____

4. List some ways God has worked through difficulties in your life, and has shown these difficulties really to be blessings._____

_____

_____

B. *Taking the proper attitude*

1. List some things the Bible guarantees when you are tempted or tested (1 Corinthians 10:13). _____

_____

_____

_____

2. How can the Bible's guarantee in Romans 8:28 about *everything* you will experience be true? _____

_____

3. What response to tribulation does God expect from you according to Romans 5:3-5? _____

_____

What are the results of tribulations? (See also James 1:3.)

_____

_____

4. Give the Bible's explanation of the purpose of unrecognized blessings in:

2 Corinthians 1:3, 4 _____

Hebrews 12:6-11 _____

5. Read 1 Thessalonians 5:18 and Hebrews 13:15.

   What response does God command in *all* situations?

   _____

   _____

   How can you rejoice and give thanks when sorrow and
   tragedy come? _____

   _____

   Describe how this contrasts with the attitude of the
   Israelites in Exodus 14:1-12. _____

   _____

Life Application

1. List the methods by which an attitude of trust can become
   a reality for you. (See Ephesians 5:18; Galatians 5:16;
   1 Thessalonians 5:17; Romans 10:17.) _____

   _____

   _____

2. With what trial in your life do you need to trust God right
   now?_____

   _____

   _____

3. What do you think the unrecognized blessings in that trial
   could be? _____

   _____

   _____

4. How can you appropriate those blessings?_____

   _____

   _____

LESSON EIGHT

RECAP

Review verses memorized.

Reread: Luke 8:4-5; Romans 6:1-16; John 15:1-17; 1 John 1:1-9.

In your own words, what does the abundant Christian life involve? _____

_____

_____

_____

Envision the abundant life you desire for yourself and describe it. _____

_____

_____

_____

How do you know your picture of the abundant life is consistent with God's view?_____

_____

_____

_____

What specific steps do you still need to take to make that life a reality for you?_____

_____

_____

_____

_____

The Christian
and the Holy Spirit

*Be sure to read this article before beginning
the lessons about the Holy Spirit.*

YOU SHALL RECEIVE POWER

by Bill Bright

Has it ever occurred to you that there could be much more to the Christian life than what you are now experiencing?

Jesus said, "I came that they (you and I and all Christians) might have life, and might have it abundantly" (John 10:10). Yet, if you are an average professing Christian, you are undoubtedly thinking, "There is certainly nothing abundant about my life. I try to witness, but no one is interested in what I have to say. I experience nothing but doubts, fears, frustrations and defeat. Surely there must be something more to this Christian life, but I have never found it."

Because of the evangelistic emphasis of Campus Crusade, we have found it absolutely imperative that each member of our staff, as well as the student leaders with whom we work, be filled with the Holy Spirit if we are to have an effective ministry for Christ on the college campus.

There was a time in my own Christian ministry when I challenged Christians to witness and live holy lives for Christ, but the results were so discouraging that I began to devote most of my time and energies to evangelism, where God blessed with much more apparent results. However, as the years have passed, the Holy Spirit has helped me to see the great potential power in lukewarm Christians, if only they are awakened and harnessed for Christ. I am now convinced that the lukewarm, carnal Christian can be changed into a vital, dynamic, witnessing Christian, if he will surrender his will to Christ and be filled with the Holy Spirit. Again and again I am reminded of the great contrast between the church of Jesus Christ today and His Church of the first century.

What is the difference? What is that strange quality that sets one man apart from another when both are Christians? Some theologians would say that it is the degree of commitment. yet there are many people all over the world who are crying out to God, dedicating their lives to Christ day after day, and yet are continuing to be impotent and defeated. Why? Are we not told in Matthew 5:6, "Blessed are those who hunger and thirst for righteousness, for they shall be satisfied"?

Did not John, the beloved disciple, quote Jesus (1 John 1:5-7) as saying that God is light, and in Him is no darkness at all, and that if we walk in the "light" we have fellowship with the Father and the Son?

Christians need not live in spiritual poverty. The many thousands of promises recorded in the Word of God apply to every Christian. These promises include: assurance of God's love (John 3:16); eternal life (Romans 6:23); forgiveness of sin (1 John 1:9); provision of material needs (Philippians 4:19); the ordering of one's steps (Psalms 37:23); the secret of successful prayer (John 15:7); promise of an abundant life (John 10:10b); God's promise to honor a holy life (2 Chronicles 16:9); assurance that everything that happens is for our own good (Romans 8:28); deliverance from temptation (1 Corinthians 10:13); victory over fear (1 John 4:18); as well as thousands of others.

The Bible promises that every Christian can possess love, joy, peace, faith and many other beneficial qualities. What is wrong? Dr. Billy Graham has stated that at least 90% of all Christians in America are living defeated lives. Others who are in a position to know the spiritual pulse of America have made similar statements. It is quite likely that, according to the law of averages, you are among the 90%. You may have a heart for God. You read your Bible faithfully, you pray, you witness, you are active in your church; yet year after year you continue to fight a losing battle. Temptations come! Half-heartedly you resist, then yield, surrender and are finally defeated. For months you journey in the slough of despondency with Mr. Christian in Bunyan's *Pilgrim's Progress*. Then you attend a spiritual retreat and you are back on the Alpine heights for a brief time. Up, down, victories, defeats! Soon you cry out with Paul in Romans 7:24, "Wretched man that I am! Who will set me free from the body of this death?"

As president of Campus Crusade for Christ, it is my privilege to speak to thousands of students each year. At the conclusion of a message which I once gave at Princeton University, a devout young man approached me in great concern over his lack of "fruit" in witnessing. "I have tried to witness," he said, "but I have had no results. I read my Bible daily and pray and memorize Scripture. I attend every Christian meeting on campus. Yet, I have never been able to introduce another to Christ. What is wrong with me?" In counseling with him, I gently probed for the answer to his problem. I knew that he meant business. He wanted to please God. He sincerely wanted his friends to know his wonderful Savior, and, according to his conduct and Christian activities, he was a model Christian.

Jesus promises in John 14:26 and 16:13 that the Holy Spirit will teach us all things and will guide us into all truth. As I counseled with this young man, we were directed to some very important passages of Scripture. When he claimed these, by faith, they unlocked the door to victory and to unspeakable joy. He left the counseling room rejoicing and with an expectant heart. At that point, he began to experience a fruitful life in Christ such as he had never before known. He knew that something had happened in his life. He was a new man — no longer afraid, impotent and defeated. Now he was bold and had power and faith to believe God. He could hardly wait to see what God was going to do through him. "Lord," he prayed, "who will be the first to whom You will lead me today?"

In the course of the day, the Holy Spirit led this young Christian to a fellow student to whom he had previously witnessed without apparent success. But today was different. God had prepared the heart of the other student and soon these two were bowed in prayer as the student friend received Christ. The next day this marvelous experience was repeated with another student responding as if drawn by an invisible hand. This is not strange, for the Word of God tells us, "No one can come to Me, unless the Father . . . draws him" (John 6:44). Through the power of the Holy Spirit, this Princeton student continued to lead fellow students to Christ day after day. His own life was so wonderfully changed and empowered, so used of God, that he eventually became a Christian minister.

The story of this Princeton student is typical of hundreds of others who have sought counsel on campus after campus across the nation and around the world. There was a young minister who had earned his bachelor's and master's degrees in one of the finest theological seminaries of America, but was ineffective in his witnessing. Upon learning how he could appropriate the power of the Holy Spirit by faith, he experienced a new spirit of expectancy and joy that resulted in a victorious and fruitful life. There was a shy, timid student at a college retreat who expressed his concern for the lost, but was utterly frustrated and defeated by his fear of man. When God's power, victory, love and faith took possession of him, he experienced joy and fruit such as he had never believed possible. Fear and defeat gave way to courage, radiance and victory. Another faithful witness who heard, believed and received, discovered that witnessing was no longer a duty, but a joy! "It is just like being released from prison," he later exclaimed.

Countless additional examples such as those cited could be given of others whose fruitless and frustrated lives became fruitful and victorious when they received by faith the power of the Holy Spirit and discovered that the promises of Jesus were for them: "Follow Me and I will make you fishers of men" (Matthew 4:19); "By this is My Father glorified, that you bear much fruit" (John 15:8); "You did not choose Me, but I chose you, and appointed you, that you should go and bear fruit, and that your fruit should remain: that whatever you ask of the Father in My name, He may give to you" (John 15:16); "And without faith it is impossible to please Him, for he who comes to God must believe that He is, and that He is a rewarder of those who seek Him" (Hebrews 11:6).

Through the centuries there have been followers of Christ who were just ordinary Christians. Nothing spectacular ever happened to them or through them. Then, as happened to Peter and the disciples, something changed their lives. They were no longer ordinary or average. They became men and women of God, instruments of power. Their defeat turned to victory. Doubts and fear turned to assurance, joy and faith. They were the ones who "turned the world upside down" (Acts 17:6). Cowardly Peter, who denied Jesus three times (you and I have denied Him many more), became the bold Peter of Pentecost who preached fearlessly. On separate occasions, 3,000 and 5,000 believed in Christ and were added to the church. The early disciples possessed a strange new quality of life, a life of power which transformed the heart of a wicked Roman Empire during the first century. Their boldness led everyone of the twelve to a martyr's grave — except John, who died in exile on the Isle of Patmos.

The change in the lives of those to whom I have just referred all began at Pentecost when those who were gathered together were filled with the Holy Spirit. Through this same power of the Holy Spirit, millions of others through the centuries have been changed into vital, dynamic Christians.

What do you know about the Holy Spirit? What does the Holy Spirit mean to you personally?

Jesus promised in His apostolic commission that the Holy Spirit would give us power to be His witnesses. "But you shall receive power when the Holy Spirit has come upon you; and you shall be My witnesses both in Jerusalem, and in all Judea and Samaria, and even to the remotest part of the earth" (Acts 1:8).

IT IS THE PURPOSE OF THIS BRIEF ARTICLE TO EXPLAIN HOW TO BE FILLED WITH THE HOLY SPIRIT AS IT RELATES

TO THE FULFILLMENT OF THE GREAT COMMISSION OF OUR LORD. THEREFORE, WE SHALL NOT DWELL ON THE MANY OTHER TRUTHS CONCERNING THE ROLE OF THE HOLY SPIRIT IN THE LIFE OF EVERY CHRISTIAN EXCEPT AS THEY CONTRIBUTE TO OUR MAJOR OBJECTIVE.

Let us now consider briefly some of these spiritual truths as they relate to the filling of the Holy Spirit.

I. WHO IS THE HOLY SPIRIT?

The Holy Spirit is the third person of the Trinity: Father, Son and *Holy Spirit*. He is not some vague, ethereal shadow nor an impersonal force. He is equal in every way with the Father and with the Son. All of the divine attributes are ascribed to the Holy Spirit. He has infinite intellect (1 Corinthians 2:11), will (1 Corinthians 12:11) and emotion (Romans 15:30).

Dr. J. Edwin Orr describes the Holy Spirit as "the Commander-in-Chief of the Army of Christ. He is the Lord of the harvest, supreme in revival, evangelism and missionary endeavor. Without His consent, plans are bound to fail. It behooves us as Christians to fit our tactical operations into the plan of His strategy, which is the reviving of the church and the evangelization of the world."

The first reference to the Holy Spirit is made in Genesis 1:2. His influence is noted throughout the Old Testament, but it becomes more pronounced in the life and ministry of our Lord. Finally, after our Savior ascended to be at the right hand of the Father, the place of power, He sent the Holy Spirit to be the "comforter" or "helper" (John 14:26 and 15:26). The Greek word for comforter or helper is *paraclete,* meaning the "one called along beside" the Christian as a companion and friend, also the one who "energizes," "strengthens" and "empowers" the believer in Christ.

The Holy Spirit is also called:

Spirit of God	1 Corinthians 3:16
Spirit of Christ	Romans 8:9
Spirit of Life	Romans 8:2
Spirit of Truth	John 16:13
Spirit of Grace	Hebrews 10:29
Spirit of Promise	Ephesians 1:13

II. WHY DID THE HOLY SPIRIT COME?

The Holy Spirit came to bear witness to the Lord Jesus Christ and to glorify Him (John 16:13, 14). As Jesus had come to exalt and reveal the Father, the Holy Spirit was sent to exalt and glorify the Son, Jesus Christ.

It logically follows, then, that the more we allow the Holy

Spirit to control our lives, the more we shall love and serve the Lord Jesus Christ, and the more we shall be conscious of His loving and abiding presence.

When we are filled with the Holy Spirit we are filled with Jesus Christ. Thus, when we are filled with the Holy Spirit — the Lord Jesus Christ — a power much greater than our own is released within us and through us for service and victorious living.

III. HOW IS THE HOLY SPIRIT RELATED TO EVERY CHRISTIAN?

(A Christian is one who has received Jesus Christ into his life as Lord and Savior, according to John 1:12; John 3:5; 2 Corinthians 5:17.)

At the time of spiritual birth:

A. The Holy Spirit regenerates men (John 3:5).

B. The Holy Spirit comes to dwell within each Christian (1 Corinthians 3:16).

C. The Holy Spirit seals every Christian in Christ (Ephesians 1:13; 4:30).

D. The Holy Spirit is the earnest or guarantee of the inheritance that each Christian will one day receive (2 Corinthians 5:5).

E. The Holy Spirit baptizes each Christian into the Body of Christ (1 Corinthians 12:13; Galatians 3:27; Romans 6:3, 4).

F. The Holy Spirit fills every yielded Christian for service.

At the moment of spiritual birth every Christian is regenerated, indwelt, sealed, guaranteed, baptized and filled with the Holy Spirit. The act of regenerating, indwelling, sealing, guaranteeing and baptizing the Christian into the Body of Christ by the Holy Spirit is a positional relationship and may or may not be accompanied by an emotional experience.

These truths do, however, acquaint the Christian with the thrilling fact of his union with Christ, ". . . you in Me, and I in you" (John 14:20). We exchange our weakness for His power, our sinfulness and defeat for His holiness and victory.

As a result of this relationship with Christ, every Christian has the potential to witness with power and to live a life of victory over sin. This potential power, the life of Jesus Christ in every believer, is released by faith as the Christian surrenders the control of his life to the Holy Spirit. Since it is the ministry of the Holy Spirit to glorify Christ, Jesus Christ now has unhindered opportunity to work in and through the believer to perform His perfect will.

Every Christian must be filled with the Holy Spirit in order to have the power to be a more effective witness for Christ. "But you shall receive power when the Holy Spirit has come upon you; and you shall be My witnesses both in Jerusalem, and in all Judea and Samaria, and even to the remotest part of the earth" (Acts 1:8). Every biblical reference to the filling of the Holy Spirit, in both the Old Testament and in the New Testament, is related to power for service and witness.

The response to the filling of the Holy Spirit may vary from a calm assurance of power and quiet realization of a greater faith in Christ and the promises of His Word to a more emotional experience.

A careful study of 1 Corinthians 12 teaches us that all Christians are members of the Body of Christ. As various parts of the human body have different functions, so various members of Christ's body will have different responsibilities in His kingdom. No Christian should belittle another's gift. Neither should any Christian seek to imitate another in the "experience of filling" or in the gifts of the Holy Spirit. Every Christian must leave the assignment of the gifts, and the manner in which they are revealed, to the Holy Spirit.

Further, according to 1 Corinthians 13, any or all of these gifts will profit little unless we are motivated by love.

We are admonished by God in Ephesians 5:17-20, "So then do not be foolish, but understand what the will of the Lord is. And do not get drunk with wine, for that is dissipation, but be filled with the Spirit, speaking to one another in psalms and hymns and spiritual songs, singing and making melody with your heart to the Lord; always giving thanks for all things in the name of our Lord Jesus Christ to God, even the Father."

The apostle Paul was suggesting that a Spirit-filled Christian will know God's will, and may give the impression of being "Spirit-intoxicated" because of the joy, radiance, boldness and courage that he frequently demonstrates. Also, as this Scripture passage suggests, a Spirit-filled Christian is continually praising God in his heart and giving thanks for all things. He realizes, in a way that he could not while in his carnal state, that all that he is and has is by the grace of God.

Beginning with the day of Pentecost and continuing through the centuries, the work of God has always been accomplished through men who were filled with the Holy Spirit — men such as Peter, Paul and all of the disciples.

In more recent times there have been men like John Wesley, Jonathan Edwards, Charles Finney, Dwight L. Moody, Charles Spurgeon, G. Campbell Morgan, R. A. Torrey and scores of other Christian leaders — some of whom are now living — who have been filled with the Holy Spirit and who have been greatly used to further the cause of Christ and His kingdom. However, the filling of the Holy Spirit is not limited to Christian leaders, but is available to all Christians who meet God's terms.

Hear what some of these men and women of God say about the importance of every Christian's being filled with the Holy Spirit:

". . . Men ought to seek with their whole hearts to be filled with the Spirit of God. Without being filled with the Spirit, it is utterly impossible that an individual Christian or a church can ever live or work as God desires . . ."

— Andrew Murray

"Christians are as guilty for not being filled with the Holy Spirit as sinners are for not repenting. They are even more so, for as they have more light, they are so much the more guilty."

— Charles G. Finney

"The Spirit-filled life, that life that permits His fullness in a sustained overflow, is the only life that can please God."

— Norman B. Harrison

"The great purpose in the filling of the Holy Spirit is power for service. The best and most-used Christians known to me have been men who have testified to a deeper experience of the filling of the Holy Spirit."

— J. Edwin Orr

"I believe that it is impossible for any Christian to be effective either in his life or in his service unless he is filled with the Holy Spirit who is God's only provision of power."

— Henrietta C. Mears

"Read the biographies of God's men and you will discover that each one sought and obtained the enduement of power from on high. One sermon preached in the anointing is worth a thousand in the energy of the flesh."

— Dr. Oswald J. Smith

I wish again to make it especially clear at this point that the Holy Spirit already indwells every believer and the special enduement of power that attends the filling of the Holy Spirit is not reserved for Christian leaders only. Every Christian not only has the prerogative of being filled with the Holy Spirit, but every Christian is admonished to be filled with the Spirit (Ephesians 5:18). Therefore, if a Christian is not filled, he is disobedient to the command of God and is sinning against God. Further, since God commands us in His Word to be filled with the Spirit, we may be certain that He has the power to fill us the very moment we invite Him to do so.

I assure you that, according to the promises of the Word of God and from observations and personal experience, Jesus is far more eager to give His love and forgiveness, His power for service, and a life of victory over sin than we are to receive them. Jesus is far more eager to fill us with the Holy Spirit than you and I are to be filled.

Why, then, are so many Christians living in defeat? Why are so few Christians effective witnesses for Christ? Why are so few Christians living lives that are filled with the Holy Spirit? These questions bring us to the next important step in preparation for being filled with the Spirit.

IV. WHAT IS THE SPIRIT-FILLED LIFE?

The Spirit-filled life is the Christ-filled life. The Spirit-filled Christian is one who, according to Romans 6:11, has considered himself to be dead to sin, but alive to God in Christ Jesus. Christ is now on the throne of the life. He is Lord! The Holy Spirit came to exalt and glorify Jesus Christ. In order to be filled with the Holy Spirit a Christian must be dead to self. When he is dead to self, the Lord Jesus Christ, who now has unhindered control of his life, can begin to express His love through him. The One to whom "all power in heaven and in earth is given," and, "in whom dwells all the fullness of the Godhead bodily," can now express that power through the Spirit-filled Christian. The One who came to seek and to save the lost, now begins to seek the lost through the Christian. He directs the Christian's steps to those who are lost and to those who are in need. He begins to use the Christian's lips to tell of His love. His great heart of compassion becomes evident in the Spirit-filled life.

Actually, in a very real sense, the Christian gives up *his* life, *his* impotence and defeat for the power and victory of Jesus Christ. This is what the great missionary statesman Hudson Taylor referred to as the "exchanged life." When a Christian is filled with the Holy Spirit, he is filled with Jesus Christ. He no longer thinks of Christ as One who helps to do some kind of Christian task but, rather, Jesus Christ does the work through the Christian. He does not want us to work for Him. He wants us to let Him do His work through us. This is that glorious experience that the apostle Paul knew when he said in Galatians 2:20, "I have been crucified with Christ; and it is no longer I who live, but Christ lives in me." The Christian's body now becomes Christ's body to use as He wills; the mind becomes His mind to think His thoughts; the will is now controlled by His will; the total personality, time and talents are now completely His.

The beloved apostle goes on to say, ". . . and the life which I now live in the flesh I live by faith in the Son of God, who loved me, and delivered Himself up for me." Whose faith? The faith of the Son of God, the One who loved us and gave Himself for us, the One to whom "all power in heaven and earth is given." Think of it! Can you grasp what this means? If you can, and if you yield your will to God the Holy Spirit and acknowledge that Jesus Christ is in your life moment by moment, you are in for a great adventure. The Lord Jesus Christ will begin to draw scores of lost men and women to Himself through your yielded, Spirit-filled life.

V. WHY ARE SO FEW CHRISTIANS FILLED WITH THE HOLY SPIRIT?

Basically, the problem involves the will. Man is a free moral agent. He was created by God with a mind and will of his own.

God would be breaking His own spiritual laws if He *forced* man to do His bidding. At the time of conversion the will of man is temporarily yielded to the will of God. In Romans 10:9, Paul tells us that, if we confess with our mouths Jesus as Lord, and believe in our hearts that God has raised Him from the dead, we shall be saved. Man must be willing to "repent," which means to turn from his own way to go God's way, before he can become a child of God. However, after conversion, the heart frequently loses its "first love." The radiance and glow that accompanied the spiritual birth experience are gone, and many Christians no longer walk in "the light as He Himself is in the light" (1 John 1:7). They no longer seek to do the will of God, but for various reasons, have chosen to go their own way. They have chosen to work out their own plan and purpose for life. Believing themselves to be free, they become servants of sin and finally they say with the apostle Paul in Romans 7:19, 20, 24: "For the good that I wish, I do not do; but I practice the very evil that I do not wish. But if I am doing the very thing I do not wish, I am no longer the one doing it, but sin which dwells in me. Wretched man that I am! Who will set me free from the body of this death?" There is no one more miserable than a Christian out of fellowship with Christ.

In this spiritual condition there is no longer any joy in the Christian walk, no longer any desire to witness for Christ, no concern for those who are desperately in need of the forgiveness and love of our Savior.

What are the reasons, then, that one who has experienced the love and forgiveness that only Christ can give, one who has experienced the joy of His presence, would reject the will of God and choose to go his own way? Why would a Christian sacrifice the power and dynamic of the Spirit-filled life in order to have his own way?

There are several reasons:

A. *Lack of knowledge of the Word of God:* God's Word contains glorious truths concerning the relationship that the Christian has with the Lord Jesus Christ, God the Father and the Holy Spirit. This lack of information has kept many from appropriating the fullness of the Holy Spirit. Think of it —

every Christian is a child of God (John 1:12). His sins have been forgiven and he may continue to be cleansed from all sin (1 John 1:7) as he continues in fellowship with Christ. God the Father, Son and Holy Spirit actually dwell in the heart of every Christian, waiting to empower and bring each child of God to his full maturity in Christ. (Review again Part III. How is the Holy Spirit related to every Christian?)

B. *Pride:* Pride has kept many Christians from being filled with the Holy Spirit. Pride was the sin of Satan (Isaiah 14:12-14). Pride was the first sin of man as Adam and Eve wanted to be something they were not. Pride is at the root of most of man's self-imposed estrangement from God. The self-centered, egocentric Christian cannot have fellowship with God: ". . . for God is opposed to the proud, but gives grace to the humble" (1 Peter 5:5).

C. *Fear:* Fear of man keeps many Christians from being filled with the Holy Spirit. "The fear of man brings a snare" (Proverbs 29:25). One of the greatest tragedies of our day is the general practice among Christians of conforming to the conduct and standards of a non-Christian society. Many are afraid to be different; ashamed to witness for the One "who loved us and gave Himself for us." Remember, in 1 Peter 2:9 we are told: "But you are a chosen race, a royal priesthood, a holy nation, a people for God's own possession, that you may proclaim the excellencies of Him who has called you out of darkness into His marvelous light." "The Lord favors those who fear (reverence which leads to obedience) Him" (Psalm 147:11). Jesus said, "For whoever is ashamed of Me and My words, of him shall the Son of Man be ashamed" (Luke 9:26).

Many Christians are fearful of being thought fanatical by their fellow Christians and others should they be filled with the Holy Spirit.

D. *Secret sin:* Unconfessed sin keeps many Christians from being filled with the Holy Spirit. Perhaps God has reminded you of a lie you have told that has damaged someone's reputation; or stolen merchandise or money that has not been returned; or an unethical transaction; or cheating on an exam, or any number of acts that He wants you to confess to Him. He may lead you to make restitution to those whom you have wronged (Matthew 5:23, 24). If so, be obedient to His leading. We may be able to hide these things from our friends and others, but we cannot hide them from God. "Would not God find this out? For He knows the secrets of the heart" (Psalm 44:21). Is there any one whom you have not forgiven? If so, God will not forgive you (Mark 11:24-26).

However, if we confess these sins to God as the Lord directs us, we are forgiven and cleansed (1 John 1:9).

E. *Worldly-mindedness:* A love for material things and a desire to conform to the ways of a secular society keep many Christians from being filled with the Holy Spirit. "Do not love the world, nor the things in the world. If any one loves the world, the love of the Father is not in him. For all that is in the world, the lust of the flesh, and the lust of the eyes and the boastful pride of life, is not from the Father, but is from the world. And the world is passing away, and also its lusts; but the one who does the will of God abides forever" (1 John 2:15-17). Man lives a brief span of years and is gone from this earthly scene. Every Christian should make careful and frequent evaluation of how he invests his time, talents and treasure in order to accomplish the most for the cause of Christ. "Only one life, will soon be past; only what's done for Christ will last."

"No one can serve two masters; for either he will hate the one and love the other, or he will hold to one and despise the other. You cannot serve God and Mammon. But seek first His kingdom, and His righteousness; and all these things shall be added to you" (Matthew 6:24, 33).

F. *Lack of trust in God:* This keeps many Christians from making a full surrender of their wills to Him and from being filled with the Holy Spirit. Many Christians have a fear that amounts almost to superstition that, if they surrender themselves fully to God, something tragic will happen to test them. They may fear that they will lose a loved one. Some fear that God will send them to some remote section of the world as a missionary to some savage tribe, against their wills.

I remember well a young lad who had such fears — he was afraid that God would change his plans. As we reasoned together, I reminded him that God's love was so great that He sent His only begotten Son to die for his sins. We spoke of a Savior who loved him so much that He gladly gave His life on the cross and shed His blood for his sins. Then I asked the question, "Can you trust a God like that?" He replied, "I had never thought of it that way — I can and will trust Him." Today this young man has finished seminary and is a member of our Campus Crusade staff. He is one of the most fruitful and victorious Christians I know.

You can trust God with your life, your loved ones, your money, your future, everything! Not only is He a loving Father, but God's love is wiser than that of any earthly father and is more tender than that of any earthly mother. So do not be afraid to trust God with your whole life, every moment of every day, and He will fill you with His Holy Spirit.

I have two sons whom I love dearly. Suppose, when they were very young, they had come to me and said, "Daddy, we love you and have been thinking about how we can show our love for you. We have decided that we will do anything that you want us to do." Now, how would I have responded? Would I have said, "boys, I have been waiting for just this moment. Now that you have relinquished your wills to mine, I am going to lock you in your rooms, give away all your favorite possessions, and make you do all of the things that you most dislike to do. You will regret the day you were born. I will make you the most miserable boys on this block."

How ridiculous! I would have responded by trying to demonstrate my love for them in an even greater way. In the same way, our heavenly Father is ready to bless and enrich our lives the moment we yield our wills, our all, to Him.

These and many other experiences of defeat have kept Christians from experiencing the joy of the Spirit-filled life. For example, do any of the following apply to you?

An exalted feeling of your own importance
Love of human praise
Anger and impatience
Self-will, stubborness, unteachability
A compromising spirit
Jealous disposition
Lustful, unholy actions
Dishonesty
Unbelief
Selfishness
Love of money, beautiful clothes, cars, houses and land

Some of you may wonder, "Is it necessary for me to gain victory over all of my defeats and frustrations before I can be filled with the Holy Spirit?" Absolutely not! Just as Jesus Christ is the only one who can forgive your sins, so the Holy Spirit is the only one who can give victory and power.

VI. HOW CAN A CHRISTIAN BE FILLED WITH THE HOLY SPIRIT?

First, we need to know that just as people have many different experiences when they receive Jesus Christ as Lord and Savior, so they have different experiences when they are filled with the Holy Spirit. For example, one man responds to the invitation to receive Christ in an evangelistic campaign, another kneels quietly in the privacy of his home and receives Christ. Both are born again, and their lives are changed by the power of Christ. Of course, there are scores of other circumstances and experiences through which sincere men meet the Savior and become "new creatures in Christ."

In like manner, and in different ways, sincere Christians are filled with the Spirit. It should be made clear at this point that to be "filled with the Spirit" does not mean that we receive more of the Holy Spirit, but that we give Him more of ourselves. As we yield our lives to the Holy Spirit and are filled with His presence, He has greater freedom to work in and through our lives, to control us in order to better exalt and glorify Christ.

God is too great to be placed in a man-made mold. However, there are certain spiritual laws that are inviolate. Since the Holy Spirit already dwells within every Christian, it is no longer necessary to "wait in Jerusalem" as Jesus instructed the disciples to do, except to make personal preparation for His empowering. The Holy Spirit will fill us with His power the moment we are fully yielded. It is possible for a man to be at a quiet retreat and become filled with the Holy Spirit. It is likewise possible for a man to be filled with the Holy Spirit while walking down a busy street in a great city. Such was the experience of Dwight L. Moody. It is even possible for a man to be filled with the Holy Spirit and know something wonderful has happened, yet be completely ignorant at the time of what has actually taken place, provided he has a genuine desire to yield his will to the Lord Jesus Christ.

I do not want to suggest that the steps which I am about to propose are the only way in which one can be filled with the Holy Spirit. This spiritual formula is offered, first, because it is scriptural, and second, because I know from experience that it works.

Do you want to be filled with the Holy Spirit? What are your motives? Are you loking for some ecstatic experience, or do you sincerely desire to serve the Lord Jesus Christ with greater power and effectiveness? Do you want, with all of your heart, to help others find Christ?

This is the spiritual formula that I urge you to prayerfully consider:

A. *We are commanded to be filled with the Spirit.*

"And do not get drunk with wine, for that is dissipation, but be filled with the Spirit" (Ephesians 5:18). This is an admonition of God. Do you think that He would ask you to do something beyond that which you are able to experience?

B. *We shall receive power for witnessing when we are filled.*

"But you shall receive power when the Holy Spirit has come upon you; and you shall be My witnesses both in Jerusalem, and in all Judea and Samaria, and even to the remotest part of the earth" (Acts 1:8). If you have no desire to be Jesus

Christ's witness or if you have no power in your witness, you may be sure that you are not filled with the Holy Spirit. The Holy Spirit came in order for the disciples — and for you and me — to receive power. Why do we need power? To be Christ's witnesses right where we are and in the remotest part of the earth. Can you sincerely say that this is your motive for wanting to be filled with the Spirit?

C. *If any man is thirsty, let him come to Me and drink.*

"Now on the last day, the great day of the feast, Jesus stood and cried out, saying, 'If any man is thirsty, let him come to Me and drink. He who believes in Me, as the Scripture said, "From his innermost being shall flow rivers of living water." ' But this He spoke of the Spirit, whom those who believed in Him were to receive; for the Spirit was not yet given, because Jesus was not yet glorified" (John 7:37-39). "Blessed are those who hunger and thirst for righteousness, for they shall be satisfied" (Matthew 5:6).

When a Christian is ready to respond to the gracious invitation of our blessed Savior, "If any man is thirsty, let him come to Me and drink," he is ready to relinquish his will for the will of God. Therefore, this third step involves a complete surrender of your will, without reservation, to the will of God. You have come to the place where you joyfully anticipate knowing and doing His will because you know God is loving and trustworthy and that His will is best.

Up until this moment the Holy Spirit has been just a "guest" in your life, for He came to live in you the moment you became a Christian. Sometimes He was locked up in a small closet, while you used the rest of the house for your own pleasure.

Now you want Him to be more than a guest — as a matter of fact, you want to turn over the title deed of your life to Him and give Him the keys to every room. You invite the Holy Spirit into the library of your mind, the dining room of your appetites, the parlor of your relationships, the game room of your social life. You invite Him into the small hidden rooms where you have previously engaged in secret, shameful activities. All of this is past. Now, He is the Master! The challenge of Romans 12:1, 2 has become clear and meaningful to you and you want to ". . . present your body a living and holy sacrifice, acceptable to God, which is your spiritual service of worship." And you no longer want to be conformed to this world, but you want to be transformed by the renewing of your mind, "that you may prove what the will of God is, that which is good and acceptable and perfect."

Now you know that your body is the temple of the Holy Spirit who lives within you. You are not your own anymore for you were bought with the precious blood of the Lord Jesus; therefore, you now want to glorify God in your body and in your spirit, which are God's (1 Corinthians 6:19, 20).

Now, with all of your heart, you want to seek first the kingdom of God (Matthew 6:33).

Now you want to seek "the things above, where Christ is, seated at the right hand of God. For you have died, and your life is hidden with Christ in God" (Colossians 3:1, 3).

Now you can say with joy unspeakable, as Paul did, "I have been crucified with Christ; and it is no longer I who live, but Christ lives in me; and the life which I now live in the flesh I live by faith in the Son of God, who loved me, and delivered Himself up for me" (Galatians 2:20). You have exchanged your life for the life of Christ.

If you can say these things and mean them with all of your heart, you are ready for the fourth step. However, before we take up the discussion of this next step, I feel constrained to call your attention to the words of our Savior found in John 15:18, 20. "If the world hates you, you know that it has hated Me before it hated you. . . . 'A slave is not greater than his master.' If they persecuted Me, they will also persecute you."

The Spirit-filled Christian life is not an easy one, though it is a life filled with adventure and thrills, the likes of which one cannot possibly experience in any other way. Whether or not we are Christians, we are going to have problems in this life. Christians or not, we will one day die. If I am going to be a Christian, I want all that God has for me and I want to be all that He wants me to be. If I am to suffer at all, and one day die, why not suffer and die for the highest and best, for the Lord Jesus Christ and His gospel!

Before we leave this thought, let me ask you a question. Have you ever heard of one of God's saints who has suffered for the cause of Christ express any regrets? I never have! I have heard only praise, adoration and thanksgiving to God for the privilege of serving Christ, no matter how difficult the task. On the other hand, I have heard many who have received Christ late in life tell how sorry they are that they waited so long. Do not develop a martyr's complex, but do not expect a "bed of roses" either.

Now for the next step in receiving the fullness of the Holy Spirit.

D. *We appropriate the filling of the Holy Spirit by faith.*

Remember that, if you are a Christian, God the Father, Son

and Holy Spirit are already living within you. Great spiritual power and resources are available to you. Like a miser starving to death with a fortune in boxes and jars about his cluttered room, many Christians are starving spiritually, living in defeat, failing to utilize the spiritual fortune that is their heritage in Christ.

In Ephesians 5:18, Paul admonishes, "And do not get drunk with wine, for that is dissipation, but be filled with the Spirit."

Further, in 1 John 5:14, 15, we are assured, "And this is the confidence which we have before Him, that, if we ask anything according to His will, He hears us. And if we know that He hears us in whatever we ask, we know that we have the requests that we have asked from Him." We know that it is God's will that we be filled with His Spirit. Therefore, as we ask the Holy Spirit to fill us, we can know according to the Word of God that our prayer is answered.

Like our salvation, the filling of the Holy Spirit is a gift of God — we do not and cannot earn either. Both are received by the complete yielding of our wills, in faith, when we have confessed our sins and met the other conditions mentioned in Lesson Four.

Here is a review of the steps that we have discussed in preparation for the filling of the Holy Spirit:

1. We are admonished to be filled.
2. We are promised power for service when we are filled.
3. We are to yield our will to God's will and seek first the kingdom of God.
4. We are to appropriate the filling of the Holy Spirit by faith.

E. *We must expect to be filled.*

"And without faith it is impossible to please Him, for he who comes to God must believe that He is, and that He is a rewarder of those who seek Him" (Hebrews 11:6).

Do you believe God wants you to be filled with the Holy Spirit?

Do you believe God has the power to fill you with the Holy Spirit?

In Matthew 9:28, 29, Jesus talked to the blind men and asked of them, "Do you believe that I am able to do this?" They said to Him, "Yes, Lord." Then He touched their eyes, saying, "Be it done to you according to your faith."

Find a quiet place where you can be alone and read again the portions of Scripture given in the preceding paragraphs. You do not have to wait for the Holy Spirit. He is already dwelling within you if you are a Christian. He is waiting for you to allow Him to fill you. Remember, "Be is done to you according to your faith." "He is a rewarder of those who seek Him."

Have you honestly yielded your life to Christ, your will to His will?

Do you believe that you are filled with the Holy Spirit at this moment? If so, thank Him that you are filled. Thank Him for His indwelling presence and power. Thank Him by faith for victory over defeat and for effectiveness in witnessing. Praise God and gives thanks continually (Ephesians 5:20; 1 Thessalonians 5:18).

VII. HOW CAN A CHRISTIAN KNOW WHEN HE IS FILLED WITH THE HOLY SPIRIT?

There are two very good ways of knowing when you are filled with the Holy Spirit.

First, by the promises of the Word of God. And second, by personal experience.

If you have faithfully yielded to the will of God and sincerely surrendered your way to Him in accordance with the steps outlined in this presentation, if you have asked Him to fill you— He has done it! "And this is the confidence which we have before Him, that, if we ask anything according to His will, He hears us. And if we know that He hears us in whatever we ask, we know that we have the requests that we have asked from Him" (1 John 5:14, 15). Is it His will that you be filled, according to Ephesians 5:18? Then, can you believe that He has heard you? Now, can you know that you have the petitions that you desired of Him?

God's Word promises us that we can know. Therefore, on the basis of His Word you can know that you are filled, if you have met the conditions which are given in His Word.

What about feelings? You may or may not have an emotional response at the time you kneel in prayer and ask for the filling of the Spirit. In counseling with many students, as well as adults, I have found that the majority experience a calm assurance that they are filled, and with this assurance comes a spirit of expectancy that God is going to use them in a way they have never been used before to introduce others to Christ. Greater faith in God and His Word is born in the hearts of those who have been filled with the Holy Spirit. Results? Greater faith, power, boldness and effectiveness in witnessing.

First, there is the fact of God's promise in His Word. Then there is the exercise of faith in the trustworthiness of God and His promises. Faith in the fact is followed by feeling. Remember: fact, faith and feelings — in that order.

VIII. WHAT RESULTS CAN ONE EXPECT
FROM BEING FILLED WITH THE HOLY SPIRIT?

Now comes the real test that will determine if you are truly filled with the Holy Spirit. As time goes on, do you find that you have a greater love for Christ? Are you more concerned for those who do not know His love and forgiveness? Are you experiencing a greater faith, boldness, liberty and power in witnessing? If so, you are filled with the Spirit. Jesus Christ is beginning to express His life and love through and in you.

Remember, Jesus promised that we would receive power after the Holy Spirit has come upon us. After receiving power we will naturally want to be His witnesses wherever we are (Acts 1:8).

It is definitely true that you will have a greater love for Christ, for your fellowman and for the Word of God when you are filled with the Holy Spirit. Also, the fruit of the Spirit, as described in Galatians 5:22, 23, will become more evident in your life.

However, we must remember that there is a difference between the fruit of the Spirit and the gifts of the Spirit.

The filling of the Holy Spirit is given for power and boldness in witnessing for Christ. Many Christian leaders agree with Dr. R. A. Torrey, who said, "I have gone through my Bible time and time again checking this subject and I make this statement without the slightest fear of successful contradiction that there is not one single passage in the Old Testament or the New Testament where the filling with the Holy Spirit is spoken of, where it is not connected with testimony for service."

We hasten to add that as a Christian abides in Christ, living in the fullness of the Spirit, the fruit of the Spirit — love, joy, peace, patience, kindness, goodness, faithfulness, gentleness and self-control, listed in Galatians 5:22, 23 — is developed and the Christian becomes more mature spiritually. The maturing of the fruit of the Spirit is a lifetime process which goes on continually as Christ is being formed in the life of the Christian. Some Christians give greater evidence of the fruit of the Spirit than do others, because of a greater degree of yieldedness to His working. The more we acknowledge ourselves to be dead to sin and give allegiance to the Lord Jesus Christ and His life within us, and the more we allow Him through the power of the Holy Spirit to live out His life through us, the more evident will be the fruit of the Spirit.

The development and maturing of the fruit of the Spirit is a long process, but the gifts of the Holy Spirit are given at the time a person becomes a Christian. Though every Christian who is filled with the Spirit receives power for witnessing, not every Christian receives the same gift, according to 1 Corinthians 12. Some are called to be apostles, some prophets, others evangelists, pastors and teachers (Ephesians 4:11). Therefore, we must let the Lord direct us into His place of service for us.

Do not try to imitate the ministry of someone else. Be patient. Do not try to decide what you should do with your life or where you should serve Christ. He will express His life in and through you as you continue to study His Word and remain obedient and sensitive to the leading of the Holy Spirit. Through God's Word and the leading of the Holy Spirit, you will discover what God's will is for you.

IX. IS THERE MORE THAN ONE FILLING OF THE HOLY SPIRIT?

Yes, there are many fillings of the Spirit for the yielded Christian. We should be filled for each new opportunity of Christian service. The admonition to be filled with the Holy Spirit in Ephesians 5:18 literally means, in the original Greek, to be filled with the Spirit constantly and continually — to keep on being filled. The Scriptures record several instances where Peter and the disciples where filled with the Spirit.

X. HOW CAN A CHRISTIAN CONTINUE TO BE FILLED WITH THE HOLY SPIRIT?

The Christian is utterly and wholly dependent upon the Holy Spirit for all spiritual victory and power. Therefore, the more yielded he is, the more liberty the Holy Spirit will have in working through his life in bringing others to Christ and bringing him to spiritual maturity in Christ.

Here are some practical suggestions that will assist you to live in the fullness of the Spirit:

A. Meditate on these glorious truths: Jesus Christ literally dwells within you. You are dead to self and sin and to all personal and selfish desires. You are alive to God through Jesus Christ (Romans 6:11). Remember, you have exchanged your life with all of its sin, frustrations and defeats for the victorious and triumphant life of Christ, in whom "all the fullness of deity dwells in bodily form, and in Him you have been made complete" (Colossians 2:9, 10). Just think, the one who dwells in your heart is the one who claims all power in heaven and in earth! This is why the apostle Paul said, "I can do all things through Him who strengthens me" (Philippians 4:13). You have buried "Old Adam," screwed the lid down on the coffin and covered him over with six feet of sod. Jesus Christ is not helping you to live the

Christian life with your old sin nature. Rather He is now using your body as His Temple, your mind to think His thoughts, your heart to express His love and compassion, your lips to speak His truths.

His will has become your will. At first you may find it necessary to acknowledge and confirm many, many times during the day that this transaction has taken place. You may find it necessary to change your whole way of thinking and praying. don't think, "What can I do for Christ?" or pray, "God, use me to do this or that for You." Pray rather, "Lord Jesus, I am Yours totally and completely without reservation. Use me as You wish. Send me wherever You will, for I am dead and my life is hid with Christ in God." Seek to abide in Christ (1 John 2:6). What is involved in abiding in Christ? Jesus said, "If you keep My commandments, you will abide in My love . . ." (John 15:10a).

To abide is to keep His commandments. To keep His commandments is to obey. The abiding life is an effortless life. How slowly do we arrive at this simple fact, that true New Testament living is effortless.

A branch does not try to produce fruit, any more than the electric light bulb tries to shine. Neither has any need to try; they simply draw upon an inexhaustible supply of life and energy. In doing so they scarcely touch the fringe of their resources. The Christian has infinitely greater resources. The one who created vegetable life and electric energy is the one who lives in us. Why do we need to try? Only because we are not abiding. The truest test of Christian living is, am I trying or am I abiding? If I find myself still trying. I am not as yet an unchoked channel through which His life may flow.

Meditate on the following portions of Scripture: John 14, 15 and 16; Matthew 6; Colossians 3; Ephesians 5; Romans 6, 8, 12 and 14; 1 Corinthians 13; 1 John 1; Hebrews 11; Galatians 5; and Psalm 37:1-7, 23, 24.

I suggest that you secure a notebook and make an outline of each of these chapters, listing especially those suggestions that you feel will aid you in abiding in Christ. Continue to use your notebook for outlining other portions of Scripture and for recording key verses you would like to memorize. There are many other portions of Scripture that will help you to abide in Christ.

B. Make it a practice to spend definite time each day in prayer for God's guidance of your life and for the souls of men. Make a list of people whom you would like to have find Christ. Pray for them daily (Ephesians 6:18 and 1 Samuel 12:23).

C. Spend time daily reading and studying the Word of God. Make a practice of memorizing key portions of Scripture (see Hebrews 4:12; 1 Corinthians 2:9-12; Psalm 119:4, 9, 15, 16, 97, 98, 103, 105, 130).

D. Do not grieve the Holy Spirit. Confess and turn from sinful practices. 1 John 1:9 says, "If we confess our sins, He is faithful and righteous to forgive us our sins and to cleanse us from all unrighteousness." The moment you do something you know is wrong, you will grieve the Holy Spirit if you do not confess it. What do we mean by grieving the Holy Spirit? The Spirit is holy and He is displeased and saddened when a Christian commits sin and continues its practice. Therefore, if you want to continue to be filled with the Holy Spirit and to have power in witnessing for Christ, live a yielded, holy life.

E. Do not quench the Holy Spirit. Be sensitive to the leading of the Holy Spirit for He is omniscient. He has infinite wisdom and knowledge and will lead us into all truth (John 16:13). Never say "no" to Him. As you grow accustomed to the Spirit-filled, Christ-directed life, you will have many wonderful experiences such as Philip had (Acts 8:26-29) when the Holy Spirit led him to speak to the Ethiopian; and as Paul had (Acts 16:9) when he was called to Macedonia to preach the gospel.

The most thrilling experiences of my entire life have been those when the still, small voice of the Spirit spoke to my heart, telling me to speak to people about Christ, and, as I have talked with them in obedience to the Spirit's leading, I have always discovered that the Holy Spirit had prepared their hearts for my witness. Many times I have been told, "Bill, the Lord sent you to me." Or "Everything you have said has been for me. Someone must have told you of my problem." The Spirit knows all things, and if you and I are filled with His presence and power, we will always have the right thing to say to those who are in need.

There have been many such thrilling leadings of the Spirit, but I shall share only one.

One day my wife, Vonette, and I were driving to the Forest Home Christian Conference Center for a session of the College Briefing Conference that has been so greatly used of God in the lives of thousands of collegians. It was an extremely hot day late in August and our car developed a vapor lock and refused to run as we started up the mountain. We waited for the motor to cool and finally, after a considerable delay, we got the car started.

We drove into the yard of a nearby rural home to ask for water to fill the radiator. The man of the house was very generous and gracious. He helped me fill the radiator with water, but even though we were there five or ten minutes, I did not speak to him about Christ. My mind was on an important meeting up the mountain that we wanted badly to attend. As I leaned over to pick up the radiator cap, which had blown off, my New Testament fell out of my shirt pocket. Still I did not hear that still, small voice of the Spirit. We had thanked the man for his kindness and were driving out of his yard when suddenly I felt a strong compulsion to return to talk with this man about Christ. "But," I argued as we discussed it, "we are late for the meeting now. Anyway, he would think we are crackpots if we were to go back. Besides, if I were going to witness to him about Christ, I should have done it when he was helping me fill the radiator with water."

Human arguments are futile against the insistent voice of the Spirit, and after we had driven a couple of miles, we turned around and headed back. As an added precaution we pulled over to the side of the road for prayer. "Lord, don't let us make a mistake — this seems so foolish. Give us the words to say. May Your will be done."

As we drove into the yard, the man came out on the porch to greet us. "Did you forget something?" he asked. "Yes, we did forget something, sir. I know this may sound a little strange, but we are Christians and we felt that the Lord wanted us to come back to talk to you about Christ." There was no need to say more for, as I spoke, tears began to gather and trickle down his cheeks. His chin began to tremble as he told us that he knew the Lord had sent us. He asked us to come inside and as we went in, he called his wife.

He said, "I used to go to church years ago, but I fell into sin and I haven't been back in many years. This week my wife has been attending a revival meeting here in town and more and more, with each passing day, I have been burdened with the weight of my sins. I want to get right with God." We all knelt there in his living room and both he and his wife committed their lives and their home to Christ. We went on our way, praising God for the leading of His Holy Spirit and for another opportunity to witness for our blessed Savior.

As you ask God to fill you with the Holy Spirit, you are about to begin the greatest adventure of your life. Remember that you are asking to be filled with the Holy

Spirit rather than filled with self. As He takes control of your life, you will become more like Christ. The Holy Spirit is not the author of confusion and emotional extremes. He has come to exalt and glorify Jesus; therefore, when you are filled with the Holy Spirit, it will be your constant desire to do the will of God and that which will please and honor Jesus Christ.

Why did Jesus come into this world? "To seek and to save that which was lost" (Luke 19:10).

What will please Him most? We shall please Him most as we help fulfill His Great Commission, by going into all the world and preaching the gospel to every creature and letting Him live His life through us.

How is this to be accomplished? By the power of the Holy Spirit.

Think of it — you and I are privileged to be used by our Savior in helping to reach a lost world with the glorious "good news"!

We dare not sin against the Lord and against those who are waiting to hear by hesitating another moment.

Ask Him to fill you now!

Bill Bright
Founder and President,
Campus Crusade for Christ International
Arrowhead Springs, San Bernardino, California

LESSON ONE

WHO IS THE HOLY SPIRIT AND WHY DID HE COME?

BE SURE YOU HAVE READ THE ARTICLE ABOUT THE HOLY SPIRIT BEFORE YOU START THIS LESSON.

Introduction

OBJECTIVE: To become acquainted with the Holy Spirit and to understand His mission.

TO MEMORIZE: John 16:13, 14.

TO READ: John 3:1-8; Romans 8.

Bible Study

A. Who the Holy Spirit is

The Holy Spirit is a person, the third person of the Trinity: Father, Son and Holy Spirit. He is not some vague, ethereal shadow, nor an impersonal force. He is a person equal in every way with the Father and the Son. All of the divine attributes ascribed to the Father and the Son are equally ascribed to the Holy Spirit.

1. Personality (a person) is composed of intellect, emotions and will. In 1 Corinthians 2:11, what indicates that the Holy Spirit has intellect? _____

    What evidence is there in Romans 15:30 that the Holy Spirit has emotion? _____

    How do you see the Holy Spirit exercising His will in 1 Corinthians 12:11? _____

2. What do you understand about the nature of the Holy Spirit from the following references?

    Romans 8:2 _____

    John 16:13 _____

    Hebrews 10:29 _____

    Romans 1:4 _____

3. What about His function or His role?

John 14:26 _____

1 Corinthians 3:16 _____

John 16:13, 14 _____

B. *Why He came*

1. What is the chief reason the Holy Spirit came (John 16:14)? _____

2. What will be a logical result when the Holy Spirit controls your life? _____

LOVE	CHRIST CENTERED
JOY	EMPOWERED BY H.S.
PEACE	INTRODUCES OTHERS TO CHRIST
PATIENCE	EFFECTIVE PRAYER LIFE
KINDNESS	UNDERSTANDS GOD'S WORD
FAITHFULNESS	TRUSTS GOD
GOODNESS	OBEYS GOD

Life Application

Write one new insight you have gained from this lesson concerning the Holy Spirit: _____

_____

_____

In what area of your life do you believe the Holy Spirit needs to be more in control? _____

_____

_____

_____

What will be the result when He is? _____

_____

_____

LESSON TWO

WHAT IS THE HOLY SPIRIT'S RELATIONSHIP WITH EVERY CHRISTIAN?

Introduction

OBJECTIVE: To realize the necessity of being filled with the Holy Spirit in order to live the Christian life.

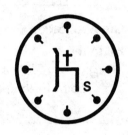

TO MEMORIZE: Ephesians 5:18.

TO READ: Romans 12:1-8; 1 Corinthians 2.

Bible Study

A. *The work of the Holy Spirit*

1. When you become a Christian (i.e., at the time of your spiritual birth), the Holy Spirit does a number of things for and in you. What are they?

   John 3:5 _____

   1 Corinthians 3:16 _____

   Ephesians 4:30 _____

   1 Corinthians 12:13 _____

   2 Corinthians 5:5 _____

2. Explain in your own words what the Holy Spirit does for the Christian according to:

   Romans 8:16 _____

   _____

   Romans 8:26, 27 _____

   _____

B. *The results of being filled with the Holy Spirit*

1. Can a person be a Christian and not have the Holy Spirit dwelling in Him (Romans 8:9)? Explain. _____

   _____

2. What is the main reason to be filled with the Spirit (Acts 1:8; 4:29, 31)? _____

_____

3. What work of the Holy Spirit is necessary for successful Christian living and service (Ephesians 5:18)?_____

_____

Life Application

Fill in the chart below:

"How I viewed the Holy Spirit in the past"	"How I view Him now"

Do you really desire to be filled with the Holy Spirit?_____
Why? _____

_____

_____

LESSON THREE

WHY ARE SO FEW CHRISTIANS FILLED WITH THE HOLY SPIRIT?

Introduction

OBJECTIVE: To understand the barriers to a Spirit-filled life.

TO MEMORIZE: 1 John 2:15-17.

TO READ: Galatians 5 and 6; Acts 5:1-11.

Bible Study

A. *The heart's battlefield*

1. How does Paul describe himself in Romans 7:19-24?

   _____

   _____

   What kind of feeling does that description arouse in you?

   _____

2. State in your own words why there are so many unhappy Christians, according to Galatians 5:16, 17. _____

   _____

B. *Why the battle is often lost*

1. Read the following Scriptures and state what you think they teach are the reasons so few Christians are filled with the Holy Spirit.

   Psalm 119:105 _____

   Proverbs 16:18 _____

   Proverbs 29:25 _____

   Luke 9:26 _____

2. What is another thing that will put a block between you and the Lord and keep you from being filled with the Spirit (Psalm 66:18)? _____

   _____

What about 1 John 2:15-17? _____

3. Lack of trust in God also will keep you from being filled with the Holy Spirit. Read John 3:16 again. Do you feel that *you* could trust a God like this? _____

Why? (Romans 8:32 and 1 John 3:16 can help you with your answer.) _____

_____

_____

Basically, the reason most Christians are not filled with the Holy Spirit is that they are *unwilling to surrender their wills to God.*

- LEGALISTIC ATTITUDE
- IMPURE THOUGHTS
- JEALOUSY
- GUILT
- WORRY
- DISCOURAGEMENT
- CRITICAL SPIRIT
- FRUSTATION
- AIMLESSNESS

- IGNORANCE OF HIS SPIRITUAL HERITAGE
- UNBELIEF
- DISOBEDIENCE
- LOSS OF LOVE FOR GOD AND FOR OTHERS
- POOR PRAYER
- NO DESIRE FOR BIBLE STUDY

Life Application

List any barriers you are aware of now between yourself and God. _____

_____

Prayerfully consider, then answer this question:

"Am *I* willing to surrender my will to God?" _____

_____

_____

LESSON FOUR

HOW CAN A CHRISTIAN BE FILLED WITH THE HOLY SPIRIT?

Introduction

OBJECTIVE: To personally appropriate the filling of the Holy Spirit.

TO MEMORIZE: Romans 12:1, 2; 1 John 5:14, 15.

TO READ: Acts 6:8 - 7:60.

YOUR LOVE FOR CHRIST

A desire to serve Him and help others find Him should be your motive for being filled with the Holy Spirit. This lesson should not be completed until the entire article, "You Shall Receive Power," starting on page 127 has been studied carefully.

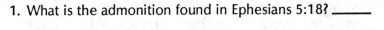

Bible Study

A. *What you must know*

1. What is the admonition found in Ephesians 5:18? _____

_____

2. Why do you need to be filled with the Spirit?

Galatians 5:22, 23 _____

Acts 1:8 _____

The fruit of the Spirit is never an end in itself, but only a means to the end that we win men and women to Christ, which in turn will bring glory and honor to Him (John 15:8).

B. *The one thing you must feel*

What is one prerequisite to being filled with the Spirit, according to Matthew 5:6? _____

_____

C. *What you must do*

1. If your desire to be filled with the Spirit is sincere, what will you do now (Romans 12:1, 2)? _____

   _____

   This means there can be no unconfessed sin in your life. The Holy Spirit cannot fill an unclean vessel. He waits to fill you with His power. Do not resist Him any longer.

2. How then are you filled with the Holy Spirit (Matthew 7:7-11; John 7:37)? _____

3. Will the Holy Spirit fill you if you ask Him? _____

   How do you know (1 John 5:14, 15)? _____

Life Application

You can be filled with the Holy Spirit only by faith. However, prayer is one way of expressing your faith. If you truly desire to be filled with the Holy Spirit, you can pray this prayer now:

"Dear Father, I need You. I acknowledge that I have been in control of my life; and that, as a result, I have sinned against You. I thank You that You have forgiven my sins through Christ's death on the cross for me. I now invite Christ to take control of the throne of my life. Fill me with the Holy Spirit as You commanded me to be filled, and as You promised in Your Word that You would do if I asked in faith. I pray this in the name of Jesus. As an expression of my faith, I now thank You for taking control of my life and for filling me with the Holy Spirit."

What must you do when you have asked Him to fill you (Hebrews 11:6)? _____

If you have asked the Holy Spirit to fill you, *thank Him.* God is dependable; His Word is true. If you are sincere, He has filled you. What should be your attitude from this day forward (1 Thessalonians 5:18)? _____

Date of filling _____

Your comments: _____

_____

_____

LESSON FIVE

HOW CAN A CHRISTIAN KNOW WHEN HE IS FILLED, AND WHAT ARE THE RESULTS OF BEING FILLED WITH THE SPIRIT?

Introduction

OBJECTIVE: To experience assurance of the filling of the Holy Spirit.

TO MEMORIZE: Galatians 5:22, 23.

TO READ: Galatians 5:16-26.

Did you sincerely follow the steps outlined in Lesson Four? Did you ask the Holy Spirit to fill you? If you did not, Lessons Five and Six will not mean much to you. Go back to Lesson Four and ask God to work in your heart. If He has filled you, you will be anxious to proceed with Lessons Five and Six.

Bible Study

A. *Results of the Spirit-filled life*

1. What will the Holy Spirit demonstrate in and through your life, as a result of His filling you (Galatians 5:22, 23)?

   _____

   Which specific fruit of the Spirit are you most in need of?

   _____

2. Read Acts 1:8. How do you see this power evidenced in your life? _____

   How does John 15:16 apply to you today? _____

   _____

3. How do you identify with 1 Corinthians 12:1-11 and Ephesians 4:11? _____

   _____

4. What mannerisms, language, activities and inconsistencies in your life do you feel are hindering the Holy Spirit's

development of His fruit, power and gifts in you? _____

_____

5. What happens as we are occupied with Christ and allow the Holy Spirit to work in us (2 Corinthians 3:18)? _____

_____

B. *Facts, faith and feelings*
   1. What is the primary way we know if we have been filled with the Spirit (1 John 5:14, 15)? _____

   _____

   2. When you asked to be filled with the Spirit, did you feel any different? _____

   Do not depend upon feeling. The promise of God's Word, not our feelings, is our authority. The Christian lives by faith (trust) in the trustworthiness of God Himself and His Word. This train diagram illustrates the relationship between *fact* (God and His Word), *faith* (our trust in God and His Word) and *feeling* (the result of our faith and obedience) (John 14:21).

   The train will run with or without the caboose. However, it would be futile to attempt to pull the train by the caboose. In the same way, we, as Christians, do not depend upon feelings or emotions, but we place our faith (trust) in the trustworthiness of God and the promise of His Word.

Life Application

Though you may not be aware of change immediately, with the passing of time there should be some evidence of your being filled with the Spirit. Ask yourself these questions now and in the future from time to time:

1. Do you have a greater love for Christ? _____

2. Do you have a greater love for God's Word? _____

3. Are you more concerned for those who do not know Christ as Savior?_____

4. Are you experiencing a greater boldness, liberty and power in witnessing?_____

If you can answer "yes" truthfully to these questions, you undoubtedly are filled with the Spirit.

What does that knowledge mean to you now? _____

_____

_____

If your answer was "no" to any of those four questions, what do you suppose that indicates? _____

_____

_____

Do you think a person can be filled with the Holy Spirit and not be aware of it?_____ Explain. _____

_____

_____

_____

LESSON SIX

HOW CAN A CHRISTIAN CONTINUE TO BE FILLED WITH THE HOLY SPIRIT?

Introduction

OBJECTIVE: To make the Spirit-filled life a moment-by-moment reality.

TO MEMORIZE: John 14:21 or John 15:10.

TO READ: Acts 10.

Bible Study

How to be filled continually

Read Ephesians 5:18. In the original Greek, "be filled" means "keep on being filled constantly and continually."

1. In prayer you must not only pray for yourself, but _____
   _____ (Ephesians 6:18 and 1 Samuel 12:23).
   What person have you stopped praying for recently who still needs your prayers? _____

2. You must _____
   What does the Word of God do for you (Psalm 119:11)?

   _____

3. You must abide in Christ. How can you do that? (John 14:21 and John 15:10)? _____
   Which two commandments do you think are the most important? _____

   _____

4. Read Ephesians 4:25-32. How do you grieve the Holy Spirit? _____

   _____

   Which commandment in that list do you need to pay

special attention to? _____

5. How can you get rid of sin in your life (1 John 1:9)? _____

_____

6. What do you think Romans 8:13 teaches that the Holy Spirit wants to do for you? _____

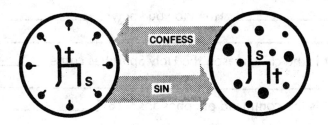

Life Application

The Spirit-filled life is an obedient and abiding life. It can be experienced daily as you:

Begin each day by asking God to cleanse your life, according to 1 John 1:9.

Present your body to the Holy Spirit according to Romans 12:1, 2 and ask Him to keep you filled with His power.

Ask the Holy Spirit to lead you to men who are lost. Be sensitive to His leading.

Expect others to come to Christ through your witness. Do not quench the Spirit by failing to respond.

Rejoice in all things, praising God even in adversity (1 Thessalonians 5:18; Romans 8:28).

1. What sin do you need to confess today? _____

_____

2. Have you realized today victory over a sin you confessed yesterday? _____

_____

LESSON SEVEN

RECAP

Review verses memorized.

Read: John 14:16-26; John 16:7-15.

Is the Holy Spirit a personality or an impersonal force? _____ _____ How do you know? _____ _____

What is the chief reason the Holy Spirit has come? _____ _____

What is the command of Ephesians 5:18? _____ _____

Name as many reasons as you can that Christians are not filled with the Holy Spirit. _____ _____ _____ _____ _____

What should be your motives for being filled with the Spirit? _____

How can a Christian be filled with the Spirit? _____ _____

How do you know you are filled with the Holy Spirit? _____ _____

How can you continue to be filled with and to walk in the Spirit? _____ _____ _____ _____

STEP FOUR
The Christian and Prayer

THE WORD AND PRAYER

"**R**evive me, O Lord, according to Thy Word" — Psalm 119:107.

"Prayer and the Word of God are inseparable, and should always go together in the quiet time of the inner chamber. *In His Word God speaks to*

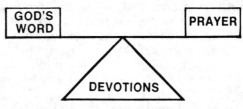

me; in prayer I speak to God. If there is to be true communication, God and I must both take part. If I simply pray, without using God's Word, I am apt to use my own words and thoughts. This really gives prayer its power, that I take God's thoughts from His Word, and present them before Him. Then I am enabled to pray according to God's Word. How indispensable God's Word is for all true prayer!

"When I pray, I must seek to know God aright. It is through the Word that the Holy Spirit gives me right thoughts of Him. The Word will also teach me how wretched and sinful I am. It reveals to me all the wonders that God will do for me, and the strength He will give to me to do His will. The Word teaches me how to pray — with strong desire, with a firm faith, and with constant perseverance. The Word teaches me not only what I am, but what I may become through God's grace. And above all, it reminds me each day that Christ is the great Intercessor, and allows me to pray in His name.

"*O Christian, learn this great lesson, to renew your strength each day in God's Word, and so pray according to His will.* Then we turn to the other side — prayer. We need prayer when we read God's Word — prayer to be taught of God to understand His Word, prayer that through the Holy Spirit I may rightly know and use God's Word — prayer that I may see in the Word that Christ is all in all, and will be all in me.

"(In my) blessed inner chamber — where I may approach God in Christ through the Word and prayer — I may offer myself to God and His service, and be strengthened by the Holy Spirit, so that His love may be shed abroad in my heart, and I may daily walk in that love."

— Andrew Murray

"If you abide in Me, and My words abide in you, ask whatever you wish, and it shall be done for you" (John 15:7).

"And this is the confidence which we have before Him, that, if we ask anything according to His will, He hears us. And if we know that He hears us in whatever we ask, we know that we have the requests which we desired from Him" (1 John 5:14, 15).

Prayer is communion with God. This is the way our heavenly Father has ordained for His children to communicate with Him.

Often prayer is misunderstood. It is thought of as a vague, mystical element in one's relationship to a holy, awesome God. The Word of God does not teach this; rather it teaches that God our Father desires the fellowship of His children.

Our relationship with God, our heavenly Father, should be a relationship of complete trust, faith and obedience. We, as children, should approach our Father in love and gratitude. Our prayer to God should be an expression of our complete trust that He will hear us, according to John 15:7 and 1 John 5:14, 15. If prayer is anything less than this, it is not prayer. Prayer is more than words; it is an attitude and an expression of the heart toward God.

The prayer life of the Christian is essential. His source of spiritual life is God in Christ. The Christian who does not utilize his resource of prayer fails, for the Christian life is an impossibility except it be lived in and through the Lord Jesus Christ.

As you study carefully the following lessons, it is our sincere desire that you will see the importance of prayer and that you will begin immediately to spend definite time daily in such fellowship with our heavenly Father. Remember, Jesus said, "... I am the way, and the truth, and the life; no one comes to the Father, but through Me ... And whatever you ask in My name, that I will do, that the Father may be glorified in the Son. If you ask Me anything in My name, I will do it" (John 14:6, 13, 14).

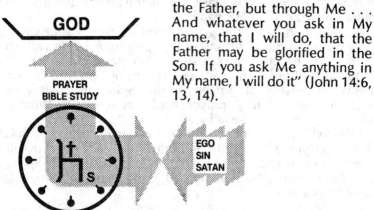

POWER THROUGH PRAYER

"No amount of money, genius, or culture can move things for God. Holiness energizing the soul, the whole man aflame with love, with desire for more faith, more prayer, more zeal, more consecration — this is the secret of power. These we need and must have, and men must be the incarnation of this God-inflamed devotedness. God's advance has been stayed, His cause crippled, His name dishonored for their lack. Genius (though the loftiest and most gifted), education (though the most learned and refined), position, dignity, place, honored names, cannot move this chariot of our God. It is a fiery one, and fiery forces only can move it. The genius of a Milton fails. The imperial strength of a Leo fails. But Brainerd's spirit could move it. Brainerd's spirit was on fire for God, on fire for souls. Nothing earthly, worldly, selfish came in to abate in the least the intensity of this all-impelling and all-consuming force and flame.

"Prayer is the creator as well as the channel of devotion. The spirit of devotion is the spirit of prayer. Prayer and devotion are united as soul and body are united, as life and heart are united. There is no real prayer without devotion, no devotion without prayer."

"The Church is looking for better methods; God is looking for better men . . . What the Church needs today is not more or better machinery, not new organizations or more and novel methods, but men whom the Holy Ghost can use — men of prayer, men mighty in prayer. The Holy Ghost does not flow through methods, but through men. He does not come on machinery, but on men. He does not anoint plans, but men — men of prayer."

— E. M. Bounds

John Quincy Adams, President of the United States, noted in his journal, in connection with his custom of studying the Bible each morning: "It seems to me the most suitable manner of beginning the day."

"Beginning the day with a devotional Bible study and prayer equips a man for the day's fight with self and sin and Satan."

— John R. Mott

LESSON ONE

DEVOTIONAL BIBLE STUDY AND PRAYER

Introduction

OBJECTIVE: To establish a consistent and effective daily prayer life.

TO MEMORIZE: Isaiah 40:31.

TO READ: Acts 1 and 2.

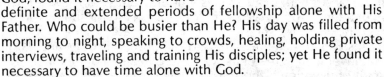

Jesus Christ, the very Son of God, found it necessary to have definite and extended periods of fellowship alone with His Father. Who could be busier than He? His day was filled from morning to night, speaking to crowds, healing, holding private interviews, traveling and training His disciples; yet He found it necessary to have time alone with God.

Down through the years the biographies and writings of men of God who have done great things for God testify to the necessity of having a devotional time. John Wesley, who shook the world for God and founded the Methodist Church, is representative of other such great spiritual leaders. He thought prayer, more than anything else, to be his business.

Just as a child needs food to grow physically, so we need food to grow spiritually. We can miss a meal, and not feel any ill effects, but, if we don't eat for a week, we begin to weaken physically. So it is in our spiritual lives. The study of the Word of God and the practice of prayer are vitally important for spiritual growth. We may miss a day without feeding on the Word of God or praying and not feel any apparent ill effects in our lives, but if we continue this practice, we shall lose the power to live the victorious Christian life.

The Christian life might be compared to a soldier in battle. He is out on the front lines but is connected with his commanding officer by radio. He calls and tells of the conditions and problems he is facing. Then his commanding officer, who from his vantage point can see the entire battle area, relays instructions. In like manner the Christian shares his joys and sorrows, his victories and defeats, and his needs, as God instructs and guides him through His Word.

It is our heavenly Father who directs our battle of life. He knows the steps we should take. We must take time to go to Him for guidance.

Bible Study

A. *Establish a definite time*

A daily devotional time in which Christians seek fellowship with the Lord Jesus Christ for the purpose of nourishing their spiritual lives should be set aside for personal worship and meditation. Once begun, this fellowship is continued throughout the day (Psalm 119:97; 1 Thessalonians 5:17).

1. In obedience to Christ's command, what did His disciples do (Acts 1:13, 14)? _____

2. Although different individuals' schedules will vary, many people prefer the morning hours, before the responsibilities of the day begin.

   David was called a man after God's own heart. What time did he set aside to communicate with God (Psalm 5:3)?

   _____

   How often do you think it was? _____

   Name two characteristics of the devotional life of Jesus (Mark 1:35). _____

3. When is your best devotional time? _____

   No one can say that he does not have time for prayer and Bible study. We can all do anything that we really want to do. Whether the period is long or short, set aside some time.

4. Make your devotional time unhurried.

   Do not think about your next responsibility. Concentrate on your fellowship with the Lord. A definite time every day will do much to help.

   An air of expectancy should pervade our devotional times. Anticipate meeting God.

   A brief period with concentration is better than a long devotional time with your mind on many things.

   How many minutes can you set aside daily for your time with God? _____

B. *Choose a definite place*

Avoid distraction by finding a quiet, private place of worship. If privacy is impossible, you will need to learn to concentrate. If you cannot have a devotional time in your own room, perhaps one of the following places will be suitable:

A nearby chapel

A corner of the school library

The library of your house

Name three other places you might find appropriate for your private prayer and Bible study.

_____

_____

_____

C. *Goal and content of the devotional time*

1. We should have a purpose, goal or reason for everything we do. "Aim at nothing and you will surely hit it." Our purpose for prayer should be fellowship with God and the meeting of our own spiritual needs.

   During the devotional time we should be concerned with learning where we have failed and with rededicating ourselves to the task before us. We should use the time to regroup our forces after the battles of the previous day, and plan for the next day's attack.

   What particular spiritual need do you feel today? _____

   _____

   What battles did you have yesterday? _____

   _____

2. The devotional time should include Bible study, prayer, personal worship and quiet meditation. All phases of the devotional time are so closely related that one can actually engage in all at one time. For example: Begin by reading a psalm of thanksgiving or praise. As you read, your heart actually responds and you continue to praise and worship God from a grateful heart. Turn now to another portion of Scripture, such as Romans 8. Interrupt your reading to thank God for each truth that applies to you as a Christian. You will be amazed at how much you have to praise and thank God for, once you get started.

   After you have read and prayed for a while, remain in an attitude of quiet, listening for instructions from God. Write down on a piece of paper any reluctant thoughts that come to mind and pray about these.

Supplementary content may include memorizing Scripture or reading from a devotional book or hymnal.

Which of these do you have available to use? _____

_____

3. Study Matthew 6:9-13. Paraphrase this prayer in your own words, using expressions meaningful to you. _____

_____

_____

_____

Life Application

Fill in the blank spaces:

1. I have set aside the following definite time in the day for my devotional time: _____

2. I have decided on the following definite place: _____

_____

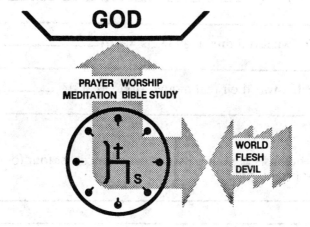

LESSON TWO

PURPOSE OF PRAYER

Introduction

OBJECTIVE: To understand the reasons for prayer.

TO MEMORIZE: 1 John 5:14, 15.

TO READ: Acts 3 and 4.

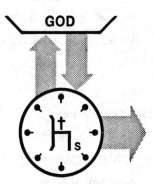

Someone has wisely said, "Satan laughs at our toiling, mocks at our wisdom, but trembles when he sees the weakest saint on his knees." Prayer is God's appointed way of doing God's work.

A. *The apostles' motive*

1. On the basis of Acts 4, what was the problem which faced the apostles? _____

   _____

2. Did they pray for God to remove the persecution? _____
   Why not? _____

   _____

3. For what did they pray (Acts 4:29)? _____

   _____

4. What was their real motive (John 14:13)? _____

   _____

B. *Your motives*

   On the basis of your personal experience, list four (or more) reasons you pray.

   _____

   _____

   _____

   _____

C. *God's motives in teaching us about prayer*

   1. Read John 4:23, 24 and John 3:5-8.

      What form does God take? _____

      What must happen to man before he can fellowship with God? _____

      What kind of worship does God desire? _____

      _____

      What is God's delight (Proverbs 15:8)? _____

      _____

   2. List some purposes of prayer from each of the following Scripture references:

      Matthew 7:7 _____

      Matthew 26:41 _____

      Luke 18:1 _____

   3. From your understanding of the above Scriptures, what do you think God wants you to realize about Him? _____

      _____

D. *Prayer meets the heart's needs*

   1. According to 2 Corinthians 3:5, what is the source of the Christian's sufficiency? _____

      How do you tap into that source? _____

   2. Read Psalm 63. Note the elements of human worship and write the word or phrase below with references (e.g., My soul thirsts for Thee — Psalm 63:1).

      _____

      _____

      _____

      _____

      _____

      _____

Life Application

1. What conclusions can you now make concerning your relationship with God in prayer? _____
_____
_____

2. Begin a prayer list. Keep a record of the things for which you pray.

DATE	REQUESTS	DATE ANSWERED

LESSON THREE

PRIVILEGE OF PRAYER

Introduction

OBJECTIVE: To understand the roles of the Father, Son and Holy Spirit in prayer.

TO MEMORIZE: Philippians 4:6, 7.

TO READ: Acts 5 and 6.

The God who created us and loved us so much that He sent His only begotten Son to die for us, the God who in spite of our sin and lack of love for Him has done everything for us, now waits anxiously for us to come to Him in prayer. We would think nothing of waiting hours at the White House to have a short appointment with the President, and it would be unthinkable to keep the President waiting even a little while.

How can we keep our great God waiting for us, as unimportant as we are? What a privilege for us to come to our heavenly Father just as a child comes to his father, and know that He will meet our needs and that He *desires* our fellowship (John 4:23).

Bible Study

A. *To whom do we pray?*

1. To whom are our prayers to be directed (Matthew 6:9)?

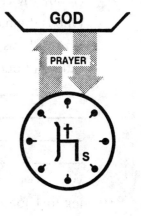

"But some will say, 'Is not all prayer unto God?' No. Very much so-called prayer, both public and private, is not unto God. In order that a prayer should be really unto God, there must a definite and conscious approach to God when we pray; we must have a definite and vivid realization that God is bending over us and listening as we pray. In much of our prayer there is little thought of God. Our mind is not taken up with the thought of the mighty and loving Father ... We are occupied neither with the need nor with the One to Whom we are praying but our mind is wandering here and there throughout the world . . . When we really come into God's presence, really meet Him face to face in the place of prayer, really seek the things that we desire *from Him,* then there is power."

— R. A. Torrey, *How to Pray*

2. Rewrite in your own words the description of God in 1 Chronicles 29:11, 12. _____

_____

_____

_____

_____

B. *Through whom do we pray?*

Read John 14:6.

1. How many mediators are there between God and man (1 Timothy 2:5)? _____

Who is the mediator? _____

2. On the basis of Hebrews 4:14-16, describe the qualifications of our great high priest._____

_____

_____

_____

_____

3. What are the requirements for prayer relationship according to 1 John 3:22, 23? _____

_____

4. What does unconfessed sin in our lives do to our prayer fellowship with God (Psalm 66:18)? _____

_____

C. *In whom do we pray?*

Read Ephesians 6:18 and Jude 20.

1. According to Romans 8:26, 27, why does the Holy Spirit need to help us pray? _____

   _____

   How does He help us pray? _____
   Why does God answer the prayers of the Holy Spirit?

   _____

2. What, then, should be our relationship to the Holy Spirit (Ephesians 5:18)? _____

   _____

   _____

3. As we exercise the privilege of prayer, what does God then do about anxiety (Philippians 4:6, 7)? _____

   _____

4. Why can we cast our troubles on Him (1 Peter 5:7)?

   _____

   _____

Life Application

1. List any new insights into prayer you have gained from this lesson._____

   _____

   _____

2. Write down one new way in which you want to apply prayer in your life right now._____

   _____

   _____

LESSON FOUR

PROCEDURE IN PRAYER

Introduction

OBJECTIVE: To apply a simple guide to your daily prayer time.

TO MEMORIZE: 1 Corinthians 14:40.

TO READ: Acts 7 and 8.

There are many procedures one may follow in prayer. It is good to follow a simple procedure but never to become bound to a ritual. God is more interested in our hearts than in our words. John Bunyan, author of *Pilgrim's Progress,* said, "In prayer it is better to have a heart without words than words without a heart." In this lesson we will consider a simple guide that you may use in your daily devotional time. It is:

Adoration, Confession, Thanksgiving, Supplication.

This order can be easily remembered by the first letter of each word — ACTS.

Bible Study

A. *Adoration*

   1. Why should we praise God?

      Jeremiah 32:17 _____

      1 John 4:10 _____

      Philippians 1:6 _____

   2. What is the best way for you to show your gratitude toward, and your faith and trust in God in all circumstances (Philippians 4:6)? _____

      _____

      What would you conclude that God expects of us (1 Thessalonians 5:16-18)? _____

      _____

If you sometimes find it hard to praise God, read some of the Psalms (Psalms 146-150 in particular).

B. *Confession*

   1. Read Isaiah 59:1, 2.

      What will hinder fellowship with God? _____

      _____

   2. Psalm 51 was David's prayer after he had fallen out of fellowship with God. What did David conclude that God

      wanted of him (Psalm 51:6, 16, 17)? _____

      _____

   3. What should you do when and if you find your fellowship

      with God is broken (1 John 1:9)? _____

      _____

C. *Thanksgiving*

   Let us never be guilty of being ungrateful to God.

   1. How often should we give thanks (Hebrews 13:15)?

      _____

      What for (Ephesians 5:20)? _____

      Why (1 Thessalonians 5:18)? _____

   2. What about a situation that seems adverse? _____

      _____

D. *Supplication*

   1. Intercession.

      An example of intercession is provided in Colossians 1:3,9. What was Paul's prayer for the Christians of Colossae?

      _____

      Many times our efforts in leading people to Christ are fruitless because we forget the necessary preparation for witnessing. The divine order is first to talk to God about men, and *then* to talk to men about God. If we follow this formula, we shall see results. Prayer is really the place where people are won to Christ; service is just gathering in the results of our prayer.

As you meditate on the above, list the requests you can make to God for Christians and non-Christians. _____

_____

_____

2. Petition.

Why should we expect God to answer our prayers (John 3:16; Romans 8:32)? _____

_____

What part does belief have in our prayers (Mark 11:24)?

_____

Faith is necessary for answered prayers. What else is necessary (1 John 5:14, 15)? _____

_____

Why will God not answer some prayers (James 1:5)?

_____

According to Psalm 84:11, 12, what has God promised to do? _____

3. Explain 2 Corinthians 12:7-10 in light of Romans 8:28.

_____

_____

What does this passage teach us about apparently unanswered prayer? _____

_____

Life Application

1. Add other requests to the prayer list you began at the end of Lesson Two.

2. Select one prayer request from your prayer request list and before you make the request, apply A-C-T. Then make the request, which completes the procedure: (S = Supplication).

LESSON FIVE

POWER IN PRAYER

Introduction

OBJECTIVE: To learn to use the great power available through prayer.

TO MEMORIZE: James 5:16.

TO READ: Acts 9 and 10.

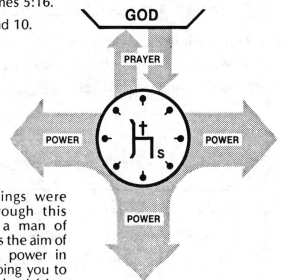

It is said of Jonathan Goforth that once he felt assured of God's will in prayer, he would continue in the power of prayer until the thing was accomplished. Great things were accomplished through this man, for he was a man of powerful prayer. It is the aim of this lesson to put power in your prayer by helping you to make it effective and satisfying.

Bible Study

A. *Power for answered prayer*

Read Acts 12:5-18.

1. How did Peter's fellow Christians respond to his imprisonment (Acts 12:5)? _____

_____

What was God's answer to their prayer (Acts 12:6-11)?

_____

What was their response to God's answer (Acts 12:13-16)?

_____

2. What do the following Scripture references tell you about the qualities God demands in a person for powerful prayer?

Hebrews 11:1, 6 _____

Romans 12:1, 3 _____

1 Corinthians 15:58 _____

1 John 3:22 _____

Ephesians 5:18 _____

B. *Conditions to answered prayer*

1. Why is it necessary to ask in accordance with the will of God (John 5:14, 15)? _____

_____

2. Write out John 15:7 in your own words and state what it teaches about conditions to answered prayer._____

_____

_____

3. What is the value of several Christians praying for something as opposed to just one (Matthew 18:19)?_____

_____

_____

C. *Prevailing prayer*

1. Example of prevailing prayer: During his lifetime, George Mueller recorded more than 50,000 answers to prayer. He prayed for two men daily for more than 60 years. One of these men was converted shortly before Mueller's death and the other about a year later. As in Mueller's experience, we do not always see the answer to our prayers. We must leave the results to God.

One of the great needs of the present day is for men and women who will begin to pray for things and then pray on and on until they obtain that which they seek from the Lord.

How long do you think we should pray for someone or something? (Read Luke 18:1-8; Matthew 15:21-28.)

_____

Why do you think God honors prevailing prayer? _____

_____

2. What did the following men accomplish through prayer?

Moses (Exodus 15:23-25) _____

_____

Samson (Judges 16:28-30) _____

_____

Peter (Acts 9:36-41) _____

_____

Elijah (James 5:17, 18) _____

_____

_____

3. In what way are all of these examples alike? _____

_____

_____

Life Application

1. Do you pray for results? _____

   Do you really believe and trust God when you pray? _____

_____

2. Write down one prayer request for which you are having to exercise "prevailing prayer." _____

_____

3. List two verses of Scripture you can claim in relation to this prayer request. _____

_____

LESSON SIX

PROMISE OF PRAYER

Introduction

OBJECTIVE: To claim God's promises for us about and in prayer.

TO MEMORIZE: Jeremiah 33:3.

TO READ: Acts 11 and 12.

Bible Study

It is estimated that there are more than 5,000 personal promises in the Bible. However, to many Christians, these promises mean little or nothing.

Why (Hebrews 4:2)? _____

_____

_____

Bags of cement sitting in a warehouse will never become concrete until they are mixed with sand, gravel and water. Even so, God's promises will never become concrete unless they are mixed with faith and action. You must make them yours by believing them and putting your faith to work.

A. *What God has promised concerning prayer*

   1. Jeremiah 33:3

      Condition: _____

      Promise: _____

   Matthew 21:22

      Condition: _____

      Promise: _____

   1 John 5:14, 15

      Condition: _____

      Promise: _____

John 14:14

    Condition: _____

    Promise: _____

2. Which promise do you need most to apply to your own prayer life right now and why? _____

_____

_____

B. *What God will provide through prayer*

  1. Material needs:

    In Philippians 4:19? _____

    In Psalm 84:11? _____

    Guidance:

    In Proverbs 3:5, 6? _____

    In Psalm 32:8? _____

    Spiritual needs:

    In Ephesians 1:3? _____

    In Philippians 4:13? _____

    In Isaiah 41:10? _____

  2. Is God dependable? _____ Can you trust Him? _____

  3. In what particular circumstance of your life do you presently need to trust Him more and for what? _____

_____

These promises are real — claim them; believe them; live by them.

Life Application

List on this chart at least three things you need to pray for, and a verse for each which promises God's provision.

NEED	PROMISE

LESSON SEVEN

RECAP

Review all memorized verses.

Read Acts 13 and 14

Have you set aside a specific place and time for daily prayer and devotions? _____ Where and when? _____

What adjustments do you need to make for it to be more effective (more time, less time, different place, etc.)? _____
_____

Why are you praying? _____
_____

What conditions are you now meeting, which you weren't before, to be more effective in prayer? _____
_____

Fill in the words to complete the suggested guide for prayer content:

A _____
C _____
T _____
S _____

Are you presently following this guide or do you have another?
_____

(Remember, a guide is not mandatory, it is just helpful.)

How has your understanding of power and promises in prayer been broadened? _____
_____
_____
_____

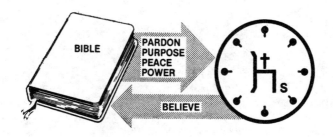

THE PRAYING CHRISTIAN

"The Christian needs strength. This we all know. The Christian has no strength of his own. This is also true. Where may strength be obtained? Notice the answer: 'Be strong in the Lord, and in the strength of His might' (Ephesians 6:10).

"Paul had spoken of this power in the earlier part of his epistle to the Ephesians (1:18-20). He had prayed to God to give them the Spirit that they might know the exceeding greatness of His power according to the working of His mighty power, which He wrought in Christ when He raised Him from the dead. This is the literal truth: The exceeding greatness of His power, which raised Christ from the dead, works in every believer. In me and in you, my reader. We hardly believe it, and still less do we experience it. That is why Paul prays, and we must pray with him, that God through His Spirit would teach us to believe in His almighty power. Pray with all your heart: 'Father, grant me the Spirit of wisdom, that I may experience this power in my life.'

"Pray for God's Spirit to enlighten your eyes. Believe in the divine power working within you. Pray that the Holy Spirit may reveal it to you, and appropriate the promise that God will manifest His power in your heart, supplying all your needs.

"Do you not begin to realize that time is needed — much time in fellowship with the Father and the Son, if you would experience the power of God within you?"

— Andrew Murray

The Christian and the Bible

GOD'S MEN AND THE WORD OF GOD

"The vigor of our spiritual life will be in exact proportion to the place held by the Bible in our life and thoughts . . . I have read the Bible through 100 times, and always with increasing delight. Each time it seems like a new book to me. Great has been the blessing from consecutive, diligent, daily study. I look upon it as a lost day when I have not had a good time over the Word of God."

— George Mueller

"I prayed for faith, and thought that some day faith would come down and strike me like lightning. But faith did not seem to come. One day I read in the tenth chapter of Romans, 'Now faith comes by hearing, and hearing by the Word of God.' I had closed my Bible and prayed for faith. I now opened my Bible and began to study, and faith has been growing ever since."

— D. L. Moody

"The Bible is truly the Word of God. He is the final and the ultimate Author; the Bible comes from God. Without Him there could have been no Bible. Without men, however, there could have been a Bible. God could have given us His Word in some other manner than that which He actually did choose. As a matter of fact, He did choose to speak through inspired men but He was not compelled to do so. In no sense was He limited. That He employed human writers was an act of grace, and the heart of faith will ever adore and revere Him that He so honored the human race as to employ lost sinners as writers of His pure and holy Word. While the human authors were true authors, nevertheless they were not the originators of the words and the thoughts that are found in the Bible. They were holy men indeed, but they were holy men who were borne by the Spirit."

— Dr. E. J. Young,
Professor of Old Testament at
Westminster Theological
Seminary: *Thy Word Is Truth.*

LESSON ONE

THE BOOK OF BOOKS

Introduction

OBJECTIVE: To recognize the unparal-
leled composition of the
Bible and to become familiar with its structure.

TO MEMORIZE: 2 Timothy 3:16, 17.

TO READ: Acts 15 and 16.

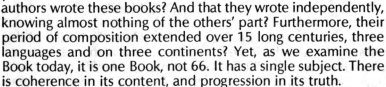

The Bible's Amazing Composition

"The way in which the Bible came into being is nothing short of a miracle.

"Everyone knows that the Bible is made up of 66 individual books. But did you know that about 40 different human authors wrote these books? And that they wrote independently, knowing almost nothing of the others' part? Furthermore, their period of composition extended over 15 long centuries, three languages and on three continents? Yet, as we examine the Book today, it is one Book, not 66. It has a single subject. There is coherence in its content, and progression in its truth.

"To see the weight of this argument, suppose you were to endeavor to assemble a comparable book from various bits of literature written since the first century of the Christian era. Take your material from the ancient papyri, pieces of ostraca, writing of the philosophers, ancient wisdom books of the East or anything you choose. Get some writing from each century, select representative material from men in various walks of life; merchants, laborers, priests, farmers. Gather it all together and bind it into one book. Now, what have you? Why it will be the most ridiculous, contradictory hodgepodge of nonsense you have ever seen.

"The Bible, on the other hand, while like that in compilation, is wholly different in result. Everything about its composition argues against its unity. There's no reason in the world why it should be one Book. Yet it is, and no honest inquirer will doubt this, if he will take the time to read it carefully.

"The human writers of the Scriptures had almost nothing in common. Look at their diverse literary qualifications. While

Moses may have been somewhat of a man of learning, having been schooled in the best universities of Egypt, Peter certainly was no writer. He was a fisherman, and there is no record that he had any education. Yet the writing of both are saturated with the wisdom of God.

"There's only one satisfactory answer. Using the ability of these men, or overcoming their disability, God *spoke through them,* and caused that they should write the Scriptures to His divine plan."

> — William W. Orr
> *Ten Reasons Why*

The Bible: A Book for Important Men

Abraham Lincoln: "I believe the Bible is the best gift God has ever given to man. All the good from the Savior of the world is communicated to us through this Book."

Immanuel Kant: "The existence of the Bible, as a book for people, is the greatest benefit which the human race has ever experienced. Every attempt to belittle it is a crime against humanity."

Sir Isaac Newton: "There are more sure marks of authenticity in the Bible than in any profane history."

Robert E. Lee: "In all my perplexities and distresses, the Bible has never failed to give me light and strength."

Daniel Webster: "If there is anything in my thought or style to commend, the credit is due to my parents for instilling in me early love for the Scriptures."

Bible Study

A. *Various names of the Bible*

List the various names the Bible is called according to the following references:

1 Corinthians 15:3, 4 _____

Ephesians 6:17 _____

B. *Construction of the Bible*

To get familiar with your own Bible, leaf through it and look at these divisions and books as you progress through this lesson.

The Bible is comprised of two main sections: the Old

Testament, containing 39 books, and the New Testament containing 27 books.

The Old Testament can be divided into five parts:

1. *Pentateuch.* The first five historical books, written by Moses, also are called the books of the Law. List these

   books: _____

   _____

   _____

2. *Historical Books.* The next 12 books tell of the establishment of the kingdom of Israel, of Israel's repeated turning from God to sin, and finally of the Assyrian and Babylonian exile — God's punishment. List these 12 books as follows:

   First three (pre-kingdom era) _____

   _____

   Next six (duration of the kingdom) _____

   _____

   _____

   _____

   Last three (exile and post-exile period) _____

   _____

3. *Poetry.* Of the next five books, Psalms — the Hebrew hymn book — is probably the best known. List the books

   of poetry: _____

   _____

4. *Major Prophets.* Written shortly before Israel was taken into captivity and during the exile, these books prophesy the coming Messiah and other world events. They also contain the record of warning of impending disaster if Israel did not turn from her wicked ways. List the five

   books of the Major Prophets. _____

   _____

5. *Minor Prophets.* These last 12 books of the Old Testament are called minor only because they are shorter, not

because they are less important. They mainly concern Israel and the coming Messiah. List all 12: _____

_____

_____

_____

_____

_____

_____

_____

The New Testament can also be divided into five parts.

6. *Gospels.* The first four books of the New Testament tell of Christ's life and ministry. List them here: _____

_____

Acts. This history of the early church which also describes the ministries of Peter and Paul consist of only one book.

For practice, write it here: _____

7. *Pauline Epistles and Hebrews.* Thirteen of the epistles were written by Paul, and named for the church or individual to whom they were sent. Although the author of Hebrews is not identified, many believe Paul also wrote

that 14th epistle. List all 14: _____

_____

_____

_____

8. *General Epistles.* There are seven of them, and they are named not for the recipients, but for the authors. List

those here: _____

_____

9. *Revelation.* The last book of the New Testament is one of prophecy. It describes the end times and the triumph of Christ in His second coming. Write the name of it here:

_____

Life Application

1. What new insight about the composition of the Bible have you gained from this study? _____

   _____

2. In order to know your Bible well and to be able to find Scripture references quickly, you should memorize the names of the books in the order in which they appear. It is easier if you learn them by division. Master one group and then go on to the next.

   Today, commit to memory the books of the first division,

   the Pentateuch, and write them again here: 1. _____

   2. _____ 3._____4. _____

   5. _____

3. NOTE: A word about different versions of the Bible:

   In his discussion of the two main texts from which the various versions have been translated, Josh McDowell says, "... areas of variation consist in only 10% of the text. There is total agreement between all text types 90% of the time ... it must always be kept in mind that the same basic story is contained both in the majority text and in the other texts and that no crucial doctrine of the Christian faith rests upon the 10% in dispute" (*Reasons*, San Bernardino: Here's Life Publishers, 1981, p. 48).

LESSON TWO

CHRIST IS THE CENTRAL PERSON OF THE BIBLE

Introduction

OBJECTIVE: To recognize the entire Bible as God's revelation of Jesus Christ to us.

TO MEMORIZE: 1 Corinthians 15:3,4.

TO READ: Acts 17 and 18.

Bible Study

A. *What Christ said about Himself and the Old Testament*

1. What did Christ say of the Scriptures in John 5:39?_____

   _____

2. Read Luke 24:25-27, 44-48.

   What was Christ's claim concerning the Old Testament teaching about Himself?_____

   _____

   What parts of the Old Testament did Christ say referred to Him (verse 44)? _____

   _____

   What do you think Christ wants you to understand about the Old Testament from verse 26? _____

   _____

   Verses 46, 47? _____

B. *What the apostles said about Christ and the Old Testament.*

1. What does Peter conclude in Acts 3:18? _____

   _____

2. How did the apostle Paul use the Old Testament to show that it contained the "good news" of Christ (Acts 17:1-3)?

_____

3. What three things occurred in Christ's life that Paul said were taught in the Old Testament (1 Corinthians 15:3, 4)?

_____

4. What does Paul conclude in Romans 15:8, 9 about the ministry of Christ? _____

C. *Old Testament prophecies concerning Christ fulfilled in the New Testament*

All of the more than 300 Old Testament prophecies about the first coming of the Messiah were fulfilled in the life of Christ. Here are a few of them.

1. Compare these Scripture references and record the prophecies fulfilled.

COMPARE	WITH	FULFILLMENT
Isaiah 11:1 1 Samuel 16:19	Luke 1:31-33	_____
Genesis 3:15	Galatians 4:4	_____
Numbers 24:17	Matthew 2:2, 9	_____
Isaiah 9:6	Matthew 1:23	_____
Isaiah 40:3	Matthew 3:1-3	_____
Zechariah 9:9	Matthew 21:1-5	_____
Psalm 69:21	Matthew 27: 34, 48	_____
Psalm 34:20	John 19:33, 36	_____
Job 19:25-27	Galatians 3:13	_____

2. What is your impression after seeing these Old Testament prophecies and their New Testament fulfillment? _____

_____

D. *Christ, the central person of the New Testament*

1. The four Gospels are the history books of Christ's ministry. (Read Matthew 1:1; Mark 1:1; Luke 1:1-4; John 20:30, 31).

   In what ways did the disciples know Jesus (1 John 1:3)?

   _____

   Do the four Gospels purport to record all that Jesus did (John 20:30)? _____

   Why were the historical facts and teachings of Jesus Christ written (verse 31)? _____

   _____

   _____

2. The book of Acts is an historical account of the acts of the Holy Spirit through the apostles.

   Who wrote it (Luke 1:1-4 and Acts 1:1)? _____

   How do you think the passage in Luke applies to the book of Acts? _____

   _____

3. The Epistles are letters written to show the church the practical outworking of the life of Christ in the lives of those who wrote them. By example, they teach us regarding our membership in the body of Christ, privileges, responsibilities and destiny.

   Read Colossians 2:6-8.

   What are Christians to do? _____

   How are we to do it? _____

   Of what are we to beware? _____

   What would you say our greatest responsibility is? _____

   _____

4. The book of Revelation is the only New Testament book of prophecy. Read Revelation 1:1-3.

This book is the revelation of whom? _____

What is its purpose? _____

Who gave such knowledge, how, and to whom? _____

_____

How will the book of Revelation affect your life and under what conditions? _____

_____

_____

Life Application

1. How will recognizing Jesus as the central figure of the entire Bible affect your Old Testament reading? _____

_____

_____

2. What do you see as your individual responsibility in fulfilling the commands of this person presented in the entire Bible? See John 15:16 and Matthew 28:19, 20. _____

_____

3. Memorize the 12 Historical books and write them again here:

Pre-kingdom era (3) _____

Kingdom era (6) _____

_____

_____

_____

_____

Exile and post-exile era (3) _____

Review those learned earlier _____

_____

_____

_____

LESSON THREE

AUTHORITY OF THE OLD TESTAMENT

Introduction

OBJECTIVE: To gain assurance of the Bible's trustworthiness by looking at the Old Testament and its validity.

"THUS SAITH THE LORD"
2,000 TIMES IN O.T.

TO MEMORIZE: 2 Peter 1:20, 21.

TO READ: Acts 19 and 20.

Bible Study

A. *Testimony of its writers*

The phrase, "Thus saith the Lord," or its equivalent, occurs more than 2,000 times in the Old Testament.

1. Write out the statements concerning inspiration made by the following writers:

   David (2 Samuel 23:2) _____

   _____

   Isaiah (Isaiah 8:1, 5, 11) _____

   _____

   Jeremiah (Jeremiah 1:9) _____

   _____

   Ezekiel (Ezekiel 3:4) _____

   _____

2. What two statements of Moses in Exodus 31:18 and 32:16 show that God actually wrote the Ten Commandments? _____

   _____

   _____

3. What statement made by David shows that the pattern
for the temple was dictated by God (1 Chronicles 28:19)?

_____

_____

B. *Testimony of Christ*

The New Testament had not been written during Christ's
earthly ministry and His references to the Scriptures refer to
the Old Testament writings. He never once denied or made
light of Old Testament Scriptures; He related Himself to
them as their fulfillment. He said, "He who has seen Me has
seen the Father" (John 14:9) and, "I and the Father are one"
(John 10:30). "The word which you hear is not Mine, but the
Father's who sent Me" (John 14:24). Christ, the God-man
said, "Search the Scripture . . . it is these that bear witness of
Me" (John 5:39).

1. How did Christ see those who did not believe the Old

   Testament prophecies (Luke 24:25)?_____

2. What did Christ say that unbelief in Him implied (John

   5:46, 47)?_____

3. What do you think Christ indicated was His responsibility concerning Old Testament prophecy (Matthew

   5:17, 18)? _____

   _____

4. What was Christ's view of the story of man's creation as

   recorded in Genesis (Matthew 19:4-6)? _____

   _____

5. What authority did Christ use to answer:

   Satan (Matthew 4:4, 7, 10)? _____

   Men (Matthew 22:29-32, 43-46)? _____

6. In John 18:37b, who did Jesus say He was and what
   connection did His purpose in coming to earth have to

   the Old Testament? _____

   _____

7. Summarize here Christ's attitude and view of the Old Testament. _____

_____

_____

_____

C. Testimony of the apostles

It is evident from their inspired writing that the apostles of Christ considered the Old Testament Scriptures prophetic of and inseparable from the authority, power and ministry of Christ.

Peter

1. From whom did the apostle Peter say the writings of the Old Testament come

   (2 Peter 1:21; Acts 1:16)?_____

   How did Peter feel about the Old Testament historical account he recorded

   in 1 Peter 3:20? _____

   _____

   Who did Peter say were inspired by God

   (Acts 3:20, 21)?_____

N.T.

FULFILLMENT

O.T.

Paul

2. How much of the Old Testament is inspired by God, according to Paul in 2 Timothy 3:16?_____

   Paul believed the Old Testament to be what (Romans 3:2)?

   _____

James

3. Acceptance of the Old Testament writing is evidenced by references concerning which person in the Book of James?

   (2:21) _____

   (2:25) _____

   (5:11) _____

   (5:17) _____

John

4. One of the many evidences that John believed the Old Testament is his acceptance of which story (1 John 3:12)?

_____

Life Application

H.S. Miller, in his book *General Biblical Introduction,* says,

"The same Old Testament books which had been received by the Jews and by Christ and the New Testament writers as inspired and authoritative were received by the early church. The church, with the exception of a few heretics, held the same high standard of inspiration. However much the fathers may have differed in other doctrines, they all, from various parts of the Empire, differing in character and training, were, with perhaps some slight variations in minor details, unanimous in this one great doctrine. They taught that in the entire Old Testament, God and Christ, the incarnate Word of God, spoke through the Holy Spirit through men, and that all Scripture is permanently fitted for our instruction. The matter was not even discussed, as some doctrines were; it was not considered debatable."

1. The writers of the Old Testament, Jesus Christ the Son of God, the apostles of Christ and the early church fathers all say of the Old Testament, "This is the inspired Word of God."

   What do you say? (See John 8:47 and 1 John 4:6.) _____

   _____

2. Write down *how* the information in this lesson gives you confidence in the authority of the Old Testament._____

   _____

3. Repeat the names of the five books of poetry until you have committed them to memory. Then write them here: _____

   _____

   _____

   Review all those learned earlier.

LESSON FOUR

AUTHORITY OF THE NEW TESTAMENT

Introduction

OBJECTIVE: To gain confidence in the Bible's authority by looking at the reliability of the New Testament.

TO MEMORIZE: Matthew 24:35.

HEAVEN AND EARTH SHALL PASS AWAY...NOT MY WORD

TO READ: Acts 21 and 22.

HOLY BIBLE

Bible Study

A. *Authority given the apostles by Christ*

1. What four things did Christ say the Holy Spirit would do for the apostles (John 16:12-15)? _____

_____

_____

_____

At that time, why do you think the apostles could not know all the truth? _____

_____

How would they in the future? _____

2. What authority did Christ give the apostles (John 17:18; 20:21)? _____

3. On what basis did Christ select the apostles to bear witness of Him (John 15:26, 27; Luke 24:46-48)? _____

_____

How did Paul fit in according to Acts 9:3-6; Acts 26:13-15

and 1 Corinthians 15:7-9? _____

How do you think we fit into this witnessing aspect?

_____

_____

4. What authority did Christ give Paul (Acts 26:15-18)?

_____

B. *The apostles wrote under Christ's authority*

1. *Paul:* What does he call himself at the beginning of the book of Romans and his other letters? _____

From whom did Paul receive what he preached (1 Corinthians 11:23; Galatians 1:11, 12)? _____

_____

What was Paul's authority and purpose (2 Corinthians 5:20)? _____

Read 2 Peter 3:15, 16. What did Peter think about Paul's writings? _____

2. *Writer of Hebrews:* Where did the writer of Hebrews get his authority (Hebrews 1:1,2)? _____

_____

3. *James:* What did this half-brother of Christ (Christ's Father is God) call himself (James 1:1)? _____

_____

4. *John:* What does John claim as the authority for writing his epistles (1 John 1:1-3)? _____

_____

_____

_____

5. *Jude:* What does this other half-brother of Christ call himself in Jude 1? _____

What do you think Paul, James and Jude meant by saying they were bondservants of Christ? _____

_____

6. *Peter:* He calls himself what (1 Peter 1:1)? _____

_____

What does Peter make known (2 Peter 1:16)? _____

_____

7. On whose writings is the foundation of the church of Jesus Christ established (Ephesians 2:20)? _____

8. What is the gospel of Christ, according to the apostles (Romans 1:16)? _____

9. Why were the apostles confident they wrote correctly about Christ (2 Corinthians 4:5, 6)? _____

_____

Life Application

RELIABILITY OF THE NEW TESTAMENT WE HAVE TODAY

"The evidence for our New Testament writings is ever so much greater than the evidence for many writings of classical authors, the authenticity of which no one dreams of questioning. There are in existence about 4,000 Greek manuscripts of the New Testament in whole or in part." — F. F. Bruce, Professor of Biblical History and Literature, University of Sheffield, England: *Are the New Testament Documents Reliable?*

"The interval between the dates of original composition and the earliest extant evidence becomes so small as to be in fact negligible, and the last foundation for any doubt that the Scriptures have come down to use substantially as they were written has now been removed. Both the authenticity and the general integrity of the books of the New Testament may be regarded as finally established." — Sir Frederic Kenyon, British classical scholar, president of the British Academy, president of the British School of Archaeology at Jerusalem: *The Bible and Archaeology.*

True, there are variant readings of some words and phrases in the New Testament. However, Bible scholars tell us that if you would put all the variants of any consequence together, they would take up about one-half of a page. Even if you chose the worst of the variant readings, no doctrine in the New Testament would be changed.

Dr. J. Harold Greenlee, Department of New Testament, Asbury Theological Seminary, says:

Although the known manuscripts of the classical writings number only a few hundred at most, there are literally thousands of known manuscripts of the New Testament. And although the oldest known manuscript of a classical writing may be an umpteenth generation copy written a thousand years or more after the original, there are manuscripts of the New Testament which were written within 300 years after the original, and some parts of manuscripts are dated to within 150 years of the original.

1. God has miraculously preserved His Word for us. Although the above study should convince any of us that the New Testament is the Word of God, what is your greatest assurance that it is God's Word (John 16:13; 8:47; 18:37b)?

_____

_____

2. How does the information in this lesson help you trust the Bible more than you may have in the past? _____

_____

_____

3. Commit to memory the names of the five books of the Major Prophets. Then write them: _____

_____

Don't forget to review all other books previously learned.

LESSON FIVE

THE POWER OF THE BIBLE

Introduction

OBJECTIVE: To experience the power of God's Word in our daily lives.

TO MEMORIZE: Hebrews 4:12.

TO READ: Acts 23 and 24.

Bible Study

A. *The Word of God*

Tell what God's Word is or what it does, or both, according to the following Scripture references (use dictionary for definition of key words if needed):

1. What it is:

    Hebrews 5:13 _____

    Philippians 2:16 _____

    Ephesians 6:17 _____

2. What it does:

    1 John 2:5 _____

    John 12:48 _____

    Romans 10:17 _____

    John 15:3 _____

3. Both:

    1 Peter 1:23 _____

    John 8:31, 32 _____

John 17:17 _____

1 Peter 2:2 _____

Hebrews 4:12 (5 things) _____

_____

_____

B. *How to understand the Word of God*

1. Read 1 Corinthians 2:14.

   No one can understand the Word of God by his own ability. Why? _____

   _____

2. Describe in your own words a natural man's reaction to spiritual things. _____

   _____

3. State again in your own words, how one must come to understand the Word of God. See verses 10-12, John 2:3, Romans 8:9. _____

   _____

   _____

4. Why do some individuals deny the authority of Scripture, the deity of Christ, the inspiration of the Bible, and other basic teachings in the printed word of the Holy Spirit?

   _____

   _____

   What should be our response to them? _____

   _____

   _____

   _____

   _____

   _____

Life Application

"I believe a knowledge of the Bible without a college course is more valuable than a college course without the Bible." — William Lyon Phelps, former professor at Yale University.

1. When we approach the Word of God, what is the first thing we should understand (2 Peter 1:20, 21)? _____

   _____

2. Name some way the power of the Bible manifests itself according to 2 Timothy 2:15-17. _____

   _____

3. How have you experienced that power in your life recently?

   _____

   _____

4. The 12 books of the Minor Prophets are probably the most difficult of all to learn. Give extra diligence to memorizing this division, then write the names here: _____

   _____

   _____

   _____

LESSON SIX

THE NEED FOR THE WORD OF GOD

Introduction

OBJECTIVE: To gain spiritual dependence on God's Word for daily Christian living.

TO MEMORIZE: Psalm 119:105.

TO READ: Acts 25 and 26.

```
            WORD OF GOD
             PSALM 119

             PARDON
             PURPOSE
             PEACE
             POWER


                MAN
```

Bible Study

Read Psalm 119.

A. *Things we need to know about the Bible*

1. What does the psalmist call God's Word in the following verses of Psalm 119?

   Verse 1 _____

   2 _____   7 _____

   3 _____   43 _____

   4 _____   72 _____

   5 _____   91 _____

   6 _____ 123 _____

2. What does this tell you of the importance of knowing God's Word? _____

3. When does God discipline (126)? _____

   _____

4. What value does the Word have for us (72)? _____

   _____

5. What is necessary in order to learn the Word (73)?

   _____

B. *How God's Word affects our feeling*

　1. The psalmist found that respecting and learning God's Word resulted in:

　　(7) _____

　　(8) _____

　　(9) _____

　2. From verses 10-16 list at least three attitudes of the psalmist that show his love for the Word of God: _____

　　_____

　　_____

　　_____

　　_____

　　_____

　　_____

　3. Why is adversity sometimes good for us (67, 71)? _____

　　_____

　4. What is the reaction of those who love Christ when His Word is not kept (136)? _____

　　(158)? _____

　5. How can we have great peace (165)? _____

　　_____

C. *Results of appropriating God's Word*

　1. What the Word does for us:

　　Knowing and memorizing the Word makes us (98) _____

　　_____

　　Meditating on it makes us (99) _____

　　_____

　　Obeying it makes us (100) _____

　　_____

Why is this (105)? _____

_____

The Word gives us (130) _____

_____

2. What we should do as a result of appropriating the Word:

   (74) _____

   (63) _____

   (11) _____

   (32) _____

   (157) _____

   (176) _____

Life Application

1. What impresses you most about Psalm 119? _____

_____

_____

2. Write *three* ways in which you recognize your personal need for God's Word today. _____

_____

_____

_____

3. Many people can recite the four books of the Gospels. Can you? _____ Add the one book of New Testament history and write all five books here: _____

_____

Since this division is quite easy, go ahead to the next division, the Pauline epistles and Hebrews. That division is much harder to learn so you should get started on it now.

LESSON SEVEN

PRIVATE BIBLE STUDY METHODS

Introduction

OBJECTIVE: To know how to and to establish good habits of regular systematic study of the Bible.

TO MEMORIZE: Colossians 3:16a and 17.

TO READ: Acts 27 and 28.

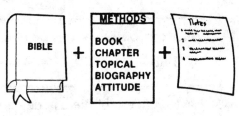

"It is a great day for a little child when he learns to feed himself; so it becomes a new era in a believer's life when he forms the habit of going daily to the original sources of spiritual truth for his own personal nourishment.

"Study the Bible as a traveler who seeks to obtain a thorough and experimental knowledge of a new country.

"Go over its vast fields to truth; descend into its valleys; climb its mountains of vision; follow its streams of inspiration; enter its halls of instruction; visit its wondrous portrait galleries.

"Remember that many doctrinal errors have grown out of a lack of spiritual perspective, or a narrow view of scriptural truth. The Savior says, 'Ye do err, not knowing the Scriptures, nor the power of God.'

"Seek to understand the deep things of God. Study 'The Word' as a miner digs for gold, or as a diver plunges into the depths of the sea for pearls.

"Most great truths do not lie upon the surface. They must be brought up into the light by patient toil" — Thompson Chain Reference Bible.

Bible Study

A. *Proper attitude for Bible study*

When you personally received Christ as your Savior and Lord, you began a great adventure. That great adventure is mapped out in the pages of the Holy Scriptures. As you read and study the Bible in the power of the Holy Spirit you will find strength and direction. You will learn and claim the many great promises God has reserved for His own.

Approach the Bible in prayer, with reverence, awe, expectancy; with a willing mind; with a thirst for truth and righteousness and fullness in the Lord Jesus Christ; with a humble and contrite heart, trusting God the Holy Spirit to engraft therein the cleansing power of His eternal Word. Above all, in the study of God's Word be eager to obey all that He commands and rejoice in the knowledge that you are an ambassador for Christ, beseeching men in His stead to be reconciled to God.

1. How do you feel about Bible study? _____

_____

2. What do you see at this point as your main purpose in studying God's Word?_____

_____

3. Have you established a definite goal regarding Bible study? _____

_____

B. Tools needed

First, obtain two translations of the Bible. Study both translations. You would not expect to learn much about the physical laws of our universe without diligent and persistent study. Should you expect to acquire much knowledge of God and the unsearchable riches of His Word without studying with equal diligence and persistence?

Other books you will need, and should plan to add to your study library as soon as possible, are a topical Bible, a concordance and a Bible dictionary. Additional Bible study books are helpful and can be added as convenient. However, always remember, Bible study involves just that — studying the *Bible*. The other things are merely tools to assist you in getting the rich truths God has for you in His Word.

As you consider each study of the Scriptures, may I suggest you record God's Word to you in a journal. This will not only help give a deeper, more serious study, it also will give you a written record of how God speaks to you and of your response to Him.

1. List the tools you now have. _____

   _____

2. List the additional tools you desire in the order in which
   you plan to obtain them. _____

   _____

   _____

C. *Suggested methods*

1. Book Study: The Bible contains many books. Yet the
   divine plan of God to redeem men in Christ Jesus runs
   through the whole of it. Be careful to consider each
   book as a part of the whole. Read it through.

   Mark and *underline* as God speaks to you through His
   Word.

   Outline it.

   List the principal characters, who they are and their
   significance.

   Select from each chapter key verses to memorize and
   copy each on a card to carry with you.

   List *teachings to obey and promises to claim.*

   Consider the characteristics revealed of God the
   Father, God the Son and God the Holy Spirit.

   What book would you particularly like to study using this
   method? (It is best to start with one of the shorter ones.)

   _____

2. Chapter Study: To get a grasp of the chapter, answer the
   following questions:

   What is the principal subject of the chapter?

   What is the leading lesson?

   What is the key verse? Memorize it.

   Who are the principal characters?

   What does it teach about God the Father? Jesus
   Christ? the Holy Spirit?

   Is there any example for me to follow?

   Is there any error for me to avoid?

   Is there any duty for me to perform?

   Is there any promise for me to claim?

   Is there any prayer for me to echo?

To what chapter of which book would you choose to apply these questions? _____

3. Topical Study: Take an important subject, such as grace, truth, prayer, faith, assurance, justification, regeneration, peace, etc., and, using a *topical Bible and concordance,* study the scope of the topic throughout the Bible. You will find it necessary to divide each topic into sub-topics as you accumulate material; e.g., forms of prayer, prayer promises, examples of prayer in Scripture, Christ's teaching on prayer, Christ's ministry as we pray, ministry of the Holy Spirit in prayer, etc.

What topic do you plan to study first? _____

How much time have you scheduled for it? _____

4. Biographical Study: There are 2,930 people mentioned in the Bible. The lives of many of these make extremely interesting biographical studies (1 Corinthians 10:11; Romans 15:4). Using a concordance, topical Bible, or the proper name index in your Bible, look up every reference to the person in question. Answer the following questions:

What was the social and political atmosphere in which he lived?

How did that affect his life?

What do we know of his family?

What kind of training did he have in his youth?

What was accomplished by him during his life?

Was there a great crisis in his life? If so, how did he face it?

What were his outstanding character traits?

Who were his friends? What kind of people were they?

What influence did they have on him? What influence did he have on them?

Does his life show any development of character?

What was his experience with God? Notice his prayer life, his faith, his service to God, his knowledge of God's Word, his courage in witnessing, and his attitude toward the worship of God.

Were any particular faults evident in his life?

Was there any outstanding sin in his life? Under what circumstances did he commit this sin? What was its nature and its effect on his future life?

What were his children like?

Was he a type or antitype of Christ?

Was there some lesson in this person's life which is outstanding to you?

Name the person you would like to study. _____

Your reason for choosing that particular person. _____

_____

Life Application

By the time you complete the studies outlined in this Handbook for Christian Maturity, you will have been introduced to each of these four methods. You already have taken the first step in the *book* study method by reading the book of Acts. Lessons 2 and 4 of Step 2, The Abundant Life, were chapter studies. You will soon be ready to apply these as well as the other two methods to more advanced work in your own individual Bible study.

1. Which method interests you most now?_____

_____

2. What do you expect serious study of the Bible to do for you?

_____

3. Complete your memorization of the Pauline epistles and the last book of prophecy. Write them all here:

Pauline epistles & Hebrews _____

_____

_____

General epistles & prophecy _____

_____

_____

LESSON EIGHT

RECAP

Write the divisions of the books of the Bible and the names of each book in each division. Go back over any division you do not know well.

_____

_____

_____

_____

_____

_____

_____

_____

_____

_____

_____

_____

_____

_____

_____

_____

_____

_____

How would you explain the statement, "Christ is the central person of the Bible"? _____

_____

_____

What do you think is the real source of the authority of the Scriptures? Explain. _____

_____

_____

Name at least three things the Word of God accomplishes that indicate its supernatural power. _____

_____

_____

Why do *you* need the Word of God? _____

_____

_____

What steps do you still need to take to be fully prepared for serious study of the Bible? _____

_____

_____

Review the names of the books of the Bible and write them one final time here. Be sure the spelling is right.

STEP SIX
The Christian and Obedience

THE OBEDIENT CHRISTIAN

Jesus refers to Himself in John 15 as the vine and to the Christian as a branch. "Abide in Me, and I in you. As the branch cannot bear fruit of itself, unless it abides in the vine, so neither can you, unless you abide in Me" (John 15:4). *To abide is to obey.* The obedient Christian abides in Christ and bears much fruit for His glory.

"The one who says he abides in Him ought himself to walk in the same manner as He walked" (1 John 2:6).

"He who has My commandments, and keeps them, he it is who loves Me . . ." (John 14:21).

"The world has yet to see what God can do *in* and *through* and *for* one individual who is completely yielded to the Lord Jesus Christ." This was the challenge that inspired Dwight L. Moody to say, "I want to be that man." God used him, as He used no other man of his time, to reach multitudes.

LESSON ONE

OBEDIENCE AND THE RESULTS OF DOING GOD'S WILL

Introduction

OBJECTIVE: To desire following God's will above all else.

TO MEMORIZE: John 14:21.

TO READ: Romans 1 and 2.

```
┌──────────────┐              ┌──────────┐
│  OBEDIENCE   │              │  BELIEF  │
└──────────────┘    LOVE      └──────────┘
                    FOR
                    CHRIST
```

The true test of our love for Christ is *obedience*. Jesus said, "He who has My commandments, and keeps them, he it is who loves Me; and he who loves Me shall be loved by My Father, and I will love him, and will disclose Myself to him" (John 14:21).

Just as there are physical laws that govern our physical lives, so are there spiritual laws that govern our spiritual lives. It is only as we are obedient to these laws that we are free. Jesus said that He had come to give us a more abundant life (John 10:10). Satan tempts us to violate the laws of the Spirit, which are confirmed by the Word of God and our hearts. Satan is the enemy of men's souls. Yet, though he wields great power, he cannot defeat us if we are completely yielded and obedient to Christ.

A successful athlete must be obedient to certain regulations. The same applies to doctors, lawyers, teachers, farmers, etc., if they are to be successful in their chosen endeavors. How then can a Christian expect to be an effective and fruitful witness unless he is obedient to the Lord Jesus Christ and to His Word (1 John 2:6, 15-17)?

Some are reluctant to trust God completely with their lives, fearing that He may wish to make a change in their plans. What if He does? Is it not logical that the one who created us knows better than we that purpose for which we were created; and since He loves us enough to die for us, is it not logical to believe that His way is best (Romans 8:32)? Obedience is the true test of our love for Christ.

Bible Study

A. *Disobedience of King Saul*

Read 1 Samuel 15.

1. What was God's command to Saul through Samuel?

_____

_____

2. How did Saul comply? _____

_____

_____

3. Summarize the results: _____

_____

_____

4. The main principle illustrated is stated in verse 22. What is it? _____

_____

B. *Obedience of Paul*

Read Acts 9:1-22.

1. What was God's command to Paul? _____

_____

_____

2. How did he comply? _____

_____

_____

3. Summarize the results listed in this passage: _____

_____

_____

4. How do you think Paul's obedience illustrates the truth of the principle listed in A. 4 above? _____

_____

_____

C. *Obedience of Ananias — and its effect*

1. What was God's command to Ananias? _____

   _____

   _____

2. What human reaction did Ananias exhibit? _____

   _____

   _____

3. How did he finally respond? _____

   _____

4. How did his simple obedience indirectly influence us?

   _____

   _____

Life Application

1. How would you have felt in Ananias' place? _____

   _____

2. What is the most important thing this lesson teaches you about obedience? _____

   _____

3. What specific area of weakness in your life do you need to bring into obedience to Christ? _____

   _____

   _____

LESSON TWO

OBEDIENCE AND PERSONAL PURITY

Introduction

OBJECTIVE: To desire a holy life.

TO MEMORIZE: 1 Corinthians 6:18.

TO READ: Romans 3 and 4.

Few areas of life are more important than our relationship to the opposite sex, and few areas are so exposed to temptation. The purpose of this lesson is:

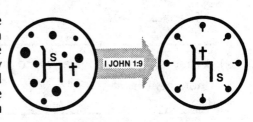

1. To show that immorality originates in the mind, and that God must give us victory there by His Holy Spirit.
2. To show that the Bible gives a healthy outlook on sex. The Bible teaches that the sexual relationship can be a source of enjoyment and blessing when confined to the proper area — marriage. The Bible never pictures sex as sinful, distasteful or dirty. Just as fire may be a great boon to man, but can bring havoc when used improperly, so is sex a great blessing, but it can ruin a life when abusively indulged.
3. To show that our gracious God forgives and cleanses in this area as He does in all others, so that we need carry no unnecessary load of guilt.
4. To show that in all our conduct toward the opposite sex we must set the highest example, and give no occasion for others to doubt our testimony.

Bible Study

A. *Purity and the mind*

1. What does Christ say of impure thought (Matthew 5:27, 28)? _____

_____

2. List the things on which we are to think (Philippians 4:8).

_____

_____

_____

Why does the human mind not want to think on these things (Romans 8:7)? _____

_____

3. How, then, do we obtain victory over impure thoughts (Galatians 5:16)? _____

_____

4. What else should we do to avoid thinking impure thoughts (Romans 13:14)? _____

_____

Note: *Temptation* is not the same as *sin* in the thought life. Evil thoughts may pass through the mind, but sin comes from dwelling on the thought. As an illustration: "You can't stop birds from flying over your head, but you can stop them from building a nest in your hair."

B. *Purity and the opposite sex*

1. What does the Bible say about the sexual relationship in its proper place (Hebrews 13:4)? _____

_____

2. When tempted by immorality, what is a Christian to do (1 Corinthians 6:18)? _____

_____

Why? _____

_____

3. List some things you can know when tempted (1 Corinthians 10:13). _____

_____

_____

4. Write in your own words the warnings against immorality found in the following Scriptures:

Proverbs 6:26 _____

_____

_____

Proverbs 6:32 _____

_____

_____

1 Thessalonians 4:3 _____

_____

_____

C. *Purity and forgiveness*

1. Write in your own words what the following verses say about God's forgiveness:

   Psalm 103:12 _____

   _____

   _____

   Isaiah 43:25 _____

   _____

   _____

   1 John 2:1, 2 _____

   _____

   _____

   Look up "propitiation" and write its meaning: _____

   _____

   _____

   _____

2. What must we do to obtain God's forgiveness (1 John 1:9)?

   _____

   _____

   _____

   _____

Life Application

1. What area of impurity in your life do you need to face and deal with? _____

   _____

   _____

2. Choose an appropriate verse or passage from this lesson, apply it to your situation and write the result you expect to attain. _____

   _____

   _____

   _____

   _____

   _____

LESSON THREE

OBEDIENCE AND THE PRIVILEGE OF SECURITY

Introduction

OBJECTIVE: To find inner security in obedience to Christ.

TO MEMORIZE: Matthew 6:33.

TO READ: Romans 5 and 6.

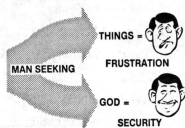

THINGS = FRUSTRATION

MAN SEEKING

GOD = SECURITY

Many people search for security and the abundant life through acquiring money and possessions, or through marriage or a career. However, security is found only in a right relationship with almighty God. Why set affections on the gift rather than on the giver? He alone owns the world. The cattle on a thousand hills are His (Psalm 50:10). He alone can supply our every need (Philippians 4:19). There is no security in the plan which denies God as Lord of our lives and of all that we possess.

Bible Study

A. *The rich fool*

Read Luke 12:13-34.

1. How did the man in verse 13 feel about spiritual areas of his life? _____

2. Why did Jesus deny his request? _____

_____

In light of this, why do you think He denies some of our requests? _____

_____

3. Why was the man in the parable a fool? _____

_____

4. How do people today make the same mistake this man made? _____

_____

5. Name some illustrations Jesus used in verses 24 - 28 to show the uselessness of worrying about material things.

_____

_____

B. *A follower of Christ*

1. Read Philippians 4:11-19.

   How did Paul react to the lack of money? _____

   _____

   Where did Paul obtain the strength to face adverse circumstances? _____

   _____

   Study verse 19. Why do you think God promises to supply our *needs*, but not necessarily our *desires*? _____

   _____

   _____

2. Read 1 Timothy 6:17-19.

   Against what things did Paul warn the rich? _____

   _____

   _____

   What did he exhort them to do? _____

   _____

   _____

   Why? _____

   _____

C. *Christ Himself*

1. In your own words, write what Jesus Christ did for us according to 2 Corinthians 8:9. _____

   _____

   _____

2. Read 2 Corinthians 9:7, 8.

   Because of what Jesus Christ has done for us, we should be willing to invest part of our income in His work. When we give toward His work, what should be our attitude (2 Corinthians 9:7)? _____

   _____

   _____

   Note the use of the words "all" and "every" in verse 8. Why can you be cheerful even though you may give sacrificially toward God's work? _____

   _____

   _____

   _____

Life Application

1. Think about the circumstances of your life. What part do they play in your search for security? _____

   _____

2. List on this chart your most important possessions and whether or not you have yielded each one to God.

POSSESSION	MINE OR GOD'S

LESSON FOUR

OBEDIENCE AND THE FEAR OF WHAT MEN WILL THINK

Introduction

OBJECTIVE: To obey God regardless of popular opinion or peer pressure.

TO MEMORIZE: Luke 9:26.

TO READ: Romans 7 and 8.

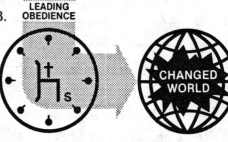

A sincere Christian will always take his stand for Christ among his friends. If we yield to fear of man, Satan may ruin our testimony substantially. If we are obedient to the leading of the Spirit of God, men and women will be won to Christ. Which shall it be?

Bible Study

A. *Peter's renunciation*

Read Matthew 26:57-75 carefully.

1. Peter knew and loved Christ in his heart, but when it came time to openly identify himself as a follower of Christ, what did he do (verse 58)? _____

_____

2. Note the contrasts between Christ and Peter:

Who accused Christ (verse 59)? _____

_____

Who accused Peter (verses 69, 71)? _____

_____

How did Christ answer His accusers (verse 64)? _____

_____

How did Peter answer his accusers (verses 71-74)? _____

What happened to Christ because He told the truth (verses 67, 68)? _____

What was the result when Peter told those lies (verse 75)?

---

3. Some have said Christ's teachings are only for weaklings, cowards, neurotics and those who demand some kind of crutch. As you look at the examples here, of Christ and Peter, how would you evaluate such a statement? _____

B. *Peter's restoration*

1. After Christ's resurrection, what did the angel announce to the women in Mark 16:7? _____

Why did the angel single out Peter's name from the rest?

---

2. Upon what basis can Christ restore you even though you have sinned against Him and denied Him? _____

C. *Peter's transformation*

1. Less than two months later at Pentecost, Peter stood up from among the disciples to give a bold defense of the Christian faith to a ridiculing crowd (Acts 2:14). What do you think made the difference? _____

---

2. What shocking thing did Peter fearlessly tell the crowd (Acts 2:36)? _____

_____

_____

3. And what resulted (Acts 2:37-42)? _____

_____

4. What do Acts 1:8 and 4:8 tell us made this dramatic difference in Peter's life? _____

_____

Life Application

1. How do you think having natural courage and boldness compares to being filled with the Holy Spirit? _____

_____

_____

_____

_____

2. Write out Proverbs 29:25 in your own words. _____

_____

_____

3. If we know and love Christ in our hearts, why must we also take a bold and open stand for Him? _____

_____

_____

4. How does Matthew 10:32 relate to your present attitudes?

_____

_____

5. To whom do you particularly need to confess Christ and take a bold stand for Him? _____

_____

LESSON FIVE

OBEDIENCE AND THE TONGUE

Introduction

OBJECTIVE: To obey God in what we say.

TO MEMORIZE: James 3:2.

TO READ: Romans 9 and 10.

Bible Study

A. *Effects of the tongue*

  1. Read James 3:1-13.

Though we may study our Bibles faithfully, attend Christian meetings regularly and even talk to our friends about Christ, one thing marks us as a really perfect (i.e., mature) Christian.

What is it? _____

_____

What does control of the tongue here indicate? _____

_____

What does the comparison of a wicked tongue to an incorrectly handled steering mechanism on a ship imply

to you? _____

_____

What does it take to start a forest fire? _____

_____

What damage can be caused by just a few words of

gossip you pass on? _____

_____

B. *Sins of the tongue*

  1. Name the sins of the tongue which are condemned in the

following references in Proverbs:

6:16-19 _____

_____

_____

11:13 _____

_____

_____

15:1 _____

_____

_____

17:9 _____

27:2 _____

2. Read Ephesians 4:29. How does this apply to profanity, obscene language, off-color jokes, etc.? _____

_____

What other things can you name that could be included here? _____

_____

C. *Significance of the tongue*

1. Read Matthew 12:33-37.

For what shall men give account? _____

_____

What illustration does Christ use? _____

_____

How does he apply it? _____

_____

What, then, is the real source of an evil tongue? _____

_____

2. What is the only solution for a believer (Galatians 5:16)?

_____

Life Application

1. How would you obey the instructions indicated in James 1:19 and 26 in your own life? _____

_____

2. Think through the attitudes expressed through your words, and ask yourself,

   Is there an attitude I need to confess and make right with God? _____

   _____

   What is it? _____

   _____

   Who has been affected by my words to whom I need to go and ask forgiveness? _____

   _____

   _____

   _____

   _____

LESSON SIX

INSINCERE OBEDIENCE

Introduction

OBJECTIVE: To recognize obedience that is external only, and become obedient from the heart.

TO MEMORIZE: Colossians 3:23.

TO READ: Romans 11-13.

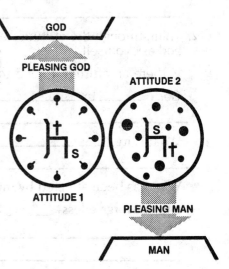

The epitaph of Amaziah reads, "And he did that which was right in the sight of the Lord, but not with a perfect heart" (2 Chronicles 25:2). Obedience involves attitude, not merely outward actions.

Bible Study

A. *An example of insincere obedience*

Read Acts 4:32 - 5:11.

1. For a short time Jerusalem Christians held goods as common property. Each Christian put his funds into a common treasury, which then supplied the needs of the Christian community. What made them willing to give up personal possessions as they did (verse 32)? _____

   _____

2. One writer has said that many today view the local church as if it were a restaurant where all kinds of people meet for a short time, sit down together in the same room, then part, not knowing or caring anything about each other. Would you say this is true? What is your estimation of the fellowship in our churches today compared with the fellowship of these Jerusalem Christians?

   _____

   _____

3. When Barnabas sold his land, which was probably valuable, and gave the money to the church, no doubt other Christians praised his devotion. How do you think Barnabas' action influenced Ananias and Sapphira?

_____

_____

_____

4. What do you suppose motivated Ananias and Sapphira to sell their possessions and give the money to the church? _____

_____

_____

5. How did their motive differ from Barnabas' motive?

_____

_____

B. *Importance of our Christian testimony*

1. How can it be possible to study the Bible, share Christ with others, attend Christian meetings, etc., for the wrong motives, and thus be committing sin when you think you are pleasing God? _____

_____

_____

2. What did Christ say was the matter with the people of His day (Mark 7:6)? _____

_____

3. Why is your heart attitude just as important to God as your outward action? _____

_____

_____

_____

_____

Life Application

1. Read 1 Corinthians 13:1-3. The word "charity" in the King James Version means "love." In terms meaningful to you, paraphrase these three verses:

_____

_____

_____

_____

_____

_____

_____

_____

2. On the basis of this passage, what would you say is the relationship between love and sincere obedience? _____

_____

_____

3. What action or activity in your life do you see as needing a change in motivation? _____

_____

4. How do you expect that change to affect other people you come in contact with? _____

_____

_____

_____

_____

_____

LESSON SEVEN

RECAP

Review all memorized verses in this step.

Read Romans 14-16.

Reread 1 Samuel 15 and Acts 4:32 - 5:11.

Complete the following statements:

True obedience to God is not _____

_____

True obedience really is _____

_____

How is your obedience expressed:

In your attitude toward God's will? _____

_____

In the sexual purity of your life? _____

_____

_____

In the degree of satisfaction you find in your possessions?

_____

_____

In your courage in witnessing for Christ? _____

_____

_____

In your speech? _____

_____

_____

In the true motivation for your action? _____

_____

_____

STEP SEVEN
The Christian and Witnessing

LESSON ONE

WHY WITNESS?

Introduction

OBJECTIVE: To understand the reasons to witness for Christ.

TO MEMORIZE: 1 Corinthians 5:14, 15.

TO READ: Galatians 1 and 2.

One friend may say to you, "I think a man's religion is such a personal matter that we should not discuss it." Another may say, "I don't like people who are dogmatic and fanatical, who try to force their views of religion on everybody they meet."

Yet, Christ considered the human soul to be of such transcendent value that He gladly exchanged the shining courts of glory for a life of poverty, suffering, shame and death as an expression of His desire to "seek and save the lost." He was "not willing that any should perish, but that all should come to repentance" (2 Peter 3:9).

Christ has a concern for the individual and for the multitude. His concern was so deep that at times the flood of manly tears could no longer be restrained, and rolled down His compassionate face. Jesus, the manliest of men, wept. Paul, the brave, besought men night and day with tears to be reconciled to God. When a young missionary who had been sent home by illness was asked why he was so eager to get back to his people, he said, "Because I cannot sleep for thinking about them."

The aim of this lesson is to discuss why it is important that we share Christ with others.

243

Bible Study

A. *What a witness is*

1. What is the greatest thing that has ever happened to you?

   _____

   _____

2. What is the greatest kindness that you can show to another? _____

   _____

3. What are you admonished to do in Psalm 107:2? _____

   _____

B. *The motivation for witnessing*

1. What did Jesus command you to do (Mark 16:15; Matthew 28:19, 20)? _____

   _____

2. Read Acts 20:24-27, 31, 32.
   How important would you say Paul's ministry of witnessing was to him? _____

3. In 2 Corinthians 5:14, 15:
   What caused Paul to witness? _____

   _____

   What effect should Christ have on people? _____

   _____

4. What does Jesus Christ say about the one who is ashamed of Him (Luke 9:26)? _____

5. If you are faithful to follow Jesus, what does He promise to do (Matthew 4:19)? _____

C. *The message*

1. What are we called, according to 2 Corinthians 5:20?*

   _____

   *An ambassador is one who is appointed to interpret the mind of his ruler to those in a foreign land.

2. As a representative of Christ, what would be your message to those who do not know Him personally (2 Corinthians 5:18-20)? _____

_____

3. Why did Jesus say He came into this world (Luke 19:10; Mark 10:45)? _____

_____

4. How does Paul express the message in 1 Corinthians 15:3, 4? _____

_____

Life Application

1. How would you define the word "witness" as it relates to Christ? _____

_____

_____

2. State one reason you feel it is important that *you*, personally, be a witness for Christ. _____

_____

_____

LESSON TWO

JESUS DEMONSTRATES HOW TO WITNESS

Introduction

OBJECTIVE: To follow Christ's example in witnessing.

TO MEMORIZE: John 4:35.

TO READ: Galatians 3 and 4.

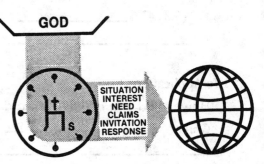

In the Gospel of John, chapter four, Jesus demonstrated how to witness in the most effective manner as He talked to the woman of Samaria. Study this passage carefully to discover new approaches and techniques of witnessing.

Bible Study

A. *Example of Jesus*

Read John 4:1-42.

1. What everyday experience did Jesus use as a situation for witnessing? _____

   _____

2. What, in your opinion, is the advantage of beginning a conversation on the level of a person's immediate interest? _____

   _____

3. List some of your natural opportunities to witness for Christ: _____

   _____

   _____

4. Why do you suppose Jesus sent all 12 of His disciples to buy provisions when two of them could have done it?

_____

_____

5. Who spoke first — Jesus or the woman of Samaria? _____

_____

Why is this significant when considering witnessing techniques? _____

_____

6. What did Jesus do repeatedly when the woman tried to divert his attention from her sin and her need? _____

_____

_____

B. *Responses of the Samaritan woman*

1. How did the woman first respond to Jesus' approach?

_____

How does verse 15 indicate that her attitude changed?

_____

What do you think brought it about? _____

_____

2. What did Jesus say that demonstrated His divine powers?

_____

3. How did Jesus describe God (verse 24)? _____

_____

What do you think is important about this statement?

_____

4. For whom was the woman looking and why? _____

_____

5. What did Jesus claim for Himself? _____

_____

C. Effectiveness of Jesus' witness

1. State briefly your analysis of the approach Jesus used in witnessing to this woman of Samaria. _____

_____

_____

2. What was the result of His witness? _____

_____

3. How did the people to whom she witnessed respond?

_____

There are three "sound barriers" to witnessing. These are much like the sound barrier through which an airplane passes. There is much stress and nervousness.

The first "sound barrier" is just starting to mention to a person the name of Jesus Christ and the value of knowing Him. Once we get the conversation around from girls, guys, the fraternity or sorority, politics, etc., to spiritual things, we have broken the first barrier. It is hard to do, and it never becomes easy. Never!

The second "sound barrier" is to ask the person if he would like to receive Christ. That nervous feeling returns once again. We must blast through this one also. Remember, many people, when they understand who Jesus Christ is and what He has done for them, will want Him in their lives.

The last barrier is the most difficult. It is to ask him to receive Christ right now. This is the most important step. Often we tell the person how and then just leave him high and dry. We have not really witnessed until we ask the person to trust Christ.

Life Application

1. State at least one thing you have learned from Christ's example that you can apply in your own witnessing. _____

_____

_____

2. What do you think most hinders your witnessing? _____

_____

_____

How can you overcome it? _____

_____

_____

_____

_____

_____

LESSON THREE

QUALIFICATIONS FOR WITNESSING

Introduction

OBJECTIVE: To take "spiritual inventory" in preparation for witnessing.

TO MEMORIZE: Matthew 4:19.

TO READ: Galatians 5 and 6.

Every sincere Christian desires to be an effective witness for Christ. A careful study of the eighth chapter of Acts will call attention to certain qualifications for witnessing. Ask the Holy Spirit to make these qualities real in your own life.

Bible Study

A. *Philip's opportunity*

Read Acts 8:25-40.

1. According to verses 25 and 26, why do you think God called Philip for this particular assignment? _____

   _____

2. To whom did Philip witness (verse 27)? _____

   _____

3. Who told Philip to join the chariot (verse 29)? _____
   Does the Holy Spirit lead us in this same way today?

   _____

4. Describe Philip's response (verse 30): _____

   _____

5. How would you describe Philip's approach in verse 30?

   _____

   _____

6. Was the man ready? _____ Why? _____

_____

_____

What was his response? _____

_____

7. What Old Testament reference was the Ethiopian reading (verses 28, 32, 33)? _____

To whom did this reference refer? _____

8. What was Philip's message? _____

_____

B. *Philip's qualifications*

There are at least eight definite qualities stated or referred to in Philip's life that contributed to his effectiveness for Christ. Place appropriate reference verses after the following words:

Knowledge of Word of God _____

Boldness _____

Compassion _____

Humility _____

Obedience _____

Receptivity, sensitivity to guidance _____

Tact _____

Enthusiasm _____

C. *Possible hindrances to our witnessing*

1. Lack of preparation. Personal dedication to Christ and understanding of how to witness and what to say are imperative.

2. Fear of man. We possibly will be persecuted by unbelievers, as well as believers, but "the fear of man bringeth a snare" (Proverbs 29:25). Christ said of those who feared to confess His name, "For they loved the praise of men more than the praise of God."

3. Fear of failure. "They won't believe; they won't accept such simple truth." Certainly some will reject or neglect

the gospel, but you should never believe the lie of Satan that people aren't interested. Christ said, "Lift up your eyes, and look on the fields, for they are (present tense . . . 'now') white already to harvest." Matthew 9:37 says, "Then saith He unto His disciples, the harvest truly is plenteous, but the labourers are few; Pray . . . that He will send forth labourers into His harvest."

4. Fear that the new Christian will not go on and grow in the Lord. Review the parable of the sower (Matthew 13:1-23). Every seed of the Word of God will fall on one of these types of soil: wayside, thorny, rocky and good. Some will be disciples. Keep up the faithful search for these disciples!

Life Application

1. What hindrance is the greatest problem to you? _____

_____

2. What steps will you take to overcome it? _____

_____

3. Look back through the list of qualities in Philip's life and list the ones you would like to have God develop in your life.

_____

_____

_____

_____

4. Spend some time in prayer, asking God for those characteristics to be shown through your life and witness. _____

_____

_____

_____

_____

_____

_____

_____

LESSON FOUR

WITNESSING AND THE WORD OF GOD

Introduction

OBJECTIVE: To learn to appropriate and use the power of the Bible in witnessing.

TO MEMORIZE: 1 Peter 3:15.

TO READ: Ephesians 1 and 2.

When the miracle of Pentecost occurred, the news spread quickly throughout Jerusalem, and a large crowd gathered, seeking the meaning of this phenomenon. Peter, under the control and in the power of the Holy Spirit, addressed the inquisitive crowd. Some of these had during Christ's trial 10 days earlier cried, "Crucify Him," and "His blood be on us, and on our children" (Matthew 27:25).

Possibly some in the front row were those before whom Peter had used profanity when he denied Christ (Matthew 26:73, 74). Under these circumstances of fear and trembling, Peter's resources had to be the Holy Spirit and God's Word. The purpose of this lesson is to demonstrate the use of the Word of God in witnessing, and its results.

Bible Study

A. *Peter's witness*

Read Acts 2.

1. Of all the disciples, why was Peter the least qualified to witness for Christ, and yet the most qualified, as suggested above and in Acts 2? _____

_____

_____

2. How much of Peter's sermon involves quotations from

the Bible (i.e., Joel, David, etc.)? _____

_____

How much Scripture memorization do you suppose Peter had done in his early life? _____

_____

3. What part does the Holy Spirit play:
   In those who share Christ's message (John 14:26)?

   _____

   In those who hear Christ's message (John 16:8-11)?

   _____

4. What did Peter say to convict them of sin (Acts 2:23, 26)?

   _____

   _____

5. Name some great things Peter preached about God (verses 24, 34, 35, 38, 39): _____

   _____

   _____

B. *The crowd's response*
   1. How many became Christians that day? _____
   2. List the emotions experienced by the hearers before and after conversion: _____

   _____

   3. What do you think caused anger toward a witnessing Christian?_____

C. *The power of the Word*
   1. Summarize Isaiah 55:11. _____

   _____

   2. How does the Word of God affect the non-Christian as you witness, according to Hebrews 4:12? _____

   _____

3. In Ephesians 6:17, what is the Bible called? _____

_____

_____

_____

As you shall see in more detail in Lesson 6, it is the Holy Spirit who brings men to grips with the issues as we witness.

D. *The value of Scripture memorization*

Committing portions of Scripture to memory is the best way to know the Word of God, and as a result, to know Christ. Also by having the promises and commands of the Word memorized, we can apply them to any life situation at a moment's notice, especially when we desire to use them in an unexpected witnessing opportunity.

1. List some things you can know from 2 Peter 1:2-4: _____

_____

_____

_____

2. List some ways having Scripture memorized will help you according to:

1 Peter 2:2, 3 and Hebrews 5:12-14 _____

_____

_____

Joshua 1:8 and Psalm 1:1-3 _____

_____

_____

Psalm 32:8 _____

_____

_____

3. List some ways in which the Scriptures will nourish your growth.

Romans 10:17 _____

Psalm 119:11 _____

Psalm 119:165 _____

4. And one thing God's Word was absolutely essential for:

1 Peter 1:23 _____

Life Application

1. List specific ways the above Scriptures will help you in your witnessing. _____

_____

2. Which one do you feel you need the most? _____

_____

3. How will you apply it? _____

_____

_____

4. Have you memorized it? _____

LESSON FIVE

WITNESSING AND PRAYER

Introduction

OBJECTIVE: To make prayer a vital part of witnessing.

TO MEMORIZE: Acts 4:31.

TO READ: Ephesians 3 and 4.

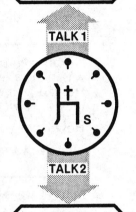

"And now, Lord, take note of their threats, and grant that Thy bond-servants may speak Thy word with all confidence ... And when they had prayed, the place where they had gathered was shaken, and they were all filled with the Holy Spirit, and began to speak the Word of God with boldness" (Acts 4:29, 31).

Many times our efforts to lead people to Christ are fruitless. The reason for this may lie in the fact that we go about it the wrong way. The divine order is *first* to talk to God about men, and *then* to talk to men about God. If we follow this formula we will see results. Prayer is really the place where people are won to Christ; service is just gathering in the fruit. The aim of this lesson is to demonstrate that prayer played a major part in the witness of the early church.

Bible Study

A. *What the early Christians prayed for*

Read Acts 4.

1. State the problem faced by these Christians. _____

   _____

   _____

2. What do you think would have happened to Christianity had they stopped witnessing? _____

3. Of what importance to the cause of Christ today is the soul-winning witness? _____

4. How did these Christians solve their dilemma:

Before magistrates? _____

In private? _____

In public? _____

5. What protected them (Acts 4:21)?_____

6. For what did they pray? _____

B. *The answer to their prayer*

1. What was the result of their prayer? _____

   _____

The answer to their prayer was immediate and definite. It was in the affirmative. They prayed, and God answered as He had promised. None could stand against them, and they were victorious in Christ.

2. How have you profited from their courage, prayer and

   effective witness? _____

   _____

3. In what ways can other people depend on your courage,

   prayer and witness? _____

   _____

C. *The Christian's opposition*

1. Were the witnessing Christians persecuted by the religious or non-religious people of their day? _____

   _____

2. Whom do you believe to be the author of resistance to Christian witness, and why? _____

   _____

Life Application

1. What specific opposition have you encountered recently, and how did you deal with it? _____

   _____

   _____

2. How could you have handled it better? _____

_____

_____

3. List at least one prospective witnessing situation and spend a few moments praying specifically for God's leading and empowering through your life. _____

_____

_____

LESSON SIX

WITNESSING AND THE HOLY SPIRIT

Introduction

OBJECTIVE: To understand and trust in the Holy Spirit's leading as you witness.

TO MEMORIZE: John 15:26, 27.

TO READ: Ephesians 5 and 6.

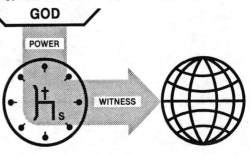

Self-consciousness and fear of what others will say are great foes to our witness. Stephen as a tablewaiter (Acts 6:2-5), not as an apostle, was brought before the most skilled and wicked opponents of Christianity. Though he might have retreated, conscious of his inadequacy, he yielded to the Holy Spirit's control of his life. By so doing, he became the first Christian martyr, mightily moved the unbelievers and laid the basis for Saul's conversion.

The purpose of this lesson is to demonstrate how the power of the Holy Spirit relates to our witness.

Bible Study

A. *Read Acts 6 and 7*

   1. Underline every mention of the Holy Spirit.

   2. What part did the Holy Spirit play in Stephen's life?

      _____

   3. What was the spiritual indictment upon his hearers which cut them to the heart? _____

      _____

   4. As a Spirit-filled man, Stephen had two purposes which were his greatest concerns, as seen in his desire to witness and in his dying prayer. What were they?_____

_____

_____

5. How do these concerns show the fullness of the Holy Spirit in Stephen (Galatians 5:22, 23 and 2 Corinthians 5:14, 15)? _____

_____

_____

B. *Work of the Holy Spirit in witnessing*

1. What is the ministry of the Holy Spirit (John 15:26; 16:13, 14)? _____

_____

2. How is it accomplished in a person who witnesses of Christ (Acts 1:8, 6:10)? _____

_____

3. What will the Holy Spirit do for the witnessing person (Acts 8:29, 4:31)? _____

_____

4. What will the Holy Spirit do for the person being witnessed to, according to 1 Corinthians 2:10-12? _____

_____

5. How would you compare that to 2 Corinthians 4:3, 4?

_____

It is the Holy Spirit who brings a man face to face with the facts regarding his condition and his need. This action is called "convicting, reproving, exposing, bringing to light." If we were to witness on our own, we would accomplish nothing, but when the Holy Spirit uses our witness, He brings a man face to face with important facts — presenting them so forcefully that these facts must be acknowledged and considered.

6. What are these basic facts (John 16:7-11)? _____

_____

_____

_____

_____

_____

7. What final result is the full responsibility of the Holy Spirit to bring about in the hearer (John 3:5, 6)? _____

_____

_____

_____

_____

Life Application

Ask the Holy Spirit of God to prepare individuals to whom you can witness. Ask Him to free the minds of specific individuals so that they can see the issues at stake and be able to make a logical, rational, intelligent choice to receive Christ as Lord and Savior. Record the names of at least three persons you feel God would have you speak to about Christ within the next week.

_____

_____

_____

_____

Ask the Holy Spirit to lead you to these individuals at the proper time, and to speak through you in confronting them with the message of Christ.

As you witness, be conscious of the fact that it is the Holy Spirit who is penetrating the mind of the other person, revealing spiritual truth.

Are you sure *you* are prepared? If not, review the earlier lessons in this step.

LESSON SEVEN

RECAP

Review all verses memorized.

Reread Galatians and Ephesians.

What is the most important reason you have learned for witnessing for Christ? _____

_____

_____

_____

_____

_____

_____

_____

Have you overcome the thing that most hinders your witnessing? _____

What is the next most effective hindrance for you and how do you plan to overcome it? _____

_____

_____

Summarize why you think a knowledge of the Word of God is important in witnessing. _____

_____

_____

_____

How will prayer specifically help you? _____

_____

_____

Why do you think the Holy Spirit does not speak of Himself?

Write a personal three-minute testimony of your personal experience with Christ. Briefly share what your life was like before your decision; how you became a Christian; and explain in greater detail what it is like to be a Christian. (Attach testimony to this lesson.)

A CHALLENGE

Some years ago at the opening of a disarmament conference, in the midst of a speech of King George of England, someone tripped over the wires of the Columbia Broadcasting Company, tearing them loose and interrupting service. The chief operator quickly grasped the loose wires in his bare hands, holding them in contact, and for 20 minutes the current passed through him while repairs were being made. His hands were slightly burned, but through them the words of the king passed on to millions of listeners, and were heard distinctly. Without his courage and endurance, the king's message would have failed to reach its destination.

Jesus Christ, the King of kings, has chosen to send His message of salvation to a lost and dying world through human means. Whatever the cost, the message must reach those who have never heard. Every faithful Christian who is willing is a human instrument through whom the King's voice is reaching the lost with a message of deliverance, freedom and peace (vastly more important than the message from London).

"And those who have insight will shine brightly like the brightness of the expanse of heaven and those who lead the many to righteousness, like the stars forever and ever" (Daniel 12:3).

HOW TO SHARE CHRIST WITH OTHERS

Every Christian desires to share Christ with his friends or with others whom he meets. The Four Spiritual Laws booklet, reproduced on the following pages, presents a clear and simple explanation of the gospel of our Lord Jesus Christ. This booklet, available from Campus Crusade for Christ, has been developed as a result of more than 30 years of experience in counseling with thousands of college students on campuses of the world as well as with a comparable number of laymen and pastors and high school students. It represents one way to share your faith effectively.

Some of the obvious benefits of using a booklet like this to share your faith in Christ are:

1. It can be used to open the conversation. You can simply say, "Have you heard of the Four Spiritual Laws?"
2. It begins with the positive, "God loves you."
3. It presents the claims of Christ clearly.
4. It includes an invitation to receive Christ.
5. If offers suggestions for growth, including the importance of the church.
6. It gives you confidence, because you know what you are going to say and how you are going to say it.
7. It enables you to stay on the subject — to control the conversation.
8. It enables you always to be prepared.
9. It makes it possible for you to be brief. Learn to present the Four Spiritual Laws without unnecessary comments, yet remaining sensitive to the leading of the Holy Spirit.
10. It represents a "transferable technique" for presenting Christ to others. Many Christians are effective in their own personal ministries, but are unable to communicate to others how to present Christ in such a way that they also may become fruitful.

Several ways you can use to introduce the Four Spiritual Laws booklet would be as follows:

"Have you heard of the Four Spiritual Laws?"

"I'm attending a seminar and we are studying a little booklet that really makes sense to a lot of people. I'd like to share it with you. Have you heard of the Four Spiritual Laws?"

"Would you help me by giving me your opinion of the Four Spiritual Laws?"

"Has anyone ever taken the time to share with you this little booklet called the Four Spiritual Laws?"

"Do you ever think about spiritual things?" (Pause for an answer.) "Have you ever heard of the Four Spiritual Laws?"

When you believe someone may be a Christian but are not really sure, you could say, "I have been a Christian for years, but I have just recently found a way to express my faith that really makes sense. I would like to share it with you. Have you heard of the Four Spiritual Laws?"

God will show you other ways to introduce the material. The important thing is to keep your introduction brief and to the point.

HOW TO PRESENT THE FOUR SPIRITUAL LAWS

1. Be sensitive to an individual's interest and the leading of the Holy Spirit. The simplest way to explain the Four Spiritual Laws is to read the booklet aloud. However, be careful not to allow the presentation to become mechanical. Remember, you are not just sharing principles — you are introducing the person to Christ. The Four Spiritual Laws are simply a tool to help you effectively communicate the gospel. Pray for God's love to be expressed through you.

2. Use the term "Four Spiritual Principles" instead of Four Spiritual Laws if there is any objection to the term "laws."

3. When questions come up that would change the subject, explain that most questions are answered as you go through the Four Spiritual Laws. Or say, "That's a good question. Let's talk about it after we have completed the Four Spiritual Laws."

4. Be sensitive to the individual. If there seems to be no response, stop and ask, "Is this making sense?"

5. Hold the booklet so that it can be seen clearly. Use a pen to focus on key points. This will help to hold attention.

6. In a group, give each person a Four Spiritual Laws booklet. Pray with those who are interested in receiving Christ. If only one is interested, be sensitive and in most cases talk with him privately.

   Make sure each one understands that Christ comes into his life by faith. If he "prays the prayer" without believing Christ will answer, nothing will result.

   Also be sensitive as to whether he wants to pray his own prayer or to use the prayer from the booklet. Some will request silent prayer.

7. If someone has already heard the Four Spiritual Laws, ask him what he thought of them, and if he has any questions. If he is interested and the gospel is not clear, go over the Four Spiritual Laws again.

8. When a person does not receive Christ during your first time together assure Him of your availability for further counsel.

   Make another appointment if he is interested. Give him a Van Dusen letter. (The Van Dusen letter may be ordered from Campus Crusade for Christ.)

   Pray for him. Occasionally ask him if he has thought further about your discussion or if he has any questions.

9. Leave a Van Dusen letter with the one to whom you have witnessed, whether or not he received Christ. Thousands have received Christ through the reading of the Van Dusen letter.

Have You Heard of the
Four Spiritual Laws?

1

Just as there are physical laws that govern the physical universe, so are there spiritual laws which govern your relationship with God.

LAW ONE

GOD **LOVES** YOU, AND OFFERS A WONDERFUL **PLAN** FOR YOUR LIFE.

(References contained in this booklet should be read in context from the Bible wherever possible.)

God's Love

"For God so loved the world, that He gave His only begotten Son, that whoever believes in Him should not perish, but have eternal life" (John 3:16).

God's Plan

(Christ speaking) "I came that they might have life, and might have it abundantly" (that it might be full and meaningful) (John 10:10).

Why is it that most people are not experiencing the abundant life? Because . . .

LAW TWO

2

MAN IS **SINFUL** AND **SEPARATED** FROM GOD. THEREFORE, HE CANNOT KNOW AND EXPERIENCE GOD'S LOVE AND PLAN FOR HIS LIFE.

Man Is Sinful

"For all have sinned and fall short of the glory of God" (Romans 3:23).

Man was created to have fellowship with God; but, because of his stubborn self-will, he chose to go his own independent way and fellowship with God was broken. This self-will, characterized by an attitude of active rebellion or passive indifference, is evidence of what the Bible calls sin.

Man Is Separated

"For the wages of sin is death" (spiritual separation from God) (Romans 6:23).

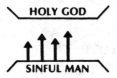

This diagram illustrates that God is holy and man is sinful. A great gulf separates the two. The arrows illustrate that man is continually trying to reach God and the abundant life through his own efforts, such as a good life, philosophy or religion.

The third law explains the only way to bridge this gulf . . .

LAW THREE

3

JESUS CHRIST IS GOD'S **ONLY** PROVISION FOR MAN'S SIN. THROUGH HIM YOU CAN KNOW AND EXPERIENCE GOD'S LOVE AND PLAN FOR YOUR LIFE.

He Died in Our Place

"But God demonstrates His own love toward us, in that while we were yet sinners, Christ died for us" (Romans 5:8).

He Rose from the Dead

"Christ died for our sins . . . He was buried . . . He was raised on the third day, according to the Scriptures . . . He appeared to Peter, then to the twelve. After that He appeared to more than five hundred . . ." (I Corinthians 15:3-6).

He Is the Only Way to God

"Jesus said to him, 'I am the way, and the truth, and the life; no one comes to the Father, but through Me' " (John 14:6).

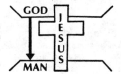

This diagram illustrates that God has bridged the gulf which separates us from Him by sending His Son, Jesus Christ, to die on the cross in our place to pay the penalty for our sins.

It is not enough just to know these three laws . . .

LAW FOUR

WE MUST INDIVIDUALLY **RECEIVE** JESUS CHRIST AS SAVIOR AND LORD; THEN WE CAN KNOW AND EXPERIENCE GOD'S LOVE AND PLAN FOR OUR LIVES.

We Must Receive Christ

"But as many as received Him, to them He gave the right to become children of God, even to those who believe in His name" (John 1:12).

We Receive Christ Through Faith

"For by grace you have been saved through faith; and that not of yourselves, it is the gift of God; not as a result of works, that no one should boast" (Ephesians 2:8,9).

When We Receive Christ, We Experience a New Birth.
(Read John 3:1-8.)

We Receive Christ by Personal Invitation

(Christ is speaking): "Behold, I stand at the door and knock; if any one hears My voice and opens the door, I will come in to him" (Revelation 3:20).

Receiving Christ involves turning to God from self (repentance) and trusting Christ to come into our lives to forgive our sins and to make us the kind of people He wants us to be. Just to agree intellectually that Jesus Christ is the Son of God and that He died on the cross for our sins is not enough. Nor is it enough to have an emotional experience. We receive Jesus Christ by faith, as an act of the will.

These two circles represent two kinds of lives:

SELF-DIRECTED LIFE
S — Self is on the throne
† — Christ is outside the life
● — Interests are directed by self, often resulting in discord and frustration

CHRIST-DIRECTED LIFE
† — Christ is in the life and on the throne
S — Self is yielding to Christ
● — Interests are directed by Christ, resulting in harmony with God's plan

Which circle best represents your life?
Which circle would you like to have represent your life?

The following explains how you can receive Christ:

YOU CAN RECEIVE CHRIST RIGHT NOW BY FAITH THROUGH PRAYER

(Prayer is talking with God)

God knows your heart and is not so concerned with your words as He is with the attitude of your heart. The following is a suggested prayer:

"Lord Jesus, I need You. Thank You for dying on the cross for my sins. I open the door of my life and receive You as my Savior and Lord. Thank You for forgiving my sins and giving me eternal life. Take control of the throne of my life. Make me the kind of person You want me to be."

Does this prayer express the desire of your heart?

If it does, pray this prayer right now, and Christ will come into your life, as He promised.

How to Know That Christ Is in Your Life

Did you receive Christ into your life? According to His promise in Revelation 3:20, where is Christ right now in relation to you? Christ said that He would come into your life. Would He mislead you? On what authority do you know that God has answered your prayer? (The trustworthiness of God Himself and His Word.)

The Bible Promises Eternal Life to All Who Receive Christ

"And the witness is this, that God has given us eternal life, and this life is in His Son. He who has the Son has the life; he who does not have the Son of God does not have the life. These things I have written to you who believe in the name of the Son of God, in order that you may know that you have eternal life" (I John 5:11-13).

Thank God often that Christ is in your life and that He will never leave you (Hebrews 13:5). You can know on the basis of His promise that Christ lives in you and that you have eternal life, from the very moment you invite Him in. He will not deceive you.

An important reminder . . .

DO NOT DEPEND UPON FEELINGS

The promise of God's Word, the Bible — not our feelings — is our authority. The Christian lives by faith (trust) in the trustworthiness of God Himself and His Word. This train diagram illustrates the relationship between **fact** (God and His Word), **faith** (our trust in God and His Word), and **feeling** (the result of our faith and obedience) (John 14:21).

The train will run with or without the caboose. However, it would be useless to attempt to pull the train by the caboose. In the same way, we, as Christians, do not depend on feelings or emotions, but we place our faith (trust) in the trustworthiness of God and the promises of His Word.

NOW THAT YOU HAVE RECEIVED CHRIST

The moment that you received Christ by faith, as an act of the will, many things happened, including the following:

1. Christ came into your life (Revelation 3:20 and Colossians 1:27).
2. Your sins were forgiven (Colossians 1:14).
3. You became a child of God (John 1:12).
4. You received eternal life (John 5:24).
5. You began the great adventure for which God created you (John 10:10; II Corinthians 5:17 and I Thessalonians 5:18).

Can you think of anything more wonderful that could happen to you than receiving Christ? Would you like to thank God in prayer right now for what He has done for you? By thanking God, you demonstrate your faith.

To enjoy your new life to the fullest . . .

SUGGESTIONS FOR CHRISTIAN GROWTH

Spiritual growth results from trusting Jesus Christ. "The righteous man shall live by faith" (Galatians 3:11). A life of faith will enable you to trust God increasingly with every detail of your life, and to practice the following:

G Go to God in prayer daily (John 15:7).

R Read God's Word daily (Acts 17:11)—begin with the Gospel of John.

O Obey God moment by moment (John 14:21).

W Witness for Christ by your life and words (Matthew 4:19; John 15:8).

T Trust God for every detail of your life (I Peter 5:7).

H Holy Spirit—allow Him to control and empower your daily life and witness (Galatians 5:16,17; Acts 1:8).

FELLOWSHIP IN A GOOD CHURCH

God's Word admonishes us not to forsake "the assembling of ourselves together. . ." (Hebrews 10:25). Several logs burn brightly together; but put one aside on the cold hearth and the fire goes out. So it is with your relationship to other Christians. If you do not belong to a church, do not wait to be invited. Take the initiative; call the pastor of a nearby church where Christ is honored and His Word is preached. Start this week, and make plans to attend regularly.

SPECIAL MATERIALS ARE AVAILABLE FOR CHRISTIAN GROWTH.

If you have come to know Christ personally through this presentation of the gospel, write for a free booklet especially written to assist you in your Christian growth.

A special Bible study series and an abundance of other helpful materials for Christian growth are also available. For additional information, please write Campus Crusade for Christ International, San Bernardino, CA 92414.

You will want to share this important discovery . . .

The Christian and Stewardship

WHAT IS A CHRISTIAN STEWARD?

Of what are we to be stewards? A steward is "a manager or superintendent of another's household." We are stewards of all that God possesses, and His possessions include our money, our talents, our minds, our bodies and the time we live in this world.

God owns everything. He is the creator and sustainer of the universe. "Christ, who is the image of the invisible God, the firstborn of every creature; for by Him were all things created that are in heaven and that are in earth, visible and invisible, whether they be thrones, or dominions, or principalities, or powers: all things were created by Him and for Him; and He is before all things and by Him all things consist" (Colossians 1:15-17).

There is just one thing that God does not, strictly speaking, own — that is, you and me. In creating the human being He allowed us to have the moral choice of whether we would subject ourselves to Him. Initially, all of us made the wrong choice. "All have sinned and come short of the glory of God" (Romans 3:23). By this choice we forfeited our love relationship with God. But, praise be to God, we who have accepted Christ "are not our own, but are bought with a price." The price is God's Son.

A Christian steward is one who realizes that as Christians "we live, and move, and have our being" in Christ. The Christian steward recognizes God as his preeminent master, and lives for Him. The whole of the Christian's life — his personality, time, talent, influence, material substance, everything — is dedicated to Christ. This is true Christian stewardship.

"Each one of us shall give account of himself to God" (Romans 14:12).

"For we must all appear and be revealed as we are before the judgment seat of Christ, so that each one may receive [His pay] according to what he has done in the body, whether good or evil [considering what his purpose and motive have been, and what he has achieved, been busy with and given himself and his attention to accomplishing]" (2 Corinthians 5:10, Amplified New Testament).

So we see that God really does own everything. Therefore we own nothing and are only stewards of what He gives us. God holds the key to every material and spiritual thing, and the only reason that we have had anything, or have it now, or will have it, is that God loves us enough to give it to us.

LESSON ONE

THE OWNERSHIP OF GOD OUR FATHER

Introduction

OBJECTIVE: To surrender every thing we have to God, because we can rest in His ownership of all.

TO MEMORIZE: 1 Chronicles 29:11.

TO READ: Genesis 1-3.

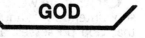

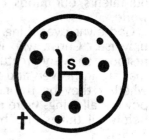

Bible Study

A. *Creation and fall of man*

1. After what pattern did God create man (Genesis 1:26)?

   _____

   Theologians have long debated just what it is in man that constitutes the image of God. That image seems to include the basic characteristics of personality — intellect, emotion and will. Adam and Eve had intellect (Genesis 2:19), emotion and will (Genesis 3:6), just as God does.

2. What did man do to bring about separation between

   himself and God (Genesis 3:1-8)? _____

   _____

   _____

   Note: This passage gives important insight into the character of sin. Adam did not get drunk or commit immoral acts — murder or the like. He and Eve merely asserted their independence from God, rebelled against His command and took control of their own lives. Sin is being independent of God and running your own life.

3. How did the sin of man affect his:

   intellect (2 Corinthians 4:2, 4)? _____

   _____

emotions (Jeremiah 17:9)? _____

_____

will (Romans 5:12; 6:20)? _____

_____

4. How did this act of rebellion affect the world (Romans 5:12)? _____

_____

_____

B. *Reconciliation.*

1. How did God bring us back and reconcile us to Himself (Romans 5:8-10)? _____

_____

2. What has God given us to enable us to live for Him (John 14:16, 17)? _____

_____

3. God now has restored us to a position of fellowship similar to what Adam had. What does that declare about our present relationship with God (1 Corinthians 6:19, 20)? _____

_____

_____

C. *Our responsibility*

1. What, then, is to be our response to God (Romans 12:1, 2)? _____

2. Many people attempt to compromise and give God less than full allegiance. How did Jesus regard that practice in Matthew 12:30? _____

3. How did Jesus describe His attitude toward those who will stand neither for nor against Him in Revelation 3:15, 16)? _____

_____

4. What logical choice did Elijah present to the people (1 Kings 18:21)? _____

_____

If Elijah's logic is true, we must take one of two positions. If we determine Jesus Christ is Lord and God, we must serve Him loyally. If He is not, Christianity is obviously a hoax, and we should dissuade men from being Christians. But it is one or the other! We must stand either with Christ or against Him, but never try to stand in between.

Life Application

1. Is there something in your life which you have not surrendered to the control of your heavenly Father? _____ What is it and how will you now deal with it? _____

_____

_____

2. How much of your life are you willing for God to control? _____

_____

How much of it does He control? _____

3. What do you think God will do with your life if you surrender it all to Him? _____

_____

4. Read Isaiah 48:17-19. What blessings would you lose by going your own way and failing to recognize God's ownership? _____

_____

_____

_____

_____

_____

God does own us — every bit of our time, talents and treasure. Scripture tells us that Christ died for us, that we should "not henceforth live unto ourselves, but unto Him who died for us and rose again" (2 Corinthians 5:15). Not to acknowledge and act upon God's total ownership of everything we are, have or will be is to rob ourselves of His blessing and make ourselves unfit for His service and use (2 Timothy 2:19-21).

LESSON TWO

EXAMPLES OF PERFECT STEWARDSHIP

Introduction

OBJECTIVE: To follow biblical examples of stewardship.

TO MEMORIZE: John 8:28.

TO READ: Luke 23, 24; Colossians 1, 2.

GOD

WHO?

MAN

1. HUMBLED HIMSELF
2. THROUGH = WITH GOD BECAME MAN
3. ENDURED CROSS

Bible Study

A. *Stewardship of God the Son*

1. List acts of Christ that were indicative of perfection in His stewardship (Philippians 2:5-8): ——————

   ————————————————————————

   ————————————————————————

   ————————————————————————

2. What was Christ's supreme purpose in life (John 6:38; Hebrews 10:7)? ————————————————

   ————————————————————————

3. Read John 12:23-33.

   As part of God's will for Jesus, what was involved (verses 32, 33)? ————————————————

   ————————————————————————

   In verse 24 Jesus uses the example of a grain of wheat which is planted in the earth. In what sense does a grain of wheat have to "die" to bring forth fruit? ——————

   ————————————————————————

   How does it apply to us (compare verse 25)? ————

   ————————————————————————

   ————————————————————————

If, as a Christian, you are unwilling to make any sacrifice to reach others for Christ, to suffer any hardship, to face any self-denial, to suffer some persecution; but rather, you want everything to be comfortable, easy and effort-

less, how much fruit will you bear? _____

_____

B. *Stewardship of God the Holy Spirit*

   1. What are some duties the Holy Spirit performs as God's steward, as revealed in the following verses?

    John 16:8-11 _____

    _____

    In what way does this convicting ministry of the Holy

    Spirit help us in evangelism? _____

    _____

    John 16:13 _____

    Note: In a general way, the Holy Spirit guides the believer into the realms of spiritual truth. In a specific way, He guided the apostles and early Christians in writing the New Testament Scriptures. This is undoubtedly what Christ had in mind.

    Romans 5:5 _____

    _____

    Romans 8:14 _____

    _____

    Romans 8:16 _____

    _____

    Romans 8:26 _____

    _____

   2. When the Holy Spirit controls a person or a group, is the evidence of it a glorifying of the Holy Spirit, or a glorifying

    of Jesus Christ (John 16:14)? _____

    _____

Life Application

1. How can you best apply to your life the example that Jesus set? Be specific. _____

_____

_____

2. What does the Holy Spirit want to do in your life at this time?

_____

_____

3. List ways you can cooperate as suggested in Acts 4:31; Ephesians 5:18-20 and Romans 12:1, 2. _____

_____

_____

_____

_____

_____

LESSON THREE

STEWARDSHIP OF OUR TIME

Introduction

OBJECTIVE: To become wise stewards of all that God has created us to be individually.

TO MEMORIZE: Galatians 2:20.

TO READ: Romans 12.

Bible Study

Read Psalm 90:12.

What should be our prayer concerning the use of time that God gives us? _____

_____

_____

A. *Right attitude about time*

1. As good stewards, what will we do (Ephesians 5:16)?

_____

2. Why is the proper use of our time today so important (James 4:14)? _____

3. What does God demand of us in the stewardship of our time (Psalm 62:8)? _____

4. What does Christ admonish us to do as stewards of time until He comes again (Mark 13:33-37)? _____

_____

5. If we are wise stewards and heed the commands of our Master, how will we use our time (Ephesians 5:15, 16)?

_____

B. *Right relationship with God*

   1. As wise stewards concerned over the use of our time, what will we want to understand (Ephesians 5:17)?

      _____

   2. What is necessary in order to know fully what is the will of God concerning the duties of our stewardship (Ephesians 5:18)? _____

   3. The Holy Spirit will enable the faithful steward to perform the duties of stewardship by giving him (Acts 1:8): _____

      _____

   4. He will perform these duties in the name of (Colossians 3:17): _____

   5. What then will be our attitude as we so utilize the time over which God has made us stewards (Ephesians 5:19, 20)? _____

      _____

   6. How would you describe such a useful and joyous life (John 10:10b)? _____

C. *Most important use of time*

   1. As wise stewards who know and are obedient to the will of God, we can be sure that we will spend much of our time aggressively doing what (Mark 16:15)? _____

      _____

   2. What does God say about a soul winner in Proverbs 11:30? _____

   3. Of what value is only one soul according to Christ in Mark 8:36? _____

      _____

      _____

   4. What then is the greatest thing you can do for another?

      _____

5. What happens in God's presence when one repents and receives Christ (Luke 15:7, 10)? _____

_____

6. How did Paul feel about those whom he had won to Christ (1 Thessalonians 2:19, 20)? _____

_____

Life Application

1. How many hours are there in a week? _____

2. Why is it that some may accomplish more than others in the same amount of time? _____

_____

The following chart can be of great value in the stewardship of your time. Fill in the hours spent on: class, sleep, Christian service, business, recreation, etc. Place the total hours per week used in each activity at the bottom of the chart. By listing the totals you can discover if you have achieved the balanced use of time required of a good steward.

	MON.	TUES.	WED.	THURS.	FRI.	SAT.	SUN.
6:00							
7:00							
8:00							
9:00							
10:00							
11:00							
12:00							
1:00							
2:00							
3:00							
4:00							
5:00							
6:00							
7:00							
8:00							
9:00							
10:00							
11:00							
12:00							

Stewardship of Time
1. Study and class _____
2. Devotional life _____
3. Christian service _____
4. Rest _____
5. Recreation and social life _____
6. Activities and athletics _____
7. Commuting _____
8. Employment _____
9. Laundry and clean-up _____
10. Miscellaneous _____

LESSON FOUR

STEWARDSHIP OF OUR BODIES

Introduction

OBJECTIVE: To surrender our
bodies to Christ,
from the heart.

TO MEMORIZE: Psalm 139:23,
24

TO READ: Psalm 51;
Galatians 5;
Ephesians 5.

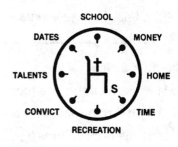

Bible Study

A. *The spirit and the body*

Read Hebrews 10:1-10.

1. Man is to be renewed in the spirit of his mind if he is to be converted to Christ. How was that conversion made possible (Hebrews 10:1-10)? _____

   _____

   _____

2. What do you learn about the body of the Christian from Romans 8:8, 9 and Romans 12:1? _____

   _____

3. Express in your own words the additional reasons given in 1 Corinthians 6:19, 20 for being a good steward of your body. _____

   _____

   _____

B. *Individual parts of the body*

1. The tongue.

   Why is it so important to be a good steward of the tongue (James 3:2-6)? _____

What should you know concerning its use (Matthew 12:36)? _____

_____

2. The heart.

What must we understand about the heart (Jeremiah 17:9)? _____

Therefore, what should a steward of God continually pray (Psalm 139:23, 24)?_____

What should be done about sin (1 John 1:9)? _____

_____

What condition of heart does God require (Psalm 51:17)?

_____

What kind of heart does God look for and why (2 Chronicles 16:9)? _____

3. The mind.

What is your responsibility in being a steward of your mind (1 Peter 1:13)? _____

_____

Whose mind and which qualities thereof should you have (Philippians 2:5-8; 1 Corinthians 2:12-16)? _____

_____

_____

What is the result of keeping your mind stayed on God (Isaiah 26:3)? _____

How can you keep your mind on Him (Philippians 4:6, 7; Proverbs 4:20-22)? _____

_____

C. *Sexual expression*

1. What do the sins spoken against in 1 Corinthians 6:9, 10, 13-18 mainly involve?_____

2. God considered David a man after His own heart, yet David's great sin was what (2 Samuel 11:14, 15, 26, 27)?

3. What is God's stern judgment against misusers and abusers of sex (1 Corinthians 6:9-11)? _____

Why is it especially tragic if a Christian becomes involved in the misuse of sex (1 Corinthians 6:15-18)? _____

How serious is sexual lust, according to Christ (Matthew 5:28)? _____

4. How can the application of the following verses enable you to overcome sexual lust?
Philippians 4:8 _____
Psalm 119:11 _____
1 Corinthians 10:13 _____
Romans 6:14 _____

Life Application

1. How would you say stewardship of each individual part of the body could affect each other part? _____

How could it affect the body as a whole? _____

2. How would you apply 1 Thessalonians 5:22 to:
the use of your tongue?   _____
the desires of your heart?   _____
the control of your mind?   _____
your conduct with members of the opposite sex? _____

LESSON FIVE

STEWARDSHIP OF OUR GIFTS

Introduction

OBJECTIVE: To recognize our talents and abilities and to surrender them to God for His use and glory.

MINISTERING
TEACHING
GIVING
HELPING
EXHORTING
FAITH
SHOWING MERCY
RULING

TO MEMORIZE: 1 Peter 4:10.

TO READ: 1 Corinthians 12.

God created man with a great variety of talents. The Christian church is composed of people endowed with different gifts and abilities. All that the Christian possesses should be dedicated fully to God to be used as He directs.

The Scriptures refer to the church as the body of Christ. Christ is its Head (1 Corinthians 12:27; Ephesians 5:23). Just as your body has many specialized parts, each having its own function, so the church is composed of many individuals, each with his own special function to perform — and contribution to make — to the rest of the body.

Every Christian possesses both natural and spiritual gifts. All men have natural gifts (abilities and talents), for they come to us at physical birth. Spiritual gifts are special abilities imparted by the Holy Spirit to Christians. These enable Christians to minister to others in behalf of Christ.

Bible Study

A. *Natural gifts*

1. What talents and natural abilities do you have? _____

_____

_____

2. How did you acquire them? _____

_____

3. According to 1 Corinthians 4:6, 7, what should your attitude be about them? _____

_____

_____

_____

4. How would you apply Colossians 3:17 to the stewardship
   of your natural gifts? _____

_____

B. *Spiritual gifts*

   1. Major passages on spiritual gifts in the Bible are:

               Romans 12:3-8
               1 Corinthians 12:1-31
               Ephesians 4:4-16
               1 Peter 4:10, 11

   From these passages make a composite list of the spiritual
   gifts (combine any two that might be identical). After each
   one you list, give your brief definition of the gift. (You may
   wish to consult a concordance or a Bible dictionary.)

Spiritual Gift	Definition
_____	_____
_____	_____
_____	_____
_____	_____
_____	_____
_____	_____
_____	_____
_____	_____
_____	_____
_____	_____
_____	_____
_____	_____

2. List additional spiritual gifts you can think of that might be included: _____

_____

_____

   Why do you think so? _____

_____

3. What are some reasons God has given gifted men to the church (Ephesians 4:11-16)?_____

_____

_____

4. Why will two people not exercise the same gift in the same manner (1 Corinthians 12:4-6)? _____

5. Though some spiritual gifts seem to be of greater value than others (1 Corinthians 12:28-31), what ideas does Paul stress to keep Christians from personal pride because of those they may possess (Romans 12:4, 5; 1 Corinthians 12:12-26; 1 Corinthians 13; Ephesians 4:11-16)?_____

_____

_____

_____

6. List the principles concerning what your attitude and responsibilities are to be toward your spiritual gifts (Romans 12:3-8). _____

_____

_____

Life Application

Realize that you have at least one spiritual gift, probably more (1 Corinthians 12:11).

To find our what they are, pray that God will make them known to you. Determine which of your activities the Lord seems to bless and inquire of other mature Christians who know you well what your spiritual gifts might be.

Seek to develop your gifts in the power of the Holy Spirit, according to the scriptural exhortations. Realize that you may have other gifts of which you are not presently aware, so exercise various gifts. Take spiritual responsibility.

Be aware that you are accountable to God for stewardship of your spiritual gifts.

List what you feel might be your spiritual gifts. _____

LESSON SIX

STEWARDSHIP OF OUR POSSESSIONS

Introduction

OBJECTIVE: To surrender all our material wealth to God, and to give in joy and gratitude.

TO MEMORIZE: Luke 16:13.

TO READ: 2 Corinthians 9;
Matthew 6:19-34; 25:14-30;
Luke 12:15-21.

Bible Study

A. *Money — the old standard*

1. What did God command those under the law of Moses to do (Malachi 3:8-10)? _____

_____

_____

_____

2. What would you say the "storehouse" is (Deuteronomy 16:11 and 12:5, 6)? _____

_____

_____

3. How much is a tithe (Hebrews 7:2)? _____

_____

B. *Money — the new standard*

1. As believers in Christ, we are under grace, rather than law. Whereas the law in itself did not provide eternal life for those who attempted to keep it (Galatians 2:16; 3:21, 22), we have received life by the favor of God — though we do not deserve it and could not possibly earn it. Therefore, do we have a *higher* or *lower* motivation and standard for stewardship of our possessions, than

those under the law? _____

2. How did Jesus regard a person's responsibility in that area (Matthew 23:33)? _____

3. Read 2 Corinthians 8, 9.

In this passage, Paul attempts to encourage the Corinthian church to give financially to help needy Christians. He first points them to the example of the Macedonian church. What did the Macedonians do before they gave their money to God (2 Corinthians 8:5)? _____

_____

In light of this, what do you think God is interested in?

_____

Nevertheless, why is giving of money an important part of our Christian life (2 Corinthians 8:7)? _____

_____

Who is the great example of giving (2 Corinthians 8:9)?

_____

In what sense does the one who "sows" (gives) sparingly reap sparingly (2 Corinthians 9:6)? _____

_____

What kind of giver does God love (2 Corinthians 9:7)?

_____

C. Other possessions

1. To whom do you and your possessions belong (1 Corinthians 6:19, 20)? _____

2. What should be your motive in the use of whatever you possess (1 Corinthians 10:31)? _____

Life Application

1. Consider your income and possessions. What should you keep for yourself as God's steward? _____

   _____

2. List some Christian groups or churches which are working to fulfill the Great Commission, in which you would like to invest financially. _____

   _____

3. Ask yourself, "Is my heart attitude one of joy and gratefulness as I give?" _____

   _____

LESSON SEVEN

STEWARDSHIP ACCOUNTING
TO OUR MASTER

Introduction

OBJECTIVE: To recognize our ultimate accountability to God.

TO MEMORIZE: 2 Corinthians 5:10.

TO READ: Luke 19:12-27;
Matthew 24 and 25.

Bible Study

A. *The Christian at Christ's coming*

1. According to 2 Corinthians 5:10, what will Christ do when He comes again? _____

   _____

   _____

2. Notice that Paul says "we all." Who is this primarily for?

   _____

   Note: A believer's sins have already been judged in Christ (Romans 8:1). The judgment here is of his works since he became a believer.

3. Read 1 Corinthians 3:11-15.

   God's judgment of our works is compared to the reaction of certain materials to fire. According to this passage, what is God most interested in regarding the works we do

   for Him (verse 13)? _____

   How is it then possible for us to spend long hours

   working for God, but have no reward whatsoever? _____

   _____

A Christian's works may be rejected, but what can he himself still be sure of (verse 15)? _____

B. *The time of Christ's coming*

1. The judgment of the Christian will take place when Christ comes again. When will that be (Acts 1:6, 7)? _____

_____

2. Upon what should we concentrate until He comes (Acts 1:8)? _____

_____

3. Why has Christ waited so long already before coming (2 Peter 3:9)? _____

_____

C. *The earth at Christ's coming*

Read Mark 13, which foretells the world conditions as Christ's coming approaches. As we see the world today becoming more like this, we know His coming is drawing nearer.

1. What will we see happening in religion (verses 5, 6)?

_____

_____

2. What will the world situation be (verses 7, 8)? _____

_____

3. What will occur in nature (verse 8)? _____

_____

4. What will the attitude be toward true believers (verses 12, 13)? _____

_____

5. Describe in your own words what you think Christ's coming will be like (verses 26, 27). _____

_____

_____

_____

Life Application

1. What are you as a believer to do as His coming draws near (verse 33)? _____

_____

2. How will obedience to that instruction affect:

Your employment?_____

Your social life? _____

Your worship? _____

LESSON EIGHT

RECAP

Review all verses memorized.

Reread Romans 12; 1 Corinthians 12; James 3:1, 2.

Define "Christian steward" in your own words. _____

_____

Why are we referred to as Christian stewards? _____

_____

_____

Summarize your responsibilities as a steward of God as you now understand them. _____

_____

_____

_____

List several things over which you exercise that stewardship.

_____

_____

_____

What is the most important thing for you to realize about your attitude toward stewardship? _____

_____

_____

In what particular area of your life have you seen a change for the better in your Christian stewardship? _____

_____

_____

_____

_____

Mr. Paul V. Brown
The Graduate House
University of California
Los Angeles, California 90024

   Re: How to Know the Will of God for Your Life.

Dear Paul:

   Thank you for your recent letter sharing some of the exciting experiences which you are having in your new and adventuresome life with Christ.

   When I read that part of your letter in which you expressed the desire to invest your life fully for Christ, I paused to give thanks to the Lord: first, for His great love and faithful direction of the lives of all who will trust Him; and second, for your response to His love and your willingness to trust Him with every detail of your life.

   It is at this crucial point that many Christians deprive themselves of the full, abundant and purposeful life which the Lord Jesus promised in John 10:10. Failing to comprehend the true character and nature of God — His absolute love, grace, wisdom, power and holiness — many Christians have foolishly chosen to live according to their own plans rather than to consider and do the will of God. Some have such a distorted view of God that they think of Him as a tyrant whom one must either appease or experience His wrath, as those who worship a pagan god. Since they are afraid of Him, they cannot love and trust Him. This is sometimes true of individuals who have transferred to God their fear of an earthly father who may have been overly strict, unduly demanding, or even tyrannical.

   In all fairness I should say that there are many sincere Christians who want to do the will of God but do not know how to go about discovering His will for their lives.

   A choice young college graduate came recently for counsel concerning God's will for his life. "How can I know what God wants me to do?" he asked. Briefly I explained the safest approach to knowing the will of God — to follow what I have chosen to call the "Sound Mind Principle" of Scripture. In less than an hour, by following the suggestions contained in this letter, this young man discovered what he had been seeking for years. He knew not only the work which God wanted him to do, but the very organization with which he was to be affiliated.

Now you may ask, "What is the Sound Mind Principle of Scripture? In 2 Timothy 1:7 we are told that "God has not given us the spirit of fear; but of power, and of love and of a sound mind." The sound mind referred to in this verse means a well-balanced mind — a mind that is under the control of the Holy Spirit — "remade" according to Romans 12:1, 2 (NEB): "Therefore, my brothers, I implore you by God's mercies to offer your very selves to Him, a living sacrifice, dedicated and fit for His acceptance, the worship offered by mind and heart. Adapt yourselves no longer to the pattern of the present world, but let your minds be remade and your whole nature thus transformed. Then you will be able to discern the will of God and to know it is good, acceptable, and perfect."

There is a vast difference between the inclination of the natural or carnal man to use "common sense" and that of the spiritual man to follow the Sound Mind Principle. The first depends upon the wisdom of man for understanding, without benefit of God's wisdom and power; the other, having the mind of Christ, receives wisdom and guidance from God moment by moment through faith.

Are your decisions as a Christian based upon unpredictable emotions and chance circumstances — upon the "common sense" of the natural man? Or do you make your decisions according to the Sound Mind Principle of Scripture?

Through the years, as I have counseled with many Christians, the question most frequently asked has been, "How can I know the will of. God for my life?" Inevitably, the majority of Christians who come for counsel are looking for some dramatic or cataclysmic revelation from God by which they will know God's plan. Without minimizing the importance of feelings, which Jesus promised in John 14:21 as a result of obedience, more emphasis needs to be placed upon the importance of the sound mind which God has given. Multitudes of sincere Christians are wasting their lives, immobile and impotent, as they wait for some unusual or dramatic word from God.

The Scripture assures us that "God has not given us a spirit of fear, but of power, and of love, and of a sound mind." Thus, a Christian who has yielded his life fully to Christ can be assured of sanctified reasoning, and a balanced, disciplined mind. Also, God has promised to give His children wisdom, according to James 1:5-7. Further, we can know with "settled and absolute assurance" that, when we pray according to the will of God, He will always hear and grant our petitions (1 John 5:14, 15). Since the Christian is to live by faith, and faith comes through an understanding of the Word of God, it is impossible to over-emphasize the importance of the Scriptures in the lives of those who would know and do the will of God.

If you would like to know the will of God for your life, according to the Sound Mind Principle of Scripture, may I suggest that you follow this bit of logic. Consider these questions: "Why did Jesus come?" (He came to seek and to save the lost" — Luke 19:10.) "What is the greatest experience of your life?" (If you are a Christian, your answer quite obviously will be, "To know Christ personally as my Savior and Lord.") "What is the greatest thing that you can do to help others? (The answer is again obvious: "Introduce them to Christ.")

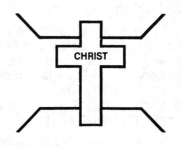

Jesus came to seek and to save the lost, and every Christian is under divine orders to be a faithful witness for Christ. Jesus said, "By this is My Father glorified, that you bear much fruit, and so prove to be My disciples" (John 15:8). It logically follows that the most important thing I can possibly do as a Christian is to allow the Lord Jesus Christ in all of His resurrection power to have complete, unhindered control of my life; otherwise He cannot continue seeking and saving the lost through me.

Thus, every sincere Christian will want to make his God-given time, talents and treasure available to Christ so that his fullest potential will be realized for Him. For one Christian, this talent which God has given him may be prophetic preaching, evangelism or teaching; for another, it may be business; for another, the ministry or missions; for another, homemaking, as expressed in Romans 12:5, 1 Corinthians 12, 14, Ephesians 4 and other Scriptures.

As you evaluate the talents that God has given you in relation to your training, personality, and other qualities, may I suggest that you take a sheet of paper and make a list of the most logical ways through which your life can be used to accomplish the most for the glory of God. With the desire to put His will above all else, list the pros and cons of each opportunity. Where or how, according to the Sound Mind Principle, can the Lord Jesus Christ through your yielded life accomplish the most in continuing His great ministry of seeking and saving the lost? Like my young friend, you will find that such a procedure will inevitably result in positive actions leading to God's perfect will for your life. But note a word of caution: the Sound Mind Principle is not valid unless certain factors exist.

1. There must be no unconfessed sin in your life; following 1 John 1:9 takes care of that: "If we confess our sins, He is faithful and righteous to forgive us our sins and to cleanse us from all unrighteousness."

2. Your life must be fully dedicated to Christ according to Romans 12:1, 2, and you must be filled with the Holy Spirit in obedience to the command in Ephesians 5:18. As in the case of our salvation, we are filled and controlled by the Spirit through faith.

3. In order to know the will of God, you must walk in the Spirit (abide in Christ) moment by moment. You place your faith in the trustworthiness of God with the confidence that the Lord is directing and will continue to direct your life, according to His promise that the "steps of a righteous man are ordered of the Lord" (Psalms 37:23). For "as you have therefore received Christ Jesus the Lord, so walk in Him" (Colossians 2:6). How? By faith — placing your complete trust in Him. Now, you must go on walking by faith. Remember, "that which is not of faith is sin," and "the just shall live by faith," and "without faith it is impossible to please God." Faith is the catalyst for all of our Christian relationships.

The counsel of others should be prayerfully considered, especially that of mature, dedicated Christians who know the Word of God and are able to relate the proper use of Scripture to your need. However, care should be taken not to make the counsel of others a "crutch." Although God often speaks to us through other Christians, we are admonished to place our trust in Him. In Psalm 37 we are told to delight ourselves in the Lord and He will give us the desires of our hearts; to commit our ways unto the Lord, to trust Him and He will bring it to pass. Also, in Proverbs 3 we are told, "Trust in the Lord with all thine heart; and lean not unto thine own under-

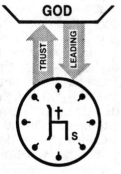

standing. In all thy ways acknowledge Him, and He shall direct thy paths."

God never contradicts Himself. He never leads us to do anything contrary to the commands of His Word; for, according to Philippians 2:13 (Phillips): "It is God who is at work within you, giving you the will, and the power to achieve His purpose."

Through the centuries sincere religious men have suggested spiritual formulas for discovering the will of God. Some are valid; others are unscriptural and misleading. For example, a young seminary graduate was investigating various possibilities of Christian service and came to discuss with me the ministry of Campus Crusade for Christ. Applying the Sound Mind Principle to his quest, I asked, "In what way do you expect God to reveal His place of service for you?" He replied, "I am following the 'closed door' policy. A few months ago I began to investigate several opportunities for Christian service. The Lord has now closed the door on all but two, one of which is Campus Crusade for Christ. If the door to accept a call to a particular church closes, I shall know that God wants me in Campus Crusade." Many sincere Christians follow this illogical and unscriptural method, often with most unsatisfactory and frustrating consequences. Don't misunderstand me. God may and often does close doors in the life of every active, Spirit-controlled Christian. This was true in the experience of the apostle Paul. As recorded in Acts 16:6-11, he was forbidden by the Spirit to go into Bithynia because God wanted him in Macedonia. My reference to "closed door" policies does not preclude such experiences, but refers to a careless hit or miss attitude without the careful evaluation of all the issues.

This approach is illogical because it allows elements of chance, rather than a careful, intelligent evaluation of all the factors involved, to influence a decision. It is unscriptural in that it fails to employ the God-given faculties of reason that are controlled by the Holy Spirit. Further, the "closed door" policy is in error because it seeks God's will through the process of elimination rather than seeking God's best first. It should be understood that true faith is established on the basis of fact. Therefore, vital faith in God is emphasized rather than minimized through employing Spirit-controlled reason. In making decisions some sincere Christians rely almost entirely upon impressions, or hunches, fearful that if they use their mental faculties they will not exercise adequate faith and thus will grieve the Holy Spirit.

There are those who assume that a door has been closed simply because of difficulties that have been encountered. Yet, experience has taught and Scripture confirms that God's richest blessings often follow periods of greatest testing. This might include financial needs, loss of health, objection of loved ones and criticism of fellow Christians. God's blessing is promised, however, only to those who are obedient — who demonstrate their faith in God's faithfulness. The apparent defeat of the cross was followed by the victory of the resurrection.

An acceptable consideration for discussing God's will contains four basic factors somewhat similar to the Sound Mind Principle: (1) the authority of Scripture; (2) providential circumstances; (3) conviction based upon reason; and (4) impressions of the Holy Spirit upon our minds. However, such an appraisal is safer with a mature Christian than with a new or carnal Christian, and there is always danger of misunderstanding "impressions."

You must know the source of "leading" before responding to it. To the inexperienced, what appears to be the leading of God may not be from Him at all but from the "rulers of darkness of this world." Satan and his helpers often disguise themselves as "angels of light" by performing miracles and signs and foretelling events, etc. The enemy of our souls is a master counterfeiter.

Remember, just as turning the steering wheel of an automobile does not alter the car's direction unless it is moving, so God cannot direct our lives unless we are moving for Him. I challenge you to begin employing the Sound Mind Principle today in all your relationships. Apply it to the investment of your time, your talents and your treasure; for this principle applies to everything you do in this life. Every Christian should take spiritual inventory regularly by asking himself these questions: Is my time being invested in such a way that the largest possible number of people are being introduced to Christ? Are my talents being invested fully to the end that the largest number of people are being introduced to Christ? Is my money, my treasure, being invested in such a way as to introduce the greatest number of people to Christ?

Every Christian is admonished to be a good steward of his God-given time, talents and treasure. Therefore, these investments must not be dictated by tradition, habit, or by emotions. Every investment of time, talent and treasure, unless otherwise directed by the Holy Spirit, should be determined by the Sound Mind Principle which is described in 2 Timothy 1:7.

Regarding the questions asked by your girl friend, the same principle applies to her. How does this Sound Mind Principle apply in the case of a secretary, homemaker, an invalid, or one who, because of circumstances beyond her control, does not have direct contact with men and women who are in need of Christ?

First, each Christian must be a witness for Christ; this is simply an act of obedience for which one need not possess the gift of evangelism. If normal day-to-day contacts do not provide opportunities to witness for Christ, an obedient Christian will make opportunities through personal contacts, church calling, letter writing, etc. Two of the most radiant, effective and fruitful Christians whom I have known were both bed-ridden invalids who, though in constant pain, bore a powerful witness for Christ to all — stranger and friend alike. "That which is most on our hearts will be most on our lips," was demonstrated in their lives. Second, a careful evaluation should be given to determine if God may not have a better position for one. Again, the Sound Mind Principle applies. For example, a secretary in a secular organization may not have much opportunity to make her life count for the Lord. It may be that God wants to use her talents in a Christian organization. One should be very careful, however, not to run from what appears to be a difficult assignment. A careful appraisal of one's present responsibilities, with this new understanding of God's leading, may well reveal a great potential for Christ.

For example, I know that there is a great scarcity of qualified secretarial help in many Christian organizations, including Campus Crusade for Christ. Quite obviously, members of an office staff do not have as much contact with men and women who are in need of our Savior as those who are actually working on the campus or conducting evangelistic meetings. However, according to the Sound Mind Principle, if their lives are fully dedicated to Christ, they can make a vital contribution to the effectiveness of any Christian ministry. By relieving others who have the gift of evangelism without the talent for business or secretarial responsibilities, the overall ministry for Christ in such an organization is strengthened greatly. In this way, they can more fully utilize their talents in helping to seek and to save the lost.

Obviously, therefore, a dedicated member of the secretarial staff of the worldwide ministry of Campus Crusade for Christ is just as vital to the success of this campus strategy as those who are working on the campus. My own personal ministry has been greatly increased by the dedicated efforts of several secretaries who are more concerned about winning students to Christ than with their own personal pleasure.

One further word of explanation must be given. It is true that God still reveals His will to some men and women in dramatic ways, but this should be considered the exception rather than the rule. God still leads men today as He has through the centuries. Philip, the deacon, was holding a successful campaign in Samaria. The Sound Mind Principle would have directed him to continue his campaign. However, God over-ruled by a special revelation, and Philip was led by the Holy Spirit to preach for Christ to the Ethiopian eunuch. According to tradition, God used the Ethiopian eunuch to communicate the message of our living Lord to his own country.

Living according to the Sound Mind Principle allows for such dramatic leading of God. But, we are not to wait for such revelations before we start moving for Christ. Faith must have an object. A Christian's faith is built upon the authority of God's Word supported by historical fact, and not upon any shallow emotional experience. However, a Christian's trust in God's will, as revealed in His Word, will result in the decisions which are made by following the Sound Mind Principle. The confirmation may come in various ways — depending upon many factors, including the personality of the individual involved. Usually, the confirmation is a quiet, peaceful assurance that you are doing what God wants you to do, with expectancy that God will use you to bear "much fruit."

As any sincere Christian gives himself to a diligent study of the Scripture and allows a loving, all-wise, sovereign God and Father to control his life, feelings will inevitably result. Thus, the end result of a life that is lived according to the Sound Mind Principle is the most joyful, abundant, and fruitful life of all. Expect the Lord Jesus Christ to draw men to Himself through you. As you begin each day, acknowledge the fact that you belong to Him. Thank Him for the fact that He lives within you. Invite Him to use your mind to think His thoughts, your heart to express His love, your lips to speak His truth. Ask Jesus to be at home in your life and to walk around in your body in order that He may continue seeking and saving souls through you.

It is my sincere prayer, Paul, that you may know this kind of life, that you may fully appropriate all that God has given to you as your rightful heritage in Christ. I shall look forward to hearing more from you concerning your personal application of the Sound Mind Principle.

Warmly in Christ,

Old Testament Highlights

INTRODUCTION

The Bible is the record of God's revelation of Himself to man. This record was written by men chosen by God, and inspired by His Spirit so that the record is free from error and free from human reasonings (2 Peter 1:21). The Old Testament is the account of man's creation, his fall because of sin, and the preparation of the world for the coming of Jesus Christ, God's Son, to redeem man from his fallen state.

This preparation of the world was accomplished through the nation Israel. In this study we shall survey the record of these happenings; we shall look at the lives of some of the men God used to live, speak and write this record; and we shall look at the truths revealed in both.

Keep in mind that we are going to cover a period of time that has been estimated to be from 4,000 to 400,000,000 years long. Naturally we shall have to be selective, but in the few incidents we look at, we shall see what God did to prepare the way for Jesus Christ.

HISTORICAL SKETCH

Date	History in the Bible	Contemporaneous History
? ADAM	The drama begins	
2,000 B. C. ABRAHAM	The spiritual race begun	The Bronze Age – the Egyptian and Babylonian civilizations had existed for centuries before Abraham
1,400 B. C. MOSES	Birth of the Hebrew nation	
		The Iron Age begins
1,000 B. C. DAVID	Height of Hebrew power	
		Rise of Assyrian power
850 B. C. ELIJAH	The nation in division: two kingdoms	
590 B. C. JEREMIAH	The nation in demolition: the Babylonian captivity	Beginning of Greek classical culture
450 B. C. EZRA	The Jewish puppet state established	Rise of Persia
		Era of Plato
	— under Persians	
400-year break between the Old and the New Testaments	— under Greeks	Alexander's conquests
	— under Romans	
		Pompey's and Caesar's campaigns

LESSON ONE

THE DRAMA BEGINS

Introduction

OBJECTIVE: To recognize how the book of Genesis relates to us today.

IN THE BEGINNING
GENESIS 1,2,3

TO MEMORIZE: Romans 5:12.

TO READ: Genesis 1, 2, and 3.

The Old Testament is an account of a Nation.

The New Testament is an account of a Man.

The Nation was founded and nurtured of God to bring the Man into the world.

Bible Study

A. *Origin of man*

1. How did our world come into existence? _____

_____

2. What was the condition of the world and everything that was in it at this time (Genesis 1:10b, 12b, 18b, 21b, and 25b)? _____

3. How did man come into existence (Genesis 1:27)?_____

_____

4. Was man an intelligent being at this time (2:20)? _____
   How do you know?_____

_____

5. How was woman brought into existence (2:21, 22)?
_____

B. *Origin of sin*

1. What was man's commission from God (1:28-30)?_____

_____

What was man's relationship with God at this time (1:28a)? _____

_____

2. How would you describe Satan's personality characteristics when he appeared as a serpent and confronted Eve? _____

How has he used these same personality characteristics in confronting you? _____

3. Whose word did Satan question (3:1)? _____
Did Eve answer truthfully (3:2, 3 — look particularly at the last phrase of verse 3, then at 2:17)? _____
To what did Satan appeal in speaking to Eve (3:5)? _____

_____

4. In the light of 1 John 2:16, analyze the temptation and give the three parts of it (3:6). _____

_____

_____

5. Why was it wrong for Adam and Eve to eat of this tree (2:17)? _____

C. Sin's result

1. What was the result of the sin of the man and the woman (3:7, 8)? _____

_____

2. What was the penalty for sin for (3:14-19):
the serpent? _____

_____

the woman? _____

_____

the man? _____

_____

How was man's relationship to God altered (3:8-10)?

_____

3. What did God promise regarding Satan's destiny (3:15)? Explain._____

_____

Life Application

1. How does Adam and Eve's sin affect you today (Romans 5:12)? _____

Man was created to have fellowship with God, but because of his stubborn self-will, he chose to go his own independent way and fellowship was broken. This is what the Bible calls sin.

The Bible says, "For all have sinned and come short of the glory of God" (Romans 3:23); "for the wages of sin is death, but the gift of God is eternal life through Jesus Christ our Lord" (Romans 6:23).

It is this first act in the drama that sets the stage for all that is to follow. If there had been no sin, there would have been no need for redemption and no need for a Bible to tell us of the need for redemption and the way of redemption.

2. Starting with Genesis 3:15, God begins to point to the time when the penalty for sin would be paid on man's behalf by the seed of the woman. In the chart on the next page, notice the prophecies pointing to Christ and their fulfillment in Him.

GOD'S PROMISED MESSIAH

PROMISE	FULFILLMENT
1. Born of a Virgin Genesis 3:15, Isaiah 7:14	Matthew 1:18-23
2. From Nation of Israel Genesis 12:3, Numbers 24:17, 19	Matthew 1:1-17
3. Tribe of Judah, Family of David Genesis 49:10, Isaiah 11:1, 10	Luke 1:31-33
4. Born in Bethlehem Micah 5:2	Luke 2:4, 6, 7
5. Time of Coming Daniel 9:24-26	Galatians 4:4
6. Part of Childhood in Egypt Hosea 11:1	Matthew 2:14, 15
7. Suffering and Atonement Isaiah 53:4-6	2 Corinthians 5:21
8. Triumphal Entry Zechariah 9:9	Matthew 21:2, 4, 5
9. Crucifixion Psalm 22	Matthew 27
10. Resurrection Psalm 16:9, 10	Acts 2:31, 32

These are only a few of the more than 300 Old Testament references to the coming of the Messiah that were fulfilled in the life, ministry, death and resurrection of Jesus of Nazareth.

Look up all the references listed above regarding the promises and their fulfillment and read them.

What is the overall picture they present to you? _____

_____

_____

_____

LESSON TWO

FROM ADAM THROUGH ABRAHAM

Introduction

OBJECTIVE: To learn from biblical example the importance of obedience in the Christian life.

ADAM— ABRAHAM
GENESIS 4-22

TO MEMORIZE: Romans 4:20, 21.

TO READ: Genesis 4, 6, 7, 12 and 22.

Bible Study

A. *Cain and Abel*

1. In Genesis 4, two sacrifices are made. Evaluate each and indicate its acceptability to God. _____
   _____
   _____

2. What do you think verse 7 is all about? _____
   _____

3. Give at least one present-day counterpart to the two types of sacrifices offered by Cain and Abel. _____
   _____

B. *Noah*

1. Why was God sorry He had made man on the earth? (See Matthew 24:37-39.) _____
   _____

2. Why was Noah chosen by God to build an ark? _____
   _____
   _____

3. What do you think God accomplished through Noah?
(See also Hebrews 11:7.) _____

_____

C. Abraham

1. Abraham holds a unique place in the history of the world.
Three religions point to Abraham as the founder of their
faiths: Judaism, Islam and Christianity. On the basis of
Genesis 12:2, 3; 16:4, 15; and 17:19, do all three have a
right to call him the founder or father of their faiths?

_____Explain._____

_____

_____

2. Why do you suppose God made the request of Abraham
recorded in Genesis 22:1, 2? _____

3. Study Genesis 22:8 thoroughly and give your explanation
of it. _____

_____

Life Application

1. What important lesson has God's response to Cain taught
you? _____

_____

_____

2. Do you think you would have boarded the ark with Noah?
_____ Upon what do you base that opinion?_____

_____

_____

3. How have you and your family been blessed in Abraham
as promised in Genesis 12:3? _____

_____

_____

LESSON THREE

MOSES, THE PASSOVER AND
THE EXODUS (EXIT)

Introduction

OBJECTIVE: To learn to walk
by faith, resting
in the Lord.

TO MEMORIZE: 1 Corinthians
10:13.

MOSES

EXODUS 3-27   ROMANS 3
DEUT 29-30   HEBREWS 11

TO READ: Exodus 1 and 2.

Jacob, the grandson of
Abraham, had taken his family
to Egypt to escape a famine.
After 400 years, his descen-
dants had multiplied greatly. A new king of Egypt arose, and
because he was concerned about their numbers he subjected
the Israelites to cruel slavery. Exodus 1 and 2 give an account of
this development, of the birth and life of Moses and of the
people's cry to God for deliverance. God heard their cry, and
sent Moses to lead them out of Egypt.

Bible Study

A. *Moses, the leader*

1. Read Hebrews 11:23-29.

   Why do you think God chose Moses to lead His people?

   _____

2. Read Exodus 3 and 4.

   When God told Moses what He wanted him to do, how
   did He say the people would react (Exodus 3:18)? _____

   _____

   In Exodus 3:17, 20, 21 and 4:12, note the "I will's" of
   God. Whose work was this going to be? _____

   _____

Where did Moses fit in? _____

_____

3. How did Moses respond and how did God handle those responses?

Exodus 4:1-9 _____

Verses 10-12 _____

Verses 13-17 _____

4. In 4:1, Moses said of the people, "They will not believe me." When Moses was obedient, how did the people respond (4:31)? _____

_____

_____

B. *The Passover*

Read Exodus 12.

1. Why was God sending plagues at this time? _____

_____

2. What was the most vital instruction given to the children of Israel? _____

_____

3. What are the correlations between Christ's death and the Passover as indicated in these Scriptures?

Exodus 12:3 _____ John 1:29 _____

Exodus 12:5, 6 _____ 1 Peter 2:22 _____

Exodus 12:6 _____ 1 Corinthians 5:7 _____

_____

Blood applied to the two doorposts (sides) and to the lintel (top) creates what kind of picture? _____

_____

4. What do you suppose happened to those who may have disobeyed the instructions given through Moses? _____

_____

What spiritual truth do you believe this illustrates? _____

_____

5. What does Exodus 12:29 teach about God being a respecter of persons? _____

How does this apply to the condition of any person who has not received Christ?_____

_____

C. *The Exodus ("going out")*

1. One of the most important events in the history of Israel occurred immediately following the Passover. What was it (Exodus 12:40, 41)?_____

_____

_____

2. Compare Exodus 3:7, 8 and John 3:16. How do you see them relating to each other?_____

_____

_____

3. One of the most remarkable and well-known miracles in the world is recorded in Exodus 14. Summarize it here.

_____

_____

_____

What spiritual truth does this experience suggest to you?

_____

_____

4. While the Israelites were in the wilderness, they had many trials and hardships; several times in the many years of wandering before coming into the land which had been promised to them, they failed God. (See Exodus 17:1-7; 32:1-6, 15-20 and Numbers 21:5-9.) What practical value do these events recorded in the Old Testament have for you today (1 Corinthians 10:5-11)? _____

_____

5. In summary of the wilderness wanderings mentioned in 1 Corinthians 10:1-15, what is God's promise to you? (Write out verse and reference and claim it.)_____

_____

_____

Life Application

1. God asked Moses a question in Exodus 4:2. What was it?

_____

2. God expects us to use what we have. Moses used a rod; David used a sling; Gideon used lanterns, pitchers and trumpets. What is in your hands? _____

_____

3. How do you think God wants you to use it? _____

_____

_____

LESSON FOUR

LAW AND GRACE

Introduction

OBJECTIVE: To understand our inability to keep the law and our need for God's grace.

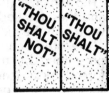

TO MEMORIZE: Romans 6:23.

TO READ: Galatians 3.

Bible Study

A. *The Law*

When "The Law" is mentioned, the thing that most commonly comes to mind is the Decalogue, or the Ten Commandments.

The Ten Commandments are listed in Exodus 20 and are repeated in Deuteronomy 5. They are:

I. You shall have no other gods before Me.

II. You shall not make for yourself an idol, or any likeness . . . You shall not worship them or serve them.

III. You shall not take the name of the Lord your God in vain.

IV. Remember the sabbath day, to keep it holy.

V. Honor your father and your mother.

VI. You shall not murder.

VII. You shall not commit adultery.

VIII. You shall not steal.

IX. You shall not bear false witness against your neighbor.

X. You shall not covet . . . anything that belongs to your neighbor.

1. Jesus condensed these ten into two in Matthew 22:37-40. What are they? 1. _____

2. _____

2. What was James' pronouncement concerning the serious-
ness of breaking even one of these laws (James 2:10)?

_____

B. What the Law does

Read Deuteronomy 29:29 and 30:11-20.

The law of Moses was a covenant of works. God said,
"Thou shalt," and, "Thou shalt not." The laws were definite
and the attached penalties were definite if the conditions
were not obeyed.

Webster defines law as "a rule of conduct or action
prescribed by the supreme governing authority and en-
forced by a sanction." Law always implies two things, a
standard and a *penalty.*

These laws were presented as *God's standard of righteousness* for that time. They were literally a yardstick for man.
The New Testament reveals that "by the law is the knowledge of sin." Jesus Christ came to "fulfill the law" and now
God's standard of righteousness is Christ Himself, a much
higher standard.

1. How are God's people to respond to the things of God
that He has revealed of Himself (Deuteronomy 29:29;

   30:11)?_____

2. Briefly, what is the summary of all the law (Deuteronomy

   30:16, 20)? _____

   _____

3. How did Jesus Christ summarize the will of God for man

   in Mark 12:29-31? _____

   _____

4. On the basis of Matthew 5:17, what do you think was

   Christ's assessment of the law? _____

   _____

5. Read Romans 3:19-26.

   What does the law reveal (3:19, 20)? _____

   _____

6. To what did the law bear witness while failing to reveal it fully (3:21)? _____

_____

7. How has a full revelation been made to us (3:22-24)?

_____

C. *Grace.*

1. You will find a modern translation of this Romans passage (3:19-26) helpful. As you read the following excerpt from Williams' translation, *underline the explanatory paraphrase* which replaces the term "the righteousness of God."

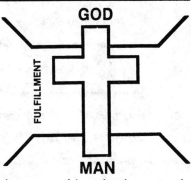

(v. 19) Now we know that everything the law says is spoken to those who are under its authority, that every mouth may be stopped and the whole world be held responsible to God; (v. 20) because no human creature can be brought in right standing with God by observing the law. For all the law can do is to make men conscious of sin.

(v. 21) But now God's way of giving men right standing with Himself has come to light; a way without connection with the law, and yet a way to which the law and the prophets testify.

(v. 22) God's own way of giving men right standing with Himself is through faith in Jesus Christ. It is for everybody who has faith, for no distinction at all is made.

(v. 23) For everybody has sinned and everybody continues to come short of God's glory.

(v. 24) But anybody may have right standing with God as a free gift of His undeserved favor, through the ransom provided in Christ Jesus.

2. Compare Romans 3:20 and Ephesians 2:8, 9 and write your conclusions. _____

_____

_____

THE JEWISH TABERNACLE

Read Exodus 25, 26, 27.

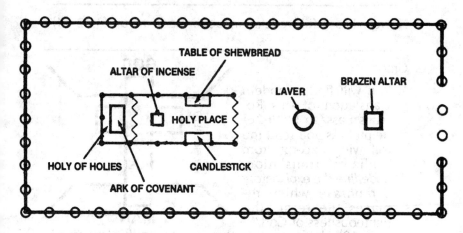

The Tabernacle and its furnishings have many lessons for us.

The first piece of furniture is the Brazen Altar, which was used for sacrifice and atonement. This teaches us the importance of having a sacrifice for our sins first.

Then came the Laver, which was used for cleansing. This shows our need for a daily cleansing from our sins.

As we proceed into the Holy Place, we observe on our right the Table of Shewbread, which teaches us two truths — Christ is our Bread come down from heaven, and the Bible is the Bread with which man is to feed his soul.

On our left is the Candlestick, which reminds us of Christ — the light of the world.

Straight ahead of us is the Altar of Incense — the reminder of our prayers which are our incense to God.

In front of us now is the veil of the tabernacle that was rent from top to bottom when Christ died. No longer is the believer's way obscured into the Holy of Holies, where God Himself dwells. Here we find the Ark which was the earthly dwelling place of God.

We must remember to keep the proper sequence in our Christian lives if we are to live victoriously for Christ.

Life Application

1. How would you explain the difference between law and grace to someone who was depending upon his own good works to please the Father? _____

   _____

2. What is Christ's relationship with:

   the law? _____

   _____

   grace? _____

   _____

   What is your relationship with:

   the law? _____

   _____

   grace? _____

   _____

3. What difference will an understanding of law and grace make in your motivation? _____

   _____

LESSON FIVE

DELIVERANCE AND FORGIVENESS

Introduction

OBJECTIVE: To maintain fellowship with God, unhindered by sin.

TO MEMORIZE: Joshua 1:9.

TO READ: Joshua 1, 7, 8, 23.

JOSHUA
JOSHUA 1-23

Bible Study

A. *Joshua and deliverence*

Joshua's name gives us some insight into the book. His name means "Jehovah is Salvation." It is carried over into the New Testament in the name of our Lord — "Jesus."

1. Read Joshua 1:1-9 and list God's promises to Joshua.

_____

_____

_____

What was the condition on which these promises would be fulfilled? _____

_____

_____

Can you apply any of these promises to your life? _____
Which, and how? _____

_____

_____

2. In Joshua 7, why did God tell Joshua to stop praying?

_____

What does God say to you in Psalm 66:18? _____

_____

Apply Numbers 32:23 to this passage. _____

_____

_____

3. What happened after the sin was taken away (Joshua 8:1)? _____

4. What was Joshua's command to the people before he died (Joshua 23:6)? _____

_____

_____

DAVID

PSALMS   I CHRONICLES
I & II SAMUEL   I KINGS

B. *David and forgiveness*

1. Read 1 Samuel 24 and 2 Samuel 5 and 12, and as you read these chapters, list the verses that indicate the following characteristics of David:

Submissiveness _____

_____

Sincerity _____

_____

Boldness _____

_____

Trust in God _____

_____

_____

_____

Sinful passion _____

_____

Sorrow for sin _____

_____

2. The nobility of David's character is seen in many of the recorded instances from his career, including some of those which you have just read. He is described as a "man after God's own heart" and as such, he occupies a high position among the heroes of the faith. Jesus' title as the ruler of God's people is "the Son of David."

   Many people, however, find the stories of David's terrible sins to be absolutely contradictory to this exalted position of spiritual leadership. How can you hold up such a man as an outstanding example of "a man after

   God's own heart"? _____

   _____

   _____

   If you can answer this question, you will have grasped the essence of biblical faith. Read 2 Samuel 12 again, and then Psalm 51, which David wrote at that time. (You might find help in Romans 4:1-8 or Luke 7:36-50; 18:9-14.)

Life Application

1. What sin, or problem, do you need deliverance from today?

   _____

2. Read Proverbs 28:13. How can you appropriate it for your

   problem? _____

   _____

3. Read Joshua 24. Circle all the "I's" in verses 3 through 13 and notice all the things God accomplished for the people of

   Israel. What do you need Him to accomplish for you? ____

   _____

4. How does your heart attitude compare with that of Joshua

   and David? _____

   _____

LESSON SIX

ELIJAH: THE POWER OF THE SPIRIT-LED MAN

Introduction

OBJECTIVE: To serve God, in power and courage.

ELIJAH
I KINGS 17-18

TO MEMORIZE: 1 Kings 18:21.

TO READ: 1 Kings 17 and 18.

Bible Study

A. *Elijah*

Read 1 Kings 17:1-7.

Indicate whether the following statements are true or false:

___1. The cessation of rain is said to rest upon *all* of these factors:

God lives.

Elijah lived in His presence.

Elijah's word controlled the rain.

___2. The Bible says that Elijah searched eagerly for the will of God.

___3. The prophet obeyed orders for the immediate future, though he did not know how it would turn out.

What step of duty have you not taken because you cannot see its outcome? _____

___4. Elijah thought the plan was absurd, and hesitated.

___5. The brook dried up, proving he was right.

B. *The widow*

Read 1 Kings 17:8-24.

___1. Strict, implicit obedience characterized Elijah.

Do you think it was humiliating to take a step of faith that made him dependent upon a very poor widow? _____ Why do you think God deals with us in such a way? _____

_____

___2. When her boy died, guilt turned the widow's eyes upon herself.

___3. God desires to remove from our lives *now* the guilt that can cripple our faith in time of crisis.

C. Ahab

Read 1 Kings 18:1-18.

___1. Ahab was at least concerned for his animals.

___2. He had refused to acknowledge the real reason for the problem (verses 17, 18).

___3. Nevertheless Elijah recognized the real reason (verses 17, 18).

D. Prophets of Baal

Read 1 Kings 18:18-40.

___1. Write in the verse number(s) in which Elijah spoke as follows:

Rebuked the people for compromise _____

Challenged the enemies of God to a contest _____

Blasted them with withering sarcasm_____

Ordered water poured_____

Prayed to God to make Himself known _____

Ordered the priests executed _____

___2. Elijah's prayer in verse 36 provides a superb revelation of the Spirit-led life. Why do you think that's true? _____

_____

_____

Life Application

1. Describe the relationship you think Elijah had with God.

_____

_____

_____

2. How does your relationship and power with God compare to Elijah's? _____

_____

3. How has God's power been exerted through you upon other lives? _____

_____

_____

4. What changes in your mental and spiritual thinking do you feel need to take place in order for you to find the power with God which you desire? _____

_____

_____

"God's promises are given, not to restrain, but to incite to prayer. . . . They are the signed check, made payable to us, which we must endorse and present for payment.

"We have an irresistible purchase power with God when we can put our finger on His own promise and say, 'Do as You have said.' . . . All prayer, like Elijah's, should be based on promise."

F. B. Meyer

LESSON SEVEN

JEREMIAH: A WITNESS WHO STOOD ALONE

Introduction

OBJECTIVE: To serve God faithfully in the face of discouragement.

JEREMIAH
JEREMIAH 1-21

TO MEMORIZE: Jeremiah 23:29.

TO READ: Jeremiah 1, 20, 21.

If you think it is difficult to stand for Christ in your house, and on your campus, or in your community, take a few lessons from Jeremiah.

Bible Study

A. *Jeremiah's call*

Read Jeremiah 1

1. When facing Scripture verses that command you to speak for Christ, have you ever said: "Why, I could never do that; I have no training for it"? What did Jeremiah say (1:6)? _____

   _____

2. To be effective in speaking, one must have something to say. Where do you get this (see 1:7-17)? _____

   _____

3. Opposition of the intensity that faced Jeremiah is unknown in America, though it is common in some parts of the world. How can a man face such overwhelming odds (see 1:8, 18, 19)? _____

   _____

B. *Jeremiah's arrest and prayer.*

Read Jeremiah 19:14, 15 for setting. In verse 14 we see that not only *what* Jeremiah said but *where* he spoke (and to *whom*) were under the Lord's direct guidance. This was also observed in Elijah's life as one of the secrets of effectiveness. We must not distribute tracts promiscuously, nor witness to every man in sight. Let God lead.

Verse 15 was Jeremiah's unpopular message in a nutshell: condemnation upon the capital city, Jerusalem; the Babylonian armies would destroy the city. He advised the people to sue for surrender terms and avoid the horrors of a siege that could not be resisted for long, since God was on the enemy's side.

Read Jeremiah 20.

1. How did punishment affect Jeremiah's testimony (20:1-6)? _____

   _____

2. Verses 7-18 are an example of the abrupt interruptions interspersed throughout the book of Jeremiah. What do these prayers reveal about the apparent fearlessness of the prophet? _____

   _____

3. Since his message brought him so much unpopularity, what did Jeremiah consider (20:8, 9)? _____

   _____

4. How did his enemies think they could get the best of him (20:10)? _____

   _____

5. What thoughts restored his confidence (20:11)? _____

   _____

6. How would you describe Jeremiah's prayer? _____

   _____

   _____

C. *Jeremiah's prophecy*

Read Jeremiah 21.

1. How do you think feelings of despair and frustration influenced the prophet's obedience to God? _____

_____

2. When asked by the government for a word of comfort and security, what response did Jeremiah make (21:1-7)?

_____

_____

3. What decision did the prophet declare his hearers must make (21:8-14)? _____

_____

Life Application

With this chart, list discouragements you may be facing, and what you have learned from Jeremiah's life that will help you cope with them.

DISCOURAGEMENT	LEARNING FROM JEREMIAH

LESSON EIGHT

RECAP

Review verses memorized.

Now that we have been through the Old Testament at a rapid pace, you have some idea of what it contains and what it teaches. Imagine yourself a Jew, possessing only the Old Testament Scriptures. Can you find God's plan for man in it?

Write it in your own words. _____

_____

_____

_____

_____

_____

_____

_____

Why did Jesus of Nazareth have to come?_____

_____

_____

_____

_____

_____

O.T. BELIEVER   BC   AD   N.T. BELIEVER

STEP TEN
New Testament Highlights

WHY THE "NEW" TESTAMENT?

The name for the last 27 books of the Bible is taken from the words of Jesus uttered on the eve of His crucifixion: "This cup which is poured out for you is the new convenant [or testament] in My blood" (Luke 22:20). This covenant, instituted at this time, was new in contrast with the Mosaic Law, or old covenant, which was instituted with the people of Israel at Mt. Sinai (Exodus 19:5; 20:1-17; Jeremiah 31:31-34). In the old covenant, God wrote His requirements for living a righteous life on tablets of stones. But because of his sinful heart, man finds it impossible to keep the commands of the law by his unaided efforts. Hence the law of the old covenant made the fact of man's sin obvious by showing him to be a transgressor of explicit commands that God had given (Galatians 3:19; Romans 7:7-25). In thus revealing man's sin, the law readies men to receive Christ, for it shows them their inability to save themselves — they must look instead to that which God does for them.

God in His mercy "did not send the Son into the world to judge the world; but that the world should be saved through Him" (John 3:17). Jesus kept the Mosaic Law perfectly. Then when He shed His blood on the cross, He made it possible for the Holy Spirit to be poured out on men who believed so they might receive not only the forgiveness of sins, but also the ability to make progress in living the holy life whose standards are set forth in the Ten Commandments (Exodus 20:1-7). In this new covenant the law is written on the heart of the believer (Jeremiah 31:33), which simply means that God graciously provides the ability to do what the law demands (Ezekiel 36:27).

Though this new covenant was officially instituted at the time of Christ's death and resurrection, it was on the basis of Christ's death (Romans 3:25) and through the Holy Spirit that God had been saving men in the ages before the cross. Hence the new covenant had really been in effect all along. However, since it was officially instituted at Christ's first advent and since the last 27 books of the Bible concern the events leading up to and following the death and resurrection of Christ, these books have been aptly titled, "The New Testament."

LESSON ONE

MATTHEW AND MARK

Introduction

OBJECTIVE: To see the relationship of Christ to
the Old Testament,
and to recognize dif-
ferent facets of Christ
presented by Matthew
and Mark.

MATTHEW
CHRIST AS KING

MARK
CHRIST AS SERVANT

TO MEMORIZE: Matthew
28:18, 19.

TO READ: Matthew 5-7.

Matthew was written to the Jews presenting Christ as King.
Mark was written to the Romans presenting Christ as Servant.
Luke was written to the Greeks presenting Him as Perfect Man,
and John was written to the world presenting Christ as Son of
God, the Savior.

Bible Study

A. *Matthew*

In presenting his record of the life of Jesus, Matthew is
careful to record the major sermons that Jesus preached.
The longest sermon on record is the "Sermon on the
Mount," which is found in chapters 5 through 7.

1. As you read and re-read this sermon, see if you can
answer the following questions which bring out some of
its more important points:

Give one reason that Jesus considers it important for His
disciples to live according to the moral standards of the

Old Testament law and prophets. _____

_____

_____

In one passage of Scripture Jesus summarized all the
moral teachings of the Old Testament (Matthew 5:21-48).

List several of them: _____

_____

_____

_____

What promise does Jesus give that helps the Christian overcome his desire for man's praise as he does good deeds (Matthew 6:1-18)? _____

_____

_____

What assurance does Jesus give that helps the Christian overcome his anxiety regarding his physical needs such as food and clothing (Matthew 6:25-34)? _____

_____

2. This Sermon on the Mount is a revelation of the moral requirements of God. In it we see what a holy God expects of man and we come to understand that by it the world is condemned to hell. The sermon gives a standard, but no enablement. The motive is fear, not love. Its value to us is that it reveals our utter inability and need. What is the only way that a human being can escape this judgment and approach the standards set forth here? _____

_____

_____

3. Read the rest of Jesus' sermons recorded by Matthew in the chapters listed below and give in your own words a phrase that would summarize each.

Chapter 10 _____

Chapter 13 _____

Chapter 18 _____

Chapters 24, 25 _____

B. *Mark*

One of the most striking ways in which the Gospel of Mark differs from Matthew is that it emphasizes more *what Jesus did than what He said.*

1. What were some of the things that Jesus did which caused the religious leaders of Jesus' day to be so angry with Him (Mark 2:1-3:5)? _____

_____

_____

_____

2. Note the four miracles Jesus performed in Mark 4:35-5:43. List the various forces which, according to these records, Jesus had complete control:

4:35-41: _____

5:1-20: _____

5:21-23, 35-43: _____

5:25-34: _____

3. What is the one thing that hinders Jesus from exercising His power in the lives of men (Mark 6:1-6)? _____

_____

Life Application

1. Which instruction from Jesus' sermons in Matthew do you need to pay particular heed to? _____

_____

2. How will you apply that teaching to the appropriate area of your life? _____

_____

3. To what degree does unbelief hinder Christ from exercising His power in your life? _____

_____

4. What other attitude of yours could be a hindrance to your Christian growth? _____

_____

_____

LESSON TWO

LUKE AND JOHN

Introduction

OBJECTIVE: To understand more deeply the ministry and person of Christ.

TO MEMORIZE: John 7:37, 38.

LUKE
CHRIST AS MAN

JOHN
CHRIST AS DEITY

The writers of the last two Gospels — Luke and John — record and arrange incidents from Christ's life according to the specific objectives they wish to achieve.

Bible Study

A. *Luke*

1. Read Luke 1:1-4.

   To whom was this Gospel originally written? _____

   _____

   What evidence is there that the recipient of this Gospel had been given some prior instruction in Christianity?

   _____

   What was Luke's objective in writing to Theophilus?

   _____

2. One of the great emphases of Luke is that Jesus, though He is the Christ, must nevertheless suffer and die at the hands of sinful men (2:33-35; 9:22-31, 43, 44; 13:31-35; 18:31-34; 24:7, 25-27, 44-47). Read Luke 20-24, the account of the last week leading up to Jesus' death and resurrection.

   What are some qualities of Jesus' character that stand

   out prominently in these chapters? _____

   _____

_____

_____

What qualities of character in Jesus' enemies stand out prominently in these chapters?_____

_____

_____

_____

Why, then, did men seek to have Jesus crucified? _____

_____

_____

How were the disciples — and thus Theophilus and all the readers of Luke — assured that Jesus' suffering and death occurred according to God's plan instead of accidently, simply because of men's evil hearts?_____

_____

What difference does that make to you? _____

_____

_____

B. *John*

1. Why did John take the trouble to relate the various signs, or miracles, found in his Gospel (John 20:30, 31)?

_____

_____

2. Skim through this Gospel and see if you can list below the seven miracles of Jesus that are recorded in John.

_____

_____

_____

_____

_____

3. What climactic event did most to confirm the disciples' — and thus the reader's — faith in Jesus as the Christ?

_____

4. Read John 13 and 14.

What attitude of heart must you demonstrate if other people are to realize that you are Christ's representative in the world (13:34, 35)? _____

_____

What is God's provision for enabling Christians to be true representatives of Christ in the world (14:16-18)?

_____

What conditions must you fulfill in order to experience fully this provision (14:15, 21, 23, 24)? _____

_____

Life Application

1. Luke presented Christ as the Son of Man. What does that say to you? _____

_____

_____

2. According to John 15:16, 27, what was to be the disciples' function after Jesus left the earth? _____

_____

How does that refer to you? _____

_____

_____

What promises can you claim from these verses? _____

_____

_____

LESSON THREE

THE ACTS OF THE APOSTLES

Introduction

OBJECTIVE: To view the dynamic establishment of the first-century church.

TO MEMORIZE: Acts 1:8.

ACTS
WORKS OF THE HOLY SPIRIT

The Book of Acts begins by referring to the material presented in the Gospels as "all that Jesus began to do and teach" (Acts 1:1). Acts tells of the works that the resurrected and ascended Christ continued to do through the Holy Spirit, poured out on His disciples at Pentecost. Acts 1:8 has often been considered as the key verse of this book. Survey the book and answer these questions: What chapters tell of the witness

of the disciples at Jerusalem? _____ At Samaria? _____

To the uttermost parts of the earth? _____

Bible Study

A. *Peter*

The following are some of the major messages that Peter gave as he witnessed for Christ: Acts 2:14-36; 3:11-26; 10:34-43.

What was the most important point about the life of Christ

that Peter was trying to get across? _____

_____

B. *Paul*

Of all the apostles, Paul stands out most prominently in Acts and the New Testament.

1. What kind of a man was Paul before he was converted

   (8:1-3; 9:1; 22:1-6; 26:4-12)? _____

_____

When Jesus appeared to Paul on the road to Damascus, what did He tell him he was to do? _____

_____

2. The first missionary journey of Paul is recorded in Acts 13 and 14. How did Paul and his friend Barnabas know they were to go forth to preach the gospel (13:1-4)?

_____

_____

To whom did Paul seek to minister first at Cypress (13:4-12), at Antioch of Pisidia (13:13-52) and at Iconium (14:1-7)? _____

_____

To whom did Paul preach after this first group rejected the gospel? _____

In preaching to the Jews, Paul was able to make a point of contact with them by referring to the Old Testament Scriptures. What was the point of contact Paul used in speaking to the pagan Gentiles at Lystra (14:8-18)? _____

_____

What did Paul do to establish his converts in the faith (14:21-23)? _____

_____

Romans 15:20 tells us one more thing about Paul's evangelism strategy. What is it? _____

_____

_____

3. Several of Paul's messages are recorded in Acts. The two major ones are found in 13:16-41 and in 17:22-31. What was the most important truth he presented in each of these? _____

_____

_____

NOTE: The places mentioned in this and the other missionary journeys of Paul may be found on maps found in the back of many Bibles.

C. *The Holy Spirit*

1. What are some of the ways in which the Holy Spirit empowered the early church?

   Acts 1:8 _____

   4:31 _____

   2:4-8; 10:46; 19:6 _____

   _____

   7:54-60 _____

   _____

   10:19-20; 13:2-4 _____

   _____

   _____

   _____

2. How did the Holy Spirit work through Paul as he ministered at Cypress (13:4-12)? _____

   _____

   At Iconium (13:52-14:3)? _____

   _____

Life Application

1. What is the most important thing you now try to tell others about Christ? _____

   _____

   _____

   How does that compare with what Peter and Paul preached?

   _____

   _____

2. What can you learn from Paul in your discipling of others?

   _____

3. What are some of the ways in which the Holy Spirit is empowering you at present? _____

_____

_____

_____

_____

_____

_____

_____

_____

_____

_____

_____

_____

LESSON FOUR

ROMANS, 1 AND 2 CORINTHIANS AND GALATIANS

Introduction

OBJECTIVE: To understand the essence of the gospel.

TO MEMORIZE: Romans 1:16.

TO READ: Galatians.

ROMANS   **1 & 2 COR**   **GAL**
LAW   **CHURCH**   **GRACE**

Out of the 27 books of the New Testament, 21 are letters and 13 of these were definitely written by Paul. They were written to meet the needs and circumstances of actual persons and communities. Paul, the man God used to write so much of the New Testament, was a Roman citizen, a Jew of Tarsus, a Hebrew of the Hebrews, brought up at the feet of a great teacher, Gamaliel, but became a bond slave and missionary to Jesus Christ. His Lord calls him "a chosen instrument of Mine, to bear My name before the Gentiles and kings and the children of Israel" (Acts 9:15). From the day of his conversion, Paul's very life was Christ (Philippians 1:21).

Bible Study

A. *Romans*

This epistle was written from the city of Corinth shortly after Paul had finished his work in Ephesus. Rome was the center of the civilized world, the great metropolis of a vast empire. The city was already the home of many Christians. The immediate reason for this letter was Paul's anticipated visit to Rome. He is telling the Romans the good news concerning the way in which God, in His infinite love, has provided free and full salvation for sinners. Paul's main insistence is that man's justification before God rests not on the Law of Moses, but on the mercy of Christ.

1. Read Romans 1:1-3, 16, 17.

   What is the main theme of Romans? _____

_____

What is the gospel of Christ? _____

_____

What does it reveal? _____

2. Read Romans 3:9-18. Man is sinful and lives a life separated from God. Man is self-centered rather than God-centered. God's Word describes how He looks at man in his sinful state.

List five characteristics of a sinful man:

verse 9 _____

verse 10 _____

verse 11 _____

verse 17 _____

verse 18 _____

According to Romans 2:11 and 3:9, 10, 23, who is included in this sinful condition? _____

What righteousness does a man have that he can offer God (Romans 3:10)? _____

3. Read Romans 3:21-28; 5:1-5.

What is it that God declared unto you (verses 25, 26)?

_____

Why has He declared this (two reasons)? _____

_____

_____

Therefore, how are you justified (1:17; 3:28; 5:1)? _____

_____

_____

What are some results of justification (5:12)? _____

_____

_____

4. Being justified by faith, what is your spiritual resource (5:5)? _____

5. Being justified by faith, what is your reasonable service (12:1)? _____

_____

6. List five ways in which this service will affect your daily walk (12:9; 13:7):

_____

_____

_____

_____

_____

B. *1 Corinthians*

This epistle was written three years after Paul left Corinth. A delegation of the leaders of the Corinthian church was sent to Ephesus to consult Paul about some very serious problems that had arisen in the church. There were thousands of Christians in Corinth and yet they had no one central meeting place. Paul dealt with individual problems and endeavored to unite the groups into units that would cooperate in the general cause of Christ.

1. Read 1 Corinthians 1:17-29. Paul makes it clear that God is wiser than men and chooses the foolish things of the world to confound the mighty.

   How has God ordained that men should hear and believe? _____

   _____

   Whom has He chosen for this task? _____

   _____

   Why? _____

2. Read 1 Corinthians 9:22-24.

   Give in your own words definite proof that Paul had forsaken all that he had to follow Christ (verse 22). _____

   _____

   To what does he liken his task? _____

   _____

Why is this so appropriate? _____

_____

3. Read 1 Corinthians 13. In verses 4-8, insert your own name in the place of "love" or "charity." As you read it, does it paint a true picture of your life? _____

Which verse does not fit you and what do you think God would have you do about it? _____

_____

C. *2 Corinthians*

Soon after Paul had written 1 Corinthians, he met Titus on his way to Corinth. Titus brought word that Paul's letter had accomplished much good but that there were still some who were disloyal and that there were problems with legalizers. Paul's condition was one of physical weakness, weariness and pain. His spiritual burdens were great: first, the maintenance of the churches; second, his concern about the legalists; and third, his anguish over the distrust felt toward him by some of the members of the churches.

1. Read 2 Corinthians 4:1-6. Paul is careful in his handling of the Word of God.

What is the tragic result of handling the Word of God deceitfully (verse 3)? _____

Why did God shine into our hearts (verse 6)? _____

_____

2. What is it that Paul fears and of which we all must be well aware (2 Corinthians 11:3)? _____

3. Paul prayed to be relieved of his "thorn in the flesh."

What was the Lord's answer to his prayer (2 Corinthians 12:9)? _____

What was Paul's attitude toward the final outcome?

_____

_____

What lesson can you learn from his experience (12:10)?

_____

D. *Galatians*

Some time after Paul had left Galatia, certain Jewish teachers began to insist that Gentiles could not be Christian without keeping the Law of Moses. The objective of this epistle is the defense of the gospel of grace that Paul had received by the revelation of Jesus.

1. Paul shows that the gospel was not of man, neither did he receive it of man nor was he taught it of man. What was its true origin (Galatians 1;12)? _____

_____

2. According to Galatians 2:20, who indwells Paul? _____ What effect does this have on his daily life? _____

_____

3. Read Galatians 5:16-21. In this passage Paul lists the works of the flesh. How can we as Christians avoid doing the works of the flesh? _____

Life Application

1. According to Galatians 5:22, 23, what will be the result in your life of this type of walk? List the definite characteristics.

_____

_____

_____

_____

Which work of your flesh do you most need to surrender to the Holy Spirit's control today? _____

_____

Why not take time right now to do that?

LESSON FIVE

THE PRISON, THESSALONIAN AND PASTORAL EPISTLES

Introduction

OBJECTIVE: To examine the character of the apostle Paul as presented in his epistles.

TO MEMORIZE: Colossians 2:6, 7.

TO READ: Ephesians.

EPH PHIL COL PHILEMON ⟱ PRISON

I & 2 THESS ⟱ LETTERS

I & 2 TIMOTHY TITUS ⟱ CO-WORKERS

Ephesians, Philippians, Colossians and Philemon are called the "prison" epistles because they were written by Paul during his first imprisonment, mentioned in Acts 28.

Bible Study

A. *Prison Epistles*

1. Ephesians.

Through his own labors, Paul had founded the church at Ephesus (Acts 19), but since, in this letter, he includes as his readers those who had never known him, most scholars agree that Paul wrote this letter not just to Ephesus, but for all Gentile Christians wherever they might be. The purpose of this letter was to show the Gentiles that they were on an equal footing with the Jews in receiving the blessings of salvation (see Ephesians 2:19-22; 3:6).

What had been the prospects of Gentiles receiving the blessings of salvation in previous times (2:11, 12)? _____

_____

_____

Through what event were the blessings of salvation made available to all (2:13-18)? _____

_____

_____

From the prayer that Paul prays in Ephesians 3:14-19, list the blessings of salvation that all Christians now enjoy. _____

_____

_____

2. Philippians.

Paul wrote this letter to the church he had founded (Acts 16) to thank them for the money they had sent him for his support while in prison. In writing it, he also sought to overcome the disunity in the church between two women, Euodia and Syntyche (4:2). With this disunity overcome, the church could stand firmly together in preaching the gospel without fear to those round about them (1:27, 28).

Read Philippians 1:12-30. What had Paul been doing in Rome that would encourage the Philippians to be bold in proclaiming the gospel (1:13, 14)? _____

How did Paul's attitude regarding the future help to encourage the Philippians to stand fearlessly for Christ (verses 18-25)? _____

_____

What was Paul's chief reason for being happy about the gift the Philippians had sent him (4:10-19)? _____

_____

3. Colossians.

Paul had never visited the church at Colossae, but reports regarding the increase of false teaching there had reached him in Rome. Since he was an apostle to all the Gentiles, he felt it was necessary to write and warn that church.

This false teaching stated that in addition to Christ being the only mediator between God and man, there were certain angelic beings through whom man must also go in order to know God. Consequently Paul's main stress in this epistle is the deity and all-sufficiency of Jesus Christ.

List at least three things Paul says about Jesus Christ which show that it is unnecessary to seek any additional way to reach God (Colossians 1:12-22). _____

_____

_____

_____

Since Christ is all-sufficient, what is the Christian to be content to do (2:6, 7)? _____

_____

What practical effect will submission to the lordship and uniqueness of Christ have upon the Christian's life (3:1-11)? _____

_____

_____

4. Philemon.

For some reason this fourth prison epistle was not joined with the other three, but rather stands by itself at the end of the Pastoral Epistles. Though the shortest of Paul's epistles, this is, nevertheless, one of the most profound and beautiful of all.

While in prison at Rome, Paul had led Onesimus, a runaway slave, to the Lord. He discovered that this slave's master was Philemon, a personal friend of Paul's, living at Colossae. In those days the penalty for a slave who had run away was either death or brutal punishment, but Paul writes Philemon to ask him to forgive Onesimus for what he had done and to receive him as a Christian brother.

This epistle stands as a great example of the profound change for good that Christ makes in all human relations. State in your own words at least three arguments Paul used to persuade Philemon to receive Onesimus in love.

_____

_____

_____

B. *The Thessalonian Epistles*

The first epistles Paul ever wrote were those to the church he had founded at Thessalonica in Macedonia. These were written from Corinth (Acts 18:1-18) soon after Paul had been at Thessalonica.

1. 1 Thessalonians.

Paul had had to leave Thessalonica very hastily because of persecution (Acts 17:10), and the enemies of the gospel there had tried to disillusion the newly won Christians by charging that Paul was only a fair-weather friend who had left them alone because of difficult circumstances. To answer this charge Paul wrote 1 Thessalonians.

What effect had the Thessalonians' conversion had on the Christians of the surrounding area (1 Thessalonians 1:7-10)? _____

_____

The lives of those to whom Paul wrote had been changed. How did this prove that those who had preached the gospel to them were godly men (1 Thessalonians 1:5,6)?

_____

_____

Give two ways in which Paul's ministry at Thessalonica made it impossible for him to be an insincere person (1 Thessalonians 2:1-10). _____

_____

_____

2. 2 Thessalonians.

Some questions regarding the circumstances of Christ's second coming had arisen after the Thessalonians had received Paul's first epistle. They were troubled because they had to endure unjustly great sufferings and persecutions for Christ (2 Thessalonians 1:3-12). Some also had become slack in doing their work because they thought that Christ's second coming would occur at any moment.

What do you think the Christian's attitude toward persecution should be (2 Thessalonians 1:3-12)? _____

_____

_____

What is to be his attitude toward work (3:6-15)? _____

_____

_____

C. *The Pastoral Epistles*

From the time of his first missionary journey, Paul had always had co-workers. The Pastoral Epistles are three letters that Paul wrote to his co-workers who were helping him to strengthen the churches already founded.

These letters were written in the period between Paul's first Roman imprisonment in A.D. 60-62 (Acts 28) and his final martyrdom under the emperor Nero in A.D. 66. 1 and 2 Timothy were written to help Timothy in his work with the church at Ephesus. Titus was written to the co-worker who was laboring on the island of Crete.

1. 1 Timothy.

Read 1 Timothy 6. What are the two things that are necessary for contentment in life (1 Timothy 6:6-8)?

_____

What great danger confronts those who seek after riches (verses 9-12)? _____

_____

What attitude should Christians who are wealthy have toward money (verses 17-19)? _____

_____

2. 2 Timothy.

Paul wrote 2 Timothy just before he was martyred. He writes as though it may be his last word to his co-worker, Timothy. What are the last commands that Paul gave Timothy (2 Timothy 4:1-5)? _____

_____

What two means will help Timothy remain true to his

calling after Paul has gone (2 Timothy 3:10,11 and 14-17)?

_____

_____

3. Titus.

What are some of the things that a Christian should be careful to do in light of the unbelieving world in which he lives (Titus 3:1,2)? _____

_____

What reason does Paul give for a Christian's living this way (3:3-7)? _____

_____

Life Application

1. Name two things you have learned from Paul's character, as you have studied him in this lesson. _____

_____

_____

2. What do you sense from Philippians 3:1 and 4:4 about an approach to life Paul would advise you to have? _____

_____

_____

_____

_____

_____

LESSON SIX

THE GENERAL EPISTLES

Introduction

OBJECTIVE: To see the gospel amplified and defined.

TO MEMORIZE: Hebrews 1:1, 2.

TO READ: James; 1 and 2 Peter; 1, 2 and 3 John; Jude.

The term "general" is at best only an imperfect way to characterize the last eight epistles of the New Testament. It has been selected because, unlike most of Paul's epistles which are written to specific churches, most of the recipients of these eight epistles are either the churches of some large area

GENERAL

HEBREWS   I, 2, 3 JOHN

JAMES   JUDE

I & 2 PETER

or are all Christians (the exceptions: Hebrews, 2 and 3 John). Again, with the exception of Hebrews, these epistles are named for their authors.

Bible Study

A. *Hebrews*

The early church called this book "Hebrews" because it was originally addressed to Jewish Christians. In the early days following their conversion through the preaching of some of Jesus' original disciples (2:3), they had become exemplary Christians, they had helped supply the needs of other Christians (6:10) and they had taken cheerfully the loss of their own possessions as they were persecuted for Christ's name (10:32-34).

However, at the writing of this letter their original teachers and leaders had died (Hebrews 13:7). Now they were on the verge of slipping back from a confession of Christ into the Judaism out of which they had been converted (13:13,14). One reason they might have wanted to do this was that the Roman government in the first century allowed

Jewish worship but deemed Christianity an illicit religion. The writer of Hebrews exhorts the readers to remain true to Christ even at the price of having to shed their own blood (12:3,4).

That writer had to have been an outstanding leader in the early Christian church, but his identity is unknown. Origen, the first Christian theologian, writing in the third century, said, "Who wrote the Epistle to the Hebrews, God alone knows." Many believe it was written by the apostle Paul, though this cannot be confirmed.

The key passage of Hebrews is 10:19-25. In verses 19,20 the writer speaks of the finality of Jesus Christ in that He is the "new and living way." This summarizes the argument from 4:14-10:18. Then in verse 21 he declares that Jesus is final because He is the great High Priest, and this was the argument of 1:1-4:13. Since Jesus Christ is final, ultimate and all sufficient, all Christians should obey the commands in Hebrews 10:22-25.

1. What are four things a Christian must do, according to Hebrews 10:22-25? _____

_____

_____

_____

_____

2. Summarize in your own words the two lines of argument that the writer uses to support these commands.

   (10:26-31) _____

   _____

   (10:32-34) _____

   _____

3. What attitude of heart did the original readers of this epistle need to have in order to remain true to Christ in the midst of persecution (Hebrews 10:35-39)? _____

_____

4. By what means did the Old Testament believers acquire this necessary quality of heart (Hebrews 11:1-39)? _____

_____

5. In view of the way these Old Testament believers lived, what should you do (Hebrews 12:1-4)? _____

_____

B. James

The writer of this epistle is thought to have been the half brother of Jesus. During the days of Jesus' earthly ministry, His brothers were unbelievers (John 7:5). However, after His resurrection, Jesus appeared to James (1 Corinthians 15:7). It would seem that this appearance affected James' conversion and perhaps that of all His brothers, for in the days prior to Pentecost we find them in the upper room praying with the apostles (Acts 1:14).

Though not counted as one of the 12 apostles, James became a prominent leader in the early Jerusalem church (Acts 15:13; Galatians 1:19; 2:9). Because the name "James" was so common in those days, it is felt that only this James who figured so prominently in the early church would have announced himself to the readers of this epistle without going into any detail as to who he was (James 1:1). The original readers of this epistle were Christians scattered abroad. Because they had suffered greatly at the hands of unbelievers (1:2-4; 2:6-7), they had tended to become cold in their devotion to Christ.

James writes this epistle to remind them about those qualities of heart and life that should characterize true Christian devotion in contrast to dead orthodoxy. In so doing, he made it clear how a Christian can find joy in Christ even when suffering for Him.

1. Why should the Christian consider adversity a reason for the greatest happiness (James 1:2-4, 12)? _____

_____

2. In what way does the Christian receive the necessary resources to stand for Christ while suffering greatly (James 1:5-8)? _____

_____

3. What two things should the Christian always remember when he feels tempted to do wrong?

(1:13-16) _____

(1:17,18) _____

4. Note the qualities of heart that should characterize true Christian devotion as opposed to dead orthodoxy:

Instead of simply hearing what God has to say in His Word, the Christian should do what (1:21-25)? _____

_____

What should we do instead of simply talk about being Christians (1:26,27)? _____

C. Peter

1 Peter. Peter addresses the various churches scattered throughout Asia Minor (present-day Turkey). But like James, Peter's purpose in writing was to strengthen Christians in standing firmly against the terrible persecutions that the Roman empire was about to unleash against the church. Thus Peter begins by pointing out the wonders of the salvation that his readers possess (1:3-12). Then he gives certain commands which when obeyed will help a person to realize the wonders of this salvation.

1. List the five commands Peter gives in 1:13-2:3:

    (1:13) _____

    (1:14-16) _____

    (1:17-21) _____

    (1:22-25) _____

    (2:1-3) _____

2. When one fulfills these commands, how does his attitude toward Christ differ from that of those who do not

    believe and obey Him (1 Peter 2:4-10)? _____

    _____

3. Chapter 2, verses 9 and 10, are in the key verses of 1 Peter. The purpose of the Christian life is not simply to enjoy the glories of salvation, but rather to enjoy these glories in order to testify of their wonders to those who do not know Christ.

    How, in general, does the Christian, by his life, witness to

    those around him (1 Peter 2:11,12)? _____

    _____

How, in relationship to the government, does the Christian demonstrate the praises of Christ (1 Peter 2:13-17)? _____

_____

How, in his relationship to an employer, can a Christian demonstrate the praises of Christ (1 Peter 2:18-25)?

_____

_____

How can a Christian wife best testify of Christ to an unbelieving husband (1 Peter 3:1-7)? _____

_____

How may the Christian be an effective witness for Christ in the midst of sufferings (1 Peter 3:8-17)? _____

_____

2 Peter. As 2 Timothy records Paul's last words before martydom, so 2 Peter was Peter's last message before his martydom (1:14; cf. John 21:19). (Tradition says he was killed by being crucified head downwards.) This epistle is a continuation of the theme of 1 Peter. The sufferings that his readers had just begun to endure when that epistle was written have continued unabated, and Peter's purpose in writing this second epistle is to encourage his readers to endure steadfastly to the end. He begins by citing the greatness of God's grace to the Christian (1:2-4). Then he follows up the first epistle by declaring certain things the Christian must do to enjoy God's blessings fully (1:5-11). In 1:14-21, Peter relates the basis for feeling so confident regarding God's grace.

1. From what two sources have the readers heard of this grace?

    (1:14-18) _____

    (1:19-21) _____

2. However, there have always been those whose teaching would keep God's people from the truth. Name three ways to recognize those who are false prophets (2 Peter 2:1-22). _____

_____

_____

_____

3. What great event should determine the present conduct of Christians (2 Peter 3:10-14)? _____

D. John

1 John. During his later years the apostle John settled at Ephesus among the Christians, who had found Christ through Paul's ministry.

While he was there a certain false teaching became popular which declared that God did not become truly incarnate in Jesus Christ and that a life of actual holiness was not essential to the Christian life. The first epistle of John was written to counteract this heresy. However, it is more than a mere refutation; it is one of the most beautiful and inspiring documents of the New Testament.

To refute this heresy John showed Christians certain tests by which they could distinguish the true from the false. The key verse is 1 John 5:13: "These things I have written to you. . . that you may know that you have eternal life." When certain things are true in a person's life he may have the assurance that he has eternal life.

See if you can find at least five tests of this assurance in the material leading up to 5:13.

(1:7) _____

(2:3) _____

(2:15) _____

(3:6) _____

(4:7) _____

2 John. It is not clear whether the recipient of this brief epistle is an individual, or whether the term "elect lady" figuratively denotes a church whose members are her "children" (verse 1). Summarize in your own words the burden of the message John gives to this church. _____

_____

_____

3 John

1. What example is Gaius to continue to follow in the future (3 John 2-8)? _____

_____

2. What is there about Diotrephes that Gaius is to avoid imitating (3 John 9-11)? _____

_____

E. *Jude*

Many Biblical scholars believe that Jude was another one of Jesus' brothers who was converted after His earthly ministry. He calls himself "the brother of James" (verse 1), and in verse 17 he indicates that he was not himself an official apostle.

1. What was Jude's reason for writing as he does in this epistle (Jude 3,4)? _____

_____

2. What are two things that Jude wants his readers to remember?

(5-16) _____

(17-19) _____

3. What is the Christian's responsibility in view of the many false teachers that exist (Jude 20-23)? _____

_____

Life Application

Have you read all these general epistles? _____

Determine one main truth from each which is particularly helpful to you and list it here:

Hebrews:_____

_____

James: _____

_____

1 Peter: _____

_____

2 Peter: _____

_____

1 John: _____

_____

2 John: _____

_____

3 John: _____

_____

Jude: _____

_____

_____

LESSON SEVEN

THE REVELATION OF JESUS CHRIST

Introduction

OBJECTIVE: To look at prophecy, and prepare for the coming of Christ.

TO MEMORIZE: Revelation 21:4.

TO READ: Revelation.

REVELATION

| 1-3 7 CHURCHES | 4-18 FUTURE PROPHECY | 19-22 FINAL REDEMPTION |

The last book of the New Testament is the record of the revelation which the apostle John received during his imprisonment on the island of Patmos for being a Christian (1:9 and following). Many of the chapters of this book are very difficult to interpret. Some of the greatest theologians in the history of the church have felt unequal to the task of expounding these Scriptures. For example, John Calvin, one of the great reformers, wrote a commentary on every book of the Bible except Revelation.

However, despite the fact that the meaning of every part of this book may not be immediately apparent, there is the promise that those who read (not necessarily understand) it will be blessed (1:3).

And though some parts may be obscure, certain ideas do stand out with unquestioned clarity. Chapters 1 through 3 are a description of Jesus as He appeared to John and a record of the messages to be sent to the seven churches of Asia Minor, and they are quite clear in their meaning. Chapters 4 through 18 are more difficult, but chapters 19 through 22, which concern those events by which God brings final redemption to the world, are clear for the most part. These four chapters are of the utmost importance for completing the history of redemption outlined since Genesis.

Bible Study

A. *Jesus Christ*

Write in your own words your impression of Jesus Christ as John describes Him in Revelation 1:9-20. _____

_____

_____

_____

B. *The churches*

Name the seven churches to whom John was to write, and tell the one main message he was to give to each.

_____

_____

_____

_____

_____

_____

_____

C. *Final events*

1. What great events are described in Revelation 19:1-21?

_____

2. What will be the fate of the devil at the beginning of Christ's thousand-year reign (Revelation 20:1-3)? _____

_____

3. What will be the devil's final fate at the end of Christ's thousand-year reign (Revelations 20:7-10)? _____

_____

4. What will be the final fate of all unbelievers (Revelation 20:11-15)? _____

5. Show three ways in which the Christian's ultimate destiny will differ from this present existence (Revelation 21:1-9)?

_____

_____

Life Application

How can you prepare spiritually for Christ's coming and the events which will be taking place? _____

_____

_____

_____

_____

LESSON EIGHT

RECAP

Review all verses memorized.

1. What is the focus in Matthew regarding the person of Christ?

_____

_____

2. How does Mark differ from Matthew? ———————

_____

_____

3. How did Luke and John each present Christ? ————

_____

_____

4. What changes took place in Paul's life after he became a Christian? _____

_____

_____

5. What are the three results of justification by faith (Romans 5:1,2)? _____

_____

_____

6. Write again the names of the books of the Old Testament, listing them by division.

_____

_____

_____

_____

_____

_____

_____

_____

_____

_____

_____

_____

_____

_____

_____

7. Write the divisions and books of the New Testament.

_____

_____

_____

_____

_____

_____

_____

_____

_____

_____

_____

_____

_____

_____

_____

HOW TO STUDY THE BIBLE

Someone has said that four things are necessary in studying the Bible: admit, submit, commit and transmit. First, admit its truth; second, submit to its teachings; third, commit it to memory; and fourth, transmit it to others. If the Christian life is a good thing for you, share it with someone else.

Use a notebook as you study the Bible. Write out the answers to the following questions as you study a portion of the Bible:

1. What persons have I read about, and what have I learned about them?

2. What places have I read about, and what have I read about them? If the place is not mentioned, can I find out where it is? Do I know its position on the map?

3. Can I relate from memory what I have just been reading?

4. Are there any parallel passages or texts that throw light on this passage?

5. Have I read anything about God the Father? or about Jesus Christ? or about the Holy Ghost?

6. What have I read about myself? about man's sinful nature? about the spiritual new nature?

7. Is there any duty for me to observe? any example to follow? any promise to claim? any exhortation to guide me? any prayer that I may echo?

8. What is the key verse of the chapter or passage? Can I repeat it from memory?

Dwight L. Moody

More Books from Here's Life Publishers

The Holy Spirit: Key to Supernatural Living by Bill Bright. A clear explanation of what the Holy Spirit can do in your life now. Available in both quality paperback and hardback.

Vonette Bright's Prayer and Praise Diary by Vonette Bright. Excellent tool for developing an effective prayer life. Paperback.

Handbook of Concepts for Living by Bill Bright. A practical book conveying the basics of the Christian life. Spiritual truths which can be communicated from one person to another and then on to others, greatly multiplying each person's ministry. For use by individuals or in group settings. Paperback. Same content is also available in nine individual books called the ***Transferable Concepts*** series. The following topics are included:

> How to Be Sure You Are a Christian
> How to Experience God's Love and Forgiveness
> How to Be Filled With the Spirit
> How to Walk in the Spirit
> How to Witness in the Spirit
> How to Introduce Others to Christ
> How to Help Fulfill the Great Commission
> How to Love by Faith
> How to Pray

The Discipleship Series. Carefully balances the study of Scripture with practical application. Builds around three levels of Christian development. For use in a group discipleship setting. Paperback. Four books are available.

> Book 1:   The Discovery Group
> Book 2:   The Discipleship Group
> Book 3:   The Leadership Group
> The Discipleship Series Leaders Guide

Ten Basic Steps Toward Christian Maturity Teacher's Manual. Guide for teaching either the complete Ten Basic Steps series or this ***Handbook for Christian Maturity.*** May be used with Christians, non-Christians or mixed Bible study groups. Paperback.

Available at Christian bookstores or from Here's Life Publishers.